Mobilizing Without the Masses

When advocacy organizations are forbidden from rallying people to take the streets, what do they do? When activists are detained for coordinating protests, are their hands ultimately tied? Based on political ethnography inside both legal and blacklisted labor organizations in China, this book reveals how state repression is deployed on the ground and to what effect on mobilization. It presents a novel dynamic of civil society contention – mobilizing without the masses – that lowers the risk of activism under duress. Instead of facilitating collective action, activists coach the aggrieved to challenge authorities one by one. In doing so, they lower the risks of organizing while empowering the weak. This dynamic represents a third pathway of contention that challenges conventional understandings of mobilization in an illiberal state. It takes readers inside the world of underground labor organizing and opens the black box of repression inside the world's most powerful authoritarian state.

Diana Fu is Assistant Professor of Asian Politics at the University of Toronto. This book builds upon her DPhil dissertation from Oxford University. Previously, she was Walter H. Shorenstein Postdoctoral Fellow at Stanford University and a pre-doctoral fellow at the Massachusetts Institute of Technology. Her research has been supported by the Harold Hyam Wingate Foundation, the Chiang Ching Kuo Foundation, and the Rhodes Trust. Her academic articles have been published in *Governance, Comparative Political Studies*, and *Modern China*. Her writing and research have appeared in *The Economist, Boston Review, PostGlobal*, and Nicholas Kristof's On the Ground Blog for *The New York Times*.

D1600859

STUDIES OF THE WEATHERHEAD EAST ASIAN INSTITUTE, COLUMBIA UNIVERSITY

The Studies of the Weatherhead East Asian Institute of Columbia University were inaugurated in 1962 to bring to a wider public the results of significant new research on modern and contemporary East Asia.

Cambridge Studies in Contentious Politics

General Editor
Doug McAdam *Stanford University and Center for Advanced Study in the Behavioral Sciences*

Editors
Mark Beissinger *Princeton University*
Donatella della Porta *Scuola Normale Superiore*
Jack A. Goldstone *George Mason University*
Michael Hanagan *Vassar College*
Holly J. McCammon *Vanderbilt University*
David S. Meyer *University of California, Irvine*
Sarah Soule *Stanford University*
Suzanne Staggenborg *University of Pittsburgh*
Sidney Tarrow *Cornell University*
Charles Tilly (d. 2008) *Columbia University*
Elisabeth J. Wood *Yale University*
Deborah Yashar *Princeton University*

(*continued after index*)

Mobilizing Without the Masses

Control and Contention in China

DIANA FU
University of Toronto

CAMBRIDGE
UNIVERSITY PRESS

CAMBRIDGE
UNIVERSITY PRESS

University Printing House, Cambridge CB2 8BS, United Kingdom

One Liberty Plaza, 20th Floor, New York, NY 10006, USA

477 Williamstown Road, Port Melbourne, VIC 3207, Australia

314-321, 3rd Floor, Plot 3, Splendor Forum, Jasola District Centre, New Delhi - 110025, India

79 Anson Road, #06-04/06, Singapore 079906

Cambridge University Press is part of the University of Cambridge.

It furthers the University's mission by disseminating knowledge in the pursuit of education, learning and research at the highest international levels of excellence.

www.cambridge.org
Information on this title: www.cambridge.org/9781108430418
DOI: 10.1017/ 9781108354707

First published 2018

A catalogue record for this publication is available from the British Library

ISBN 978-1-108-42054-9 Hardback
ISBN 978-1-108-43041-8 Paperback

Cambridge University Press has no responsibility for the persistence or accuracy of URLs for external or third-party internet websites referred to in this publication, and does not guarantee that any content on such websites is, or will remain, accurate or appropriate.

For my family and for those at the front lines

Contents

Figures and Tables

Preface

Behind every book is another untold story – this is mine. This book originates from my undergraduate years at the University of Minnesota. Under the tutelage of Raymond Duvall, Daniel Kelliher, Ann Waltner, Sharilyn Geistfled, and many others, I struck out in my junior year to do "fieldwork" in Beijing. I was only dimly aware of what this consisted, but I knew one thing for certain: I was and continue to be drawn to the everyday experiences of marginalized people. Every other day, I crammed into a sweat-stenched bus that jammed its way through the Beijing traffic and dropped me off at a *hutong* in the second ring of the city. There, I talked, played, and traded stories with participants of one of China's first migrant NGOs. It was also there that I tried my hand at ethnography – the neck-deep immersion of oneself into the culture of one's "subjects." It was hard; it was exhilarating. I came back with a fistful of field notes and a "stomach full of words," as the migrant women would often say. With the unflagging support of my mentors, this project became my first publication and set my research trajectory for the next decade.

During my first year of graduate study at Oxford University, I felt terribly lost in the city of spires. Lost among restless, active minds, the swooshing gowns at Rhodes House, and the Latin recitations at formal dinner. My supervisors Vivienne Shue, Rachel Murphy, and Maria Jaschok (M.Phil) helped me to stay on course, as did Rana Mitter and Patricia Thornton. Vivienne advised me to do what I was good at regardless of what type of research was a la mode, advice that I have echoed to my own students. For all of its dynastic traditions, Oxford gave me the chance to think unfettered by conventions, which brought its own burdens. Dear friends including Rachel and Deborah carried me through dark times, as did my dance partner.

Oxford also allowed me to disappear into fieldwork for nearly two years, supported by the Rhodes Trust, the Harold Hyam Wingate Foundation, and the Chiang Ching-kuo Foundation. Back in China, I encountered new mentors and friends including Ching Kwan Lee, Guang Lei, Pun Ngai, Shen Yuan, Zhu Jiangang, Zheng Guanghuai, and Huang Yan. Through their guidance, I discovered a new world of labor activism. I met some of the most tenacious and committed activists and workers during this period. I admired their resilience, humor, and wiliness in tough circumstances. I also realized just how little I could offer them besides an empathetic ear and some company. This book is really their stories, which deserve to be recorded.

But alas, scholarship demands more than storytelling – it must provide explanations of social realities and theorize hidden political processes. Many inspired me throughout this painstaking process. In Boston, I benefited from the intellectual might of Richard Locke, Elizabeth Perry, Roger Petersen, Edward Steinfeld, David Singer, as well as other faculty members and students at MIT.

As a postdoctoral fellow at Stanford University, I tapped into the brilliant minds of Francis Fukuyama, Jean Oi, Gi-Wook Shin, Andrew Walder, and Zhou Xueguang who helped me to go beyond the immediate case studies. I am especially indebted to Gi-Wook Shin at the Shorenstein Asia-Pacific Center for his support in book writing and to Andrew Walder for his incisive commentary.

I also benefited enormously from Kevin O'Brien, whose own work inspired me to draw connections between Chinese politics and contentious politics. Kevin also integrated me into a dynamic network of young scholars, including Rachel Stern and Daniel Mattingly who provided insightful critique.

The book would also not be in its current form if Sidney Tarrow had not challenged me to think "big" by linking my ideas to contentious politics. It would also have been impossible without Jessica Teets, whose unmatched problem-solving skills helped me to cut through uncertainties. Likewise, senior colleagues including Mary Gallagher, William Hurst, Andrew Mertha, James Scott, Susan Shirk, Elisabeth Wood, and Lesley Wood gave penetrating critique at various seminars at Yale, Cornell, the University of California San Diego, and the University of Toronto.

I am blessed with terrific colleagues at the University of Toronto. My chairs, Grace Skogstad and Louis Pauly, gave me unwavering support and candid advice. My colleagues including Chris Cochrane, Carolina De Miguel, Victor Falkenheim, Matt Hoffman, Paul Kingston, Peggy Kohn, Sida Liu, Kanta Murali, Neil Nevitte, Lynette Ong, Edward Schatz, Phil Triaphildophilous, Lucan Way, Melissa Williams, Joe Wong, and Yiching Wu navigated me through the writing and publication process. My doctoral student and stellar research assistant, Emile Dirks, tirelessly edited and gave feedback on the chapters.

I would also like to thank David Samuels and Ben Ansell, editors at *Comparative Political Studies*, for their confidence in my work and for allowing me to draw upon my 2017 *CPS* article in the book. Parts of Chapter 3 also draw from an article published in *Governance*.

I am also grateful to my editors Robert Dreesen and Doug McAdam for their thoughtful guidance in getting me to the finish line. Thanks also to Andrew Nathan and Ross Yelsey for including this book in the Studies of the

Weatherhead East Asian Institute. Andrew Nathan also provided invaluable commentary on the manuscript.

The book's tale ends where it began – at home with my family and friends. It started with mama, who taught me to "set off my own kind of fireworks," and baba, from whom I inherited a stubborn ambition. Along the way, I also picked up a fast-talking and sensitive guy in China who became my lifelong adventure buddy. In Toronto, friends from City Dance Corps and my faith community buoyed my spirit. Together with my dear friends Diana, Laura, and Christine, they walked me through the valleys and the peaks. They remind me that after all, a book is just a book. And that life is more than the mind.

Organizing under Duress

I first observed mobilizing without the masses while studying labor organizations in China. While a few of these organizations have gained official status, the majority operated under the radar. Keenly aware of this precarious status, leaders were quick to assure me that their organizations harbored no anti-state agenda, and that they were not independent labor unions. On the contrary, they insisted that these were grassroots non-governmental organizations (NGOs) that assisted the country's 270 million migrant workers in attaining their legally guaranteed rights. As such, these organizations acted to preserve social stability and harmony, goals which aligned with the Chinese state's interests.

It was true that these organizations bore little resemblance to independent unions such as Poland's "Solidarity" trade union. They were small, poorly resourced, and did not involve themselves in popular protests. Activists also complained about the lack of solidarity among workers and described the organizing process as "grabbing a fistful of sand that slipped through one's fingers." Moreover, the state security apparatus' vigilance and harassment of grassroots labor organizations kept activists on edge. Organizations were disbanded from time to time, and the ones that moved and resurrected themselves in other jurisdictions learned to self-censor. Whether operating in Beijing, the Pearl River Delta, or the Yangtze River Delta, few of the groups I studied involved themselves in worker strikes or protests because doing so would be seen as a flagrant defiance of the state. Under such conditions, mobilization seemed unlikely.

Had I unquestioningly recorded these observations and activists' initial claims, I would not be writing this book. As it happened, however, my subsequent eighteen months of participant observation inside these organizations across China revealed a wholly unexpected political process. In fact, these organizations *were* mobilizing participants in remarkable, if unconventional, ways. Instead of organizing migrant workers to engage in collective strike action, activists coached them to confront the state as individuals or in small groups in a dynamic that I term "mobilizing without the masses." In doing so, organizations strategically hid behind the audacious contender.

To illustrate this dynamic in action, take the example of a female worker from Sichuan who was in desperate straits because her employer refused to pay her work injury compensation as stipulated by the labor law. While working without protective gear at a small car manufacturer, she had caught her upper arm in a machine, causing severe injuries. Factory management sent her to the hospital but refused to pay for subsequent treatment. Without surgery, she might have become disabled for life. When informal mediation with factory management failed, she sought assistance from the township labor bureau. After being turned away repeatedly by officials who told her that she would have to wait for arbitration, she visited the local state-run union as well as the Women's Federation, but to no avail; officials "passed the ball" from one unresponsive bureau to another. Despairing, she visited the local labor bureau again. This time, she threatened the labor bureau official: "If you don't solve my problem, I'm going to take *extreme measures*!"

To a casual observer, this lone challenger at the labor bureau may have been indistinguishable from the masses of aggrieved workers who had reached their tipping points. But to the participant observer, this individual challenger's actions represented the outcome of an organized process. In fact, a labor activist in a grassroots labor organization was coaching her via text messaging, telling her when, where, and how to make these threats against her employer.

Through embedding myself in these organizations, I observed this hidden coaching process, which was integral to the work of these groups. In the semi-private sphere of the organization, activists – many of whom were themselves migrant workers – facilitated discussions of labor exploitation, growing socioeconomic disparity, and the failures of China's political and legal institutions in protecting workers' rights. Such discussions inculcated in their participants a sense of belonging to a much larger community of migrant workers who also faced the same unresponsive local states and inefficient legal systems. Thus, even without rallying participants to take part in collective strike action, activists provided workers with the moral support and strategic resources for contention.

This behind-the-scenes mobilizing was not one that activists articulated to me in interviews or recorded in handbooks distributed to workers. It was the unspoken modus operandi of grassroots activists working in a repressive authoritarian setting who were forced to experiment with innovative tactics. This kind of innovative organizing emerged as a political compromise with local authorities that were themselves caught in a bind: if they repressed such organizations stridently, they risked driving activists further underground. If they openly tolerated such groups, they would be held responsible for the multiplication of organizations that threatened a key pillar of the ruling Chinese

Communist Party's legitimacy – social stability. Seizing upon such opportunities, activists devised a range of tactical innovations that allowed them to operate in a repressive political environment.

In a nutshell, this book theorizes this type of unorthodox mobilization and the political conditions that gave rise to it. In doing so, it revises our understanding of the role that organizations can play in encouraging and directing popular contention. It suggests that despite high risks, it is nevertheless possible for weak civil society organizations to facilitate popular contention under certain conditions. Contrary to assumptions, civil society's hands are not entirely tied; organizations can provide critical strategic, cognitive, and moral resources to popular contenders, thereby shaping the very grammar of popular contention.

ORGANIZING UNDER DURESS IN CHINA

How do organizations mobilize popular contention under repressive political conditions in an authoritarian state? While much has been written about civil society's role in challenging authoritarian incumbents (Bunce and Wolchik 2011; Beissinger 2007; Almeida 2003; Diamond 1994; Weigle and Butterfield 1992; Gold 1990), the micro-politics of organizing contention on an everyday basis in authoritarian political settings remain relatively obscure. This book casts a spotlight on one seemingly counterintuitive dynamic of organizing contention: *mobilizing without the masses*. In this dynamic, civil society organizations[1] refrain from mobilizing aggrieved citizens to take up large-scale collective contention. Instead, they coach participants to contend as individuals or as small groups. The process of coaching contention is a collective endeavor that takes place in the private harbors of organizational headquarters. In these relatively safe spaces, activists construct and disseminate pedagogies of contention that foster collective identity and consciousness. In conventional forms of mobilization, the fostering of collective identity and oppositional consciousness facilitates collective action (Snow 2013; Gamson 1992; Melucci 1989). Yet in mobilizing without the masses, only a single individual or a small band of the aggrieved engages in overt contention. While the organizational process is a collective one, it remains concealed behind a repertoire of small-scale or individualized contention.

---

[1] The term "civil society" is conceptually slippery and has been the subject of much scholarly debate (Evans and Heller 2015: 691–713; Foley and Edwards 1996; Diamond 1994). In the Chinese context, debates have centered around the level and type of autonomy civil society has gained vis-à-vis the state (Lu 2009; Howell 2003; Foster 2001; Saich 2000; White, Howell, and Shang 1996; Gold 1990). This book follows recent studies (Teets 2014: 14; Simon 2013) that define civil society broadly as composed of a diverse array of organizations with voluntary membership and some degree of operational autonomy from the state, defined as the ability to set a self-determined agenda (Wang 2006).

This dynamic of contention allows organizations to facilitate popular contention while reducing potential political risks to the organization itself. Through channeling discontent into individual forms of contention, organizations strike a middle ground between being obedient to the authoritarian state and becoming rebellious social movement vehicles. On the one hand, organizations are not entirely obedient; they coach citizens to disrupt social order in an effort to demand redress from the local government. On the other hand, they also refrain from inciting large-scale protests and strikes, which are risky endeavors in authoritarian settings, particularly when they are coordinated by civil society organizations. The small-scale contentious performances that activists coach participants to deploy do not constitute a serious collective challenge to the state. Instead, by disguising the collective coordinating behind a façade of individual contention, activists signal to the state that they understand the boundaries of organized contention. In such a manner, even weak organizations can serve as mobilizing vehicles for limited contentious political activity, despite the threat of state harassment and periodic organizational closures. In doing so, they deliver tangible benefits to participants seeking to claim rights from an otherwise unaccountable authoritarian state.

Theoretically, mobilizing without the masses suggests an alternative pathway through which civil society organizations in repressive political environments can facilitate contention. As such, this dynamic is situated between individual contention (Bayat 2013; Scott 1987) and collective contention (Tarrow 2011; McAdam et al. 2001). It bears some resemblance to "everyday resistance" in that aggrieved citizens take matters into their own hands to contest the status quo without resorting to collective defiance. To the casual observer, the participants in mobilizing without the masses resemble any number of self-inspired, atomized protestors seeking redress from the state. Yet beneath the surface, there exists an organization that is instrumental in inspiring such individual contention. This organizational element is similar to the dynamic of collective contention in that mobilizing vehicles play a key role in coaching contention. During the pedagogical process of mobilizing without the masses, activists construct diagnostic, prognostic, and motivational frames (Snow and Benford 1988) that encourage participants to identify themselves with a broader group of disadvantaged citizens. However, activists are careful to ensure that these collective frames ultimately do not translate into large-scale collective action. Instead, they coach participants to contain the scale of contention in the interest of minimizing political risk to the organization.

Empirically, mobilizing without the masses emerged from a close study of state repression and civil society contention in China. Contemporary China is an instructive case for examining the dynamics of organizing under duress because while the Party-led state has permitted the growth of civil society, it continues to repress organizational activism. For the most part, civil society organizations in China do not openly oppose the party-state or disrupt social stability on a large scale. For example, environmental NGOs have spearheaded an emergent "green civil society" movement with transnational ties and have successfully pushed for changes to China's environmental policies, but it is risky for them to openly challenge the state's policies on energy or the environment (Mertha 2008; Sun and Zhao 2008; Ho 2001). Likewise, citizen rights advocacy organizations and religious organizations also face periodic repression even when they do not explicitly mobilize participants to oppose the state's agenda. For example, authorities disbanded the Open Constitution Initiative in 2009, presumably because of its involvement in high-profile civil rights cases.[2] The ensuing "new citizens' movement" that was initiated by leaders of the disbanded Open Constitution Initiative was also subject to intense state harassment.[3] Similarly, the Beijing Women's Legal Aid and Research Center was disbanded in 2016 despite its leadership's decision to refrain from handling politically sensitive cases.[4] Likewise, underground Protestant churches that have largely restricted their activities to private home meetings also experience state harassment. The state continues to limit the organizational activity by pressuring landlords not to lease to religious organizations and by putting church leaders and members under house arrest (Vala 2012).

In this operating environment, aggrieved citizens have typically mobilized without the aid of formal organizations. This is reflected in a range of popular contention that has erupted in rural and urban areas alike, from peasants protesting land grabs (Heurlin 2016) to workers striking for higher pay to the middle-class advocating for environmental protection and food safety (Yasuda 2017: 15–16; Stern 2013: 8–9; Mertha 2008; Sun and Zhao 2008). Although these "mass incidents" have not yet forced the party-state into a crisis point (Slater and Wong 2013: 729–30), they have contributed to a level of social instability that is unnerving to the regime. More importantly, this surge of popular contention is characterized by a lack of organizational bases (Reny and Hurst 2013; Chen 2012: 9; Lee 2007b; Zhou 1993: 55). For example, "rightful resisters" cleverly use the language of the law to press for their legal rights as citizens, but they do so without the help of formal organizations (O'Brien and Li 2006). Under certain conditions, these "temporary communities" (Cai 2010: 16) of protestors have successfully won compensation from the state, in part due to their avoidance of formal mobilizing structures. In fact, having visible leaders in protests can increase the likelihood of repression, as the state knows which individuals to round up in order to demobilize contention.

Meanwhile, most civil society organizations stay in the relatively secure space of social services provision through partnering with local states (Howell 2015; Hsu and Hasmath 2014; Teets 2014; Hildebrandt 2013; Simon 2013; Lu 2009; Shieh 2009). Some NGOs even "beg to be co-opted" by the state

---

[2] *Economist*, Open Constitution Closed. July 25, 2009.

[3] A. Jacobs and C. Buckley, Chinese Activists Test New Leader and Are Crushed, January 15, 2014, *New York Times*.

[4] K. D. Tatlow, China Is Said to Force Closing of Women's Legal Aid Center, January 29, 2016, *New York Times*.

(Foster 2001) while others form a "contingent symbiosis" with the local state in which officials tolerate these organizations so long as they provide beneficial services and refrain from challenging social stability (Spires 2011). To the extent that organizations are engaged in advancing social change, they mainly do so through policy advocacy at local levels of government. Civil society's participation in policy debates in China has been analyzed through the lenses of "consultative authoritarianism" (Teets 2014), "authoritarian deliberation" (He and Warren 2011), and "policy entrepreneurship" (Mertha 2008). NGOs have forged alliances with local state agencies to push for environmental protection (Mertha 2008; Ho 2001), provide disaster relief (Teets 2012, 2009), defend the rights of sexual minorities (Hildebrandt 2013), and advocate for migrant workers (Spires 2011). This co-dependent relationship allows the government to reap the benefits of an active civil society while simultaneously allowing organizations to secure their survival and influence policy-making (Hildebrandt 2013; Spires 2011; Shieh 2009; Lu 2009). Whether providing social services or policy consultation, civil society organizations have proven themselves adept at working within the limits of China's authoritarian political system.

Yet, this study shows that Chinese civil society organizations can and do play a far more active role in shaping state–society relations than delivering social services and providing policy consultation. Under certain conditions, some grassroots organizations coach participants to make rights claims against the state. In turn, they are essentially engaged in a form of mobilization, defined as the process through which individuals are recruited and spurred to engage in contentious actions against the state. The next section examines the broader set of political conditions that make this form of mobilization possible.

CHINA'S ASSOCIATIONAL REVOLUTION

Since the 1990s, China has experienced an associational revolution in which civil society organizations have blossomed under the vigilance of the party-state (Teets 2014; Hildebrandt 2013; Dillon 2011; Howell 2003; Ho 2001; Gold 1998; Brook and Frolic 1997; White et al. 1996). During this period, as many as eight million formal and informal organizations surfaced (Wang and He 2004: 524).[5] This revolution has resulted in a pluralization of civil society organizations in a variety of sectors such as labor, environment, HIV/AIDS, and disaster relief, among others. It also represented a shift in state control from a strict corporatist system of regulation that permitted only state-run mass organizations to one that relied on indirect and variegated forms of control over civil society (Teets 2014: 70).

---

[5] Eight million is a higher bound estimate. The Ministry of Civil Affairs reports that in 2009, there were 400,000 registered social organizations and an estimated additional 2–3 million informal organizations registered as commercial enterprises.

This associational revolution stemmed from the party-state's goal of down-sizing the government and pluralizing civil society, expressed in the official slogan "small government, big society" (*xiaozhengfu, dashehui*). It unfolded as China was transitioning out of a command economy into a partially liberalized economy. Marketization also demanded parallel adjustments to the structure of governance, as the party-state sought to downsize the government and to make it more efficient. As the central state placed pressures on local states to innovate new models of governance to address the problems created by rapid economic growth, the latter turned to civil society for assistance in providing public goods and services (Teets 2014: 47). Thus, the push to pluralize civil society in the early 1990s reflected the party-state's desire to shift responsibil-ities for social welfare, economic development, and disaster relief to the private sector (Ma 2006: ch. 2).

In response, a plethora of social organizations emerged. Together with exist-ing social organizations, they can be located along a spectrum according to the degree of the threat they pose to the Chinese Communist party-state. The least threatening include state-run mass organizations such as the All-China Federation of Trade Unions (ACFTU) and the All-China Women's Federation (ACWF), which remain tethered to the state. Further down the spectrum is the panoply of social organizations, non-profits, and philanthropic foundations that often partner with local governments to improve the quality of governance through the provision of social services. The most extreme are organizations that threaten social stability either due to political goals such as advocating for democratization or human rights or due to their mobilizing tactics, which may involve coaching participants to deploy illegal means to advocate for their rights. In reality, civil society organizations may shift on this spectrum of con-tention in both directions. Organizations that are contentious at one point in time may become co-opted by the state and change their tactics and goals to be more accommodating. Conversely, organizations that enjoy synergistic relationships with the state may also transgress into disruptive politics as they develop, thus developing a more antagonistic relationship with the state.

This study recognizes the dynamic movement of civil society organizations along a continuum. However, for analytical purposes, it divides civil society organizations into two sectors: the aboveground and the underground sector. This approach captures the dynamic relationship between the state and the organization at a particular moment in time. The aboveground sector entails organizations that, at the time of analysis, do not directly threaten social sta-bility in their stated objectives and mobilizing tactics. These organizations are typically registered with the Bureau of Civil Affairs or with the Bureau of Commerce and partner with local states to deliver critical social services such as disaster relief, education, health provision, and environmental protection (Hildebrandt 2013; Lu 2009; Shieh 2009). Some organizations in this sector also have opportunities to serve as policy consultants on diverse issues related to local governance (Teets 2014; He and Warren 2011; Mertha 2008).

In contrast, the underground sector is composed of organizations that, at the moment of study, harbor goals beyond social services delivery and limited policy consultation. These include a wide range of organizations that threaten the party-state's legitimacy either because they engage in rights advocacy on behalf of marginalized populations or because they organize participants around principles or belief systems that challenge the party-state's ideologies. For example, organizations such as the New Citizens Group,[6] networks of human rights lawyers as well as certain legal aid and labor rights organizations, may be seen by the state to undermine social stability by encouraging vulnerable citizens to make rights claims. In addition, religious organizations such as informal Protestant churches and sects such as the Falun Gong may be seen to rally participants around belief systems that ultimately challenge the ideologies that the party-state propagates. Although these organizations largely refrain from directly mobilizing protests, their collective action potential is nevertheless problematic to the party-state.

Together, the emergence of these two sectors of civil society posed a dire governance dilemma for the party-state: how to foster civil society growth while simultaneously monitoring its potential to mobilize opposition? The party-state must walk a fine line between promoting organizations that can assist the state while keeping threatening organizations at bay (Howell 2012: 287). On the one hand, a vibrant civil society sector could assist the party-state in delivering social services to the population and allow the state to downsize the government.

On the other hand, an unbridled civil society could challenge state power, as the resurrection of civil society in Eastern Europe, Latin America, and elsewhere has shown (Alagappa 2004: 16; Ekiert and Kubik 2001; Bernhard 1993; O'Donnell and Schmitter 1986: ch. 5).[7] For a brief period during the 1989 Tiananmen Democracy Movement, Chinese civil society organizations faced off with the ruling Communist Party to demand liberal reforms (Nathan 2001; Wright 2001; Zhao 2001; Gold 1990). Among the civil society groups was the Beijing Workers' Autonomous Federation, which, in the week leading up to June 4, mobilized 150 activists to Tiananmen Square and also issued calls for a general strike which went unanswered (Walder and Gong 1993). Although the scale of this independent workers' organization was miniscule compared to the Polish Solidarity Trade Union, it represented a "new species of political protest" in that it fit neither with the factional mobilization model in the 1970s nor with the traditional model of intellectual dissidents (Walter and Gong 1993: 3–4). The 1989 democracy movement alarmed the party-state because organizations implicitly

---

[6] The New Citizens Group was formerly known as the Open Constitution Initiative or *Gongmeng*.
[7] While this study examines the rise of social organizations in China, it does not argue that the rise of civil society is the only or necessarily the most important factor that contributes to political change in authoritarian regimes.

challenged the state's monopoly on defining and solving social and political problems (Manion 1990). While the party-state successfully demobilized the Tiananmen protestors with infamous crackdown on June 4, 1989, it remained all too aware that it must carefully balance the need for civil society against the threat that it poses to illiberal state power.

Traditionally, the party-state has governed civil society through a state corporatist system of regulation, which limited the types of organizations that were legally permitted (Economy 2004; Pearson 1997; Unger and Chan 1995; Whiting 1991). Ironically, the Chinese state's embrace of state corporatism in the 1980s reflected a gradual "relaxing" of control from a party system that previously dominated society directly via state institutions (Unger and Chan 1995: 39). In what has been called a "state-led civil society," the Chinese state controlled society not through direct domination but through a disciplined and unequal partnership with civic organizations (Frolic 1997:58).

Although the corporatist regulatory structures remained throughout the 2000s, there was also a high degree of informality as well as local variations in terms of governing civil society organizations. For example, the party-state actively encouraged local states to experiment with relaxing the registration requirements for certain types of social organizations (Simon 2013). In keeping with its tradition of "guerrilla policy-making" (Heilmann and Perry 2011), at least four municipalities or cities including Beijing, Changsha, Foshan, and Guangzhou have spearheaded reforms aimed at the "one-stop registration" of civil society organizations (Simon 2013: 316). In addition, local states often relied on informal and erratic practices of policing civil society organizations that crossed the line of political acceptability. Local bureaus of civil affairs periodically launched "rectification campaigns" to de-register certain organizations based on parochial political goals. In contrast to abiding by a rigid corporatist system, the party-state actively experimented with versatile approaches to controlling civil society.

FLEXIBLE REPRESSION OF CIVIL SOCIETY

Part I of this book argues that under the Hu Jintao administration (2003–13), the party-state adopted "flexible repression" to govern civil society, which provided the opportunities for mobilizing without the masses to emerge. This type of state control permitted civil society groups to operate with a degree of maneuverability so long as these same groups did not directly mobilize collective contention. Flexible repression was part of a broader adaptive governance style that characterized the Chinese political system. Since the end of the Mao era (1949–76), the party-state has embraced a style of governance that emphasizes adaptability and agility. Instead of abiding by formal regulations and policies, the party-state encouraged political actors of all ranks and especially in the localities to experiment with innovative ways of managing society (Heilmann and Perry 2011: 9).

Three main features characterized flexible repression: decentralization, improvisation, and fragmentation. First, flexible repression entailed the decentralization of control. The central state gave considerable discretion to local states to experiment with policies governing civil society, so long as they aligned with the central state's broad mandate to maintain social stability. Decentralization was an enduring tradition of Chinese governance under the Chinese Communist Party (Landry 2008). While strategic decisions were reserved for the top leadership, the implementation and operationalization of these decisions were left to local leaders (Heilmann and Perry 2011: 13). In governing civil society, local authorities had a wide degree of latitude when deciding which organizations should be permitted to register, which should be tacitly tolerated, and which should be disbanded.

The second feature of flexible repression was improvisation. Local state actors did not necessarily follow a tightly scripted set of procedures in governing civil society groups. Instead, they adapted their repertoire of control to specific situations. In the absence of clear "rules of the game," local state agents combined a diverse range of hard and soft control tools to keep organizations in check. Furthermore, they relied not only on the security apparatus but also on other bureaucratic and societal actors including gangsters, landlords, and officials to pressure organizations into compliance (Deng and O'Brien 2013; Lee and Zhang 2013). Together, this heterogeneous network of actors devised the specific practices of control. This decentralization of control was in keeping with the central state's "guerrilla policy style," which encouraged "diverse and flexible responses" to domestic challenges (Heilmann and Perry 2011: 22–3).

Finally, flexible repression was characterized by fragmentation across different agencies within a single local state. Because the local state is composed of different agencies with competing agendas, inter-agency conflict arose over how to effectively control civil society organizations. These conflicts directly influenced how control was carried out. Working at cross-purposes, various agencies working within a single local state pursued contradictory strategies.

These three features of flexible repression were manifested in the specific practices of state control, which entailed constraining underground organizations' mobilization capacity while channeling aboveground organizations into social services delivery. Unlike their aboveground counterparts, underground organizations were much more difficult to govern through institutionalized channels. In practice, the state exercised fragmented control to govern groups that threatened social stability. "Fragmented control" highlights local states' horizontal fragmentation within a single administrative level into a myriad of agencies with different bureaucratic mandates (Chapter 3). Although every agency had an incentive to maintain social stability, local state agencies interpreted and operationalized this broad mandate differently. Driven by varying bureaucratic missions, agencies within the local state pursued divergent control tactics. Where one would have expected the local state to be united in repressing underground groups, certain government agencies attempted to co-opt potentially threatening groups while others actively repressed or neglected them. Fragmented control, in turn, shaped the mobilizing strategies of underground organizations by creating political opportunities for activists to mobilize outside of legal channels in a process that I call "censored entrepreneurialism."

In turn, the state exercised "competitive control" over the aboveground sector of civil society organizations – those that provided social services and did not typically threaten social stability (Chapter 4). In accordance with the broad political objective to outsource some social services to "society," local states created markets for sub-contracting social services delivery to particular organizations. Different state agencies and Party organs competed for control over these markets and the regulatory power to manage organizations. Because the central party-state did not necessarily delineate the specific division of labor between different agencies and Party organs, local state actors clashed over new methods and regulations of managing civil society. In response to competitive control, civil society organizations that partnered with one state agency were more likely to accrue political legitimacy with other agencies. For example, partnering with the Bureau of Civil Affairs in Beijing sent political signals to the same bureau in other localities that the organization in question was politically "safe" to collaborate with. This triggered a "cascade effect" in terms of gaining political legitimacy, allowing the organization to expand its operations to different cities with the explicit approval of local state officials. Fragmented control and competitive control together constituted the broader operating environment for mobilizing without the masses.

BETWEEN COLLECTIVE AND INDIVIDUAL CONTENTION

Mobilizing without the masses provides a pathway to political agency for activists and participants of civil society organizations that is situated in between collective and individual contention. On the one hand, this dynamic departs from collective contention because its goal is not to coordinate mass protests or demonstrations. Rather, organizations participate behind the scenes by coordinating *non-collective* contention in the form of coaching individual workers to threaten social stability or by organizing small-scale contention such as flash demonstrations. At the same time, this dynamic also departs from individual contention because organizational vehicles are actively involved in directing these acts of contention. Moreover, it makes use of a repertoire of individual action that is far more confrontational and public than that of "everyday resistance" (Scott 1987). As such, mobilizing without the masses falls within the ecosystem of "boundary-spanning contention" (O'Brien 2003) that straddles the border between transgressive and contained actions (Figure 1.1).

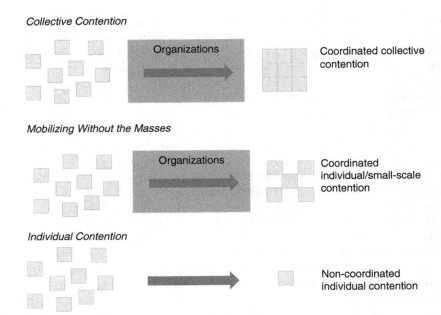

FIGURE 1.1 Comparing dynamics of contention

The Dynamic of Collective Contention

Mobilizing without the masses is situated in between two familiar modes of contention: collective contention and individual contention. In the "dynamics of contention" framework, collective action is the ultimate aim of mobilization (Tilly and Tarrow 2015; Tarrow 2011; McAdam et al. 2001). This focus on collective action is expressed in the definition of contentious politics: "discontinuous, public *collective* claim making in which one of the parties is a government" (McAdam et al. 2001: 9, emphasis added). This definition emerged from the study of social movements in which the mobilizing process culminates in collective action by both challengers and their opponents. To achieve their goals, challengers either create new organizational vehicles or appropriate and transform existing vehicles into instruments of contention. The mobilization process is set in motion when challengers perceive an opportunity or a threat and begin to press for change (McAdam et al. 2001: 45). Each link in the mobilizing process builds towards a moment of climactic collective action – an iterative exchange between challengers and opponents that disrupts status quo politics. In this model, tactical innovations – protests, demonstrations, petition drives, or boycotts – by challengers are by nature collective acts that offset their lack of institutionalized power (McAdam 1983: 735). Contentious activities peak at moments of tactical innovation and ebb when the opposition (the state) adopts successful counter-tactics (McAdam 1983).

In this dynamic, mobilizing structures are the ties that bind movement participants together. Mobilizing structures include meso-level groups, informal networks, and professional social movement organizations (Zald and McCarthy 1987: 23). Given the right set of structural opportunities, challengers can appropriate existing organizations that were not originally intended to be used for contention and transform them into instruments of social movements that serve several major functions. For example, these organizations may play a key role in amassing the human, material, and cognitive resources needed for mobilizing sustained collective action. Mobilizing structures facilitate the "bloc recruitment" of participants into the movement (McAdam 1982: 129). They also furnish leaders with the communication networks necessary for disseminating tactics and growing the movement beyond its local origins. Mobilizing structures then re-define the collective identities of movement participants in accordance with the movement's goals (McAdam et al. 2001). Organizers construct collective identities and provide motivation for collective action by building frames, which is generally understood to be interpretations of the struggle and of possible solution (Snow 2013; Benford and Snow 2000: 232; Gamson 1975). Once participants come to identify themselves as the constituents of a group with a common goal, they are more likely to engage in collective action. Finally, mobilizing structures are also laboratories for devising and disseminating tactical innovations. For example, in the American civil rights movement of the 1950s and 1960s, three key institutions – black churches, black colleges, and the southern wing of the North American Association for the Advancement of Colored People (NAACP) – were critical in disseminating then-novel tactics such as lunch counter sit-ins, freedom rides, and bus boycotts (McAdam 1983).

In authoritarian settings, informal networks can substitute for formal mobilizing structures (Beinin and Vairel 2011; Wiktorowicz 2003; Denoeux 1993). In the dense urban settings of Egypt, informal ties essentially form an "organizational grid ... a type of associational life that remains outside of the surveillance of the state" (Singerman 2004: 156). Among left-wing groups in Italy, kinship and friendship ties were critical to recruitment into networks carrying out political violence (Della Porta 1995: 167–8). Similarly, informal networks including kinship, friendship, religious and social ties have played a key role in facilitating collective action in China. For example, informal networks facilitated student activism during the 1989 Democracy Movement (Wright 2001; Zhou 1993) as well as workers' protests (Becker 2012; Hurst 2009; Lee 2007b) and church recruitment (Vala and O'Brien 2008). Virtual informal networks created by online chat rooms and social media also served as a mobilizing vehicle (Yang 2009). Regardless of the type of network, the primary purpose of mobilizing structures is assumed to be facilitating collective action. Moreover, collective action can be considered a part of a broader social movement process to the extent that it "challenges the behavior or the legitimacy of specific social or political actors, not of single individuals" (Diani and Bison 2004).

The power to effect social and political change derives from the disruption created by sustained collective action. Defined as "the application of a negative sanction [or] the withdrawal of a crucial contribution on which others depend" (Piven and Cloward 1979: 24–5), disruptive collective action can take the form of blockades, sit-ins, and strikes which can be an explosive source of power because they reinforce solidarity among demonstrators, obstruct the daily routine of opponents, and broaden the conflict (Tarrow 2011: 99–105). However, disruptive collective action alone is insufficient to effect long-term political change; such action must be sustained. This can be challenging because activists may eventually be absorbed into conventional politics while participants may defect from the movement or become demobilized by state repression (Tarrow 2011: 104–5). Alternatively, organizations that are established to sustain a movement may also paradoxically become impediments to advancing social movement goals as they succumb to what Robert Michels famously termed "the iron law of oligarchy" (Michels 1911). Large bureaucratic organizations can get in the way of organizing disruptive politics, thus becoming a hindrance to the continuation of collective contention (Piven and Cloward 1978). The discontinuation of all forms of collective action, either due to repression or due to the inability of the movement to sustain momentum, is seen as a failure of mobilization, leading social movements to "evaporate" into individual resistance (Tarrow 2011: 12). To summarize, in the dynamic of collective contention, mobilizing structures – whether in the form of organizations or informal networks – can enable disruptive collective action.[8]

The Dynamic of Individual Contention

In contrast, studies of contention in authoritarian states shed light on a wholly different dynamic of individual contention (Bayat 2013; Rev 1987; Scott 1985). Perhaps the most renowned conception of individual contention is James Scott's "weapons of the weak" – "a repertoire of individual acts ranging from foot dragging, dissimulation, desertion, false compliance, pilfering, feigned ignorance, slander, arson, sabotage" (Scott 1985: preface, xvi). Driven by the most basic need to survive, the oppressed draw upon a repertoire of individual contention to thwart their oppressors without assembling en masse and without challenging the symbolic class structures in society (Scott 1987; 1985). In this dynamic, there is no need for organizations because actions are taken in informal, non-institutionalized settings. Furthermore, because the immediate goal of everyday resisters is to improve their own livelihoods rather than to challenge the structural conditions of oppression, resisters do not need organizations to

---

[8] This is of course not always the case. Scholars such as Piven and Cloward (1978) have argued that mobilizing structures such as formal organizations may prevent disruptive collective action. In any case, the analytical focus of social movement literature is on whether or not mobilizing structures facilitate *collective* action.

mobilize them (Scott 1985). Due to this individualistic nature, participants do not confront the types of collective action problems faced by those in conventional social movements (Olson 1965). The possibility for free riding is minimal, as each contender reaps individual rather than collective rewards. While these individual actions may over time produce an accumulated effect that may trigger wider social change, these individual contenders do not explicitly coordinate their actions in order to mobilize for the purposes of attaining a shared goal.

Bypassing formal organizations is also a feature of the "social non-movements" observed in the urban areas of the Middle East (Bayat 2013). In polities where the state limits the scope and type of organizational life, citizens resort to a set of "collective practices by non-collective actors … *rarely guided by an ideology or recognizable leadership and organizations*" (Bayat 2013: 15; emphasis added). These may include illegally tapping into the electricity grid, street vending, squatting, and other such informal activities that are not explicitly sanctioned by the state. For example, when rural migrants become urban squatters in Cairo and Istanbul, they do so without necessarily consulting each other and also without apparent leadership (Bayat 2013: 16). Instead, each actor decides to occupy land out of their own initiative and to meet their own needs of survival. Because actors do not explicitly identify themselves as sharing a common goal with like-minded individuals, they do not see the need to make use of organizing vehicles. The absence of an organization enables participants to dodge state crackdowns on urban activism as it becomes more difficult for the state to identify and punish contenders (Bayat 2013: 23).

Passive networks (Bayat 2013) play a pivotal role in forging a sense of common identity among urbanites participating in social non-movements. However, these passive networks differ from organizations in that they do not pull bystanders into the conflict, nor do they actively coordinate contention. These networks have been conceived as "instantaneous communications between atomized individuals, which are established by tacit recognition of their commonalities directly in public spaces or indirectly through mass media" (Bayat 2013: 23). Individuals recognize each other's similar social positions through noticing "similar hairstyles, blue jeans, hang-out places, food, fashions, and the pursuit of public fun" (Bayat 2013: 19). This mutual recognition, for example, between contenders engaged in the same act of street vending in urban slums, enables them to form common identities.

The power of individual contention derives from the aggregation of atomized acts over time. In his study of Hungarian peasants resisting the centralized agricultural production, Istavan Rev argued that the advantages of being atomized included a tacit and shared understanding between individuals that they were not completely isolated, despite not having a formal organizational structure:

They were atomized, but not completely lonely. They knew that they were part of a secret mass of more than two million. They knew that even the apparatus joined them secretly, that individual officials hoped that the peasants' resistance would provide the necessary alibi for their survival. There were government agents, secret police, military in the villages, too. But the peasants had their own language of gestures, which was common to all; it was not necessary to ask questions, since the discourse referred to immediate, concrete things. They just lived their lives and their way of living gradually changed the political system around them.

(Rev 1987: 348)

The combined power of millions of peasants acting on their own accord to hide produce from central state collectors resulted in systemic changes as the state had to accommodate peasant resistance. Rev saw the Hungarian peasants as taking part in what Charles Tilly called a "reactive form of collective action" (Tilly 1976: 369, cited in Rev 1987: 343–4).[9] In other words, Hungarian peasants' power was found in their prolonged, uncoordinated but extensive atomized actions that inadvertently pulled local state officials into their web of resistance and dissimulation (Rev 1987: 339).[10]

Examining urban dwellers' resistance in the contemporary Middle East, Asef Bayat makes a similar argument that the cumulative effect of everyday action results in social change when there is a certain threshold of people engaged in the same acts of "quiet encroachment" (2013: ch. 2). The power to bring about social change accumulates through disparate individuals performing ordinary acts of transgression over a long period of time (2013: 22). Similarly, in "weapons of the weak," power also comes from the aggregation of small acts such as foot-dragging, sabotage, arson, petty theft, and others (Scott 1987: xvi). To borrow James Scott's analogy, "just as millions of anthozoan polyps create, willy nilly, a coral reef, so do thousands of individual acts of insubordination and evasion create a political and economic barrier reef of their own" (Scott 1987: 422). The power of individual contention lies not in its explosiveness but in its ability to change the status quo through the accumulated effect of minute acts.

Beyond weapons of the weak and social non-movements, structural constraints in many authoritarian states limit the scope and forms of mobilization. When collective action does erupt, it often appears as "flashes in the pan" rather than as sustained social movements. In these polities, mobilization can take on self-limiting forms (Beinin and Vairel 2011). In communist Eastern Europe, citizens devised "oppositional speech acts" against authorities,

---

[9] According to Tilly, a reactive collective action is defined as "group efforts to reassert established claims when someone else challenges or violates them" (1976: 367).

[10] Local state officials in Hungary contributed to peasant resistance by turning a blind eye to their illegal behaviors of withholding produce from the central state. Officials also abetted peasants in selling their produce on the black market and falsified information in their reports of local production to superiors, all with the goal of maintaining their own survival in the system (Rev 1987: 339).

including political graffiti, hit-and-run protests, joke-telling, and making comments about or critiques of the regime in private spheres (Johnston 2005: 108–34; 2006). In Syria under the regime of President Hafiz al-Asad (1971–2000), citizens used underground short stories, jokes, cartoons, and other such popular media to subvert the regime's symbolic and rhetorical power (Wedeen 1999: 25).

In China, where the party-state forbids independent collective organizing (Zhou 1993: 55; Walder 1986: 19),[11] citizens have long learned to contend without organizations, instead devising creative forms of individual contention. For example, between 1978 and 1989, Chinese peasants who pushed for de-collectivization of farmland had few available organizational resources apart from the Chinese Communist Party. According to Daniel Kelliher, "Most alternative organizations were suppressed, surviving only underground or behind closed doors of private homes. Peasants were left standing alone to face the new state they had brought to power" (1992: 22). Consequently, millions of peasants defied state policies by de-collectivizing agricultural production through individual actions such as bribing officials to permit an individual family to farm land (Zhou 1996). These practices gained traction as peasants across the country began to adopt them, eventually creating a bottom-up push for de-collectivization (Zhou 1996; Kelliher 1992). In addition, aggrieved citizens have also repurposed official institutions such as the petitioning system to press for claims as individuals (X. Chen 2008). Increasingly, the party-state has channeled citizens (particularly workers) away from the petitioning system into settling disputes through the legal system (Gallagher 2007). However, given the continued restrictions on collective contention outside of the official trade union and the repression of NGOs and law firms that facilitate activism, workers have resorted to individual legal mobilization according to the labor dispute system (Gallagher 2014). In some cases, they have also resorted to taking extreme actions including self-directed or other-directed violence aimed at garnering the attention of the media and the public which, in turn, place pressure on authorities to respond (Gallagher 2014). Finally, aggrieved individuals have also turned to collective inaction such as absenteeism or inefficiency at the workplace, evasion of public duties, and expressing lack of enthusiasm for state-initiated campaigns (Zhou 1993: 66). Others have devised creative means of expression such as posting traditional rhyming couplets at the entrance of their homes that satirize the Communist Party (Thornton 2002) and posting online critiques of authorities (King et al. 2013; Yang 2009). All of these forms of individual contention bypass the need for formal organizational vehicles.

---

[11] In his study of work and authority in Chinese industry, Walder (1986: 19) argued that a defining feature of communist regimes is their "extra-ordinary ability to prevent organized political activity even from reaching the stage of collective action."

Dynamic of Mobilizing Without the Masses

Mobilizing without the masses is situated between the dynamics of collective and individual contention. It begins with individuals who share a common grievance; despite repeatedly seeking redress from the state and from employers, they are thwarted at every turn. However, instead of deploying individual resistance, the aggrieved turn to civil society organizations for assistance in making claims for legally guaranteed rights. Within these organizations, leaders assemble the aggrieved individuals and reframe their individual complaints into a problem shared by millions of their brethren. By bringing participants face-to-face with similarly disadvantaged individuals, organizers construct a collective identity as citizens of a polity that has denied them their legal rights. Recognizing the high risks to mobilizing en masse, activists coach participants to contend individually or as a small group. Thus, while the organizational process frames a collective problem and fosters collective identity, the contentious action is individualistic.

Participants are taught to deploy a repertoire of contentious performances against state officials or employers. According to Charles Tilly, "participants in contentious politics learn, follow, and innovate within rough scripts for claim-making" (Tilly 2008: 201). However, whereas Tilly's analytical focus is on the range of contentious performances that make up *collective* contention, mobilizing without the masses highlights individualistic contentious performances. In the context of contemporary China, organizers train individuals to adopt a repertoire of contentious performances including but not limited to verbally threatening state officials; contacting journalists with their grievances; staging sit-ins at government offices; holding flash demonstrations; and, in extreme cases, threatening to commit suicide in a public space. In contrast to the weapons of the weak (Scott 1985) and "social non-movements" (Bayat 2013), which silently eat away at structures of power, the performances of mobilizing without the masses are purposefully loud and public. Despite the fact that the contenders act alone or in small groups, their purpose is to attract bystanders and to encourage media coverage of their performances.

In mobilizing without the masses, the power to effect change derives from threatening the political incentives of otherwise unresponsive authorities and from the pedagogical process of training citizens to engage in individual contention. One might suspect that a single individual's contentious performance lacks the disruptive power that comes from collective action. However, individual contention can be powerful when it threatens the interests of authorities. In the context of contemporary China, the power to change state officials' behaviors comes from threatening a key bureaucratic incentive to maintain social stability. The "one veto rule" (*yipiao fojue*) stipulates that any outbreak of "mass incidents" (*quntixing shijian*) or collective contention would negatively affect the evaluation of local cadres, who are expected to maintain social stability in their jurisdiction (Wang and Minzner 2015; Sun et al. 2010). In other words, local leaders are incentivized to settle threats to social stability as quickly as possible. Because local bureaucrats' performances are evaluated based on their ability to keep order in their jurisdiction, this mandate can be a powerful weapon for citizens. In mobilizing without the masses, activists coach individuals to stage contentious performances such as performances of suicide ("suicide shows") or flash protests that directly threaten social stability. As a result, even though the contender may be an individual, they can induce authorities to address their claims by threatening local social order. Fearing that the scale of social disruption may grow when it is covered by the media, state officials are incentivized to respond to a citizen's demands.

Mobilizing without the masses also derives power from the pedagogical process itself, which fosters collective consciousness through constructing frames – shared interpretations of a problem and of a solution (Benford and Snow 2000). When activists teach participants to engage in acts of individual contention, they are simultaneously reframing individual grievances as part of broader common problems shared by millions of others. Snow and Benford (1988) divide core framing tasks into three types: diagnostic framing; prognostic framing; and motivational framing. In terms of diagnostic frames, activists encourage participants to attribute their problems to such structural factors as the collusion between business and the state, lax implementation of laws, and the state policies that contribute to socio-economic inequality. In terms of prognostic and motivational frames, activists narrate cases of successful contention in order to inspire their participants to confront power-holders in similar ways. Through the pedagogical process, participants begin to identify as citizens with equal rights to healthcare, labor protection, and social security. They learn to claim their rights as equal citizens in a polity with unelected political leaders, weak legal institutions, and a government mired in corruption.

This transformation in citizenship consciousness is especially important in China. Since imperial times, social citizenship – the protection of the basic right to subsistence – has been the cornerstone of the Chinese state's legitimacy (Perry 2008; Perry and Goldman 2007). In post-reform China (1979–present), the party-state has championed lifting hundreds of millions out of poverty as its primary achievement. Yet the state has not been able to provide equal social citizenship to a variety of groups. Among them are the hundreds of millions of migrant workers who suffer social exclusion under China's national household registration system. In this context, civil society organizations play a critical role in teaching migrant workers to demand the right to *equitable* distribution of social and economic resources. Importantly, this claim goes beyond the right to a basic level of subsistence. Activists teach rural citizens that they should enjoy the same rights as urban citizens and that the poor should be treated by the state the same way as the rich. Thus, although mobilizing without the masses may be individualistic in terms of the contentious action, its ambitions can be as broad as changing participants' grammar of contention so that they demand rights as equal citizens rather than as subjects of a benevolent authoritarian state.

TACTICAL INNOVATION

Under flexible repression, civil society organizations in China devised three tactics: the pedagogy of micro-collective action; the pedagogy of atomized action; and the pedagogy of discursive action. All three fall under the broader dynamic of mobilizing without the masses. They emerged from activists' experimentation with different methods of rights advocacy that reduces organizational risk but still facilitates rights claims. They can be placed on a continuum from most to least risky for both the organization and its participants. In the pedagogy of micro-collective action, the riskiest of the three, activists organize small bands of citizens to engage in flash demonstrations which are limited in scale and duration. Because these tactics pose an immediate, public threat to social stability, they often result in organizational closure or the harassment of activists involved. During the pedagogical process, activists coach participants to attribute their grievances to broader structural factors such as the state's collusion with business interests. At the same time, activists construct motivational frames that provide participants with the rationale for taking collective action. The combination of diagnostic and motivational frames inspires participants to stage small-scale collective action, which involves only a handful of contenders. The distinguishing characteristic of micro-collective action is its symbolic nature; participants' primary aim is not to extract specific concessions from the state but to demonstrate that it is possible to act in solidarity for a common cause.

The pedagogy of atomized action, the second riskiest tactic, involves training individuals to threaten state officials with the possibility of disrupting social order should the latter continue to delay or prevent redress for the aggrieved contender. This tactic can win concrete gains for participants while building their collective consciousness of belonging to a broader population who share similar grievances and obstacles in seeking redress. While the collective element of organizing takes place at the headquarters of the organization, it is by no means the heart of the contentious process. It is atomized action – suicide shows, sit-ins, soliciting media coverage, stalking factory bosses – that induces bureaucrats to respond. Atomized action brings aggrieved and powerless citizens face-to-face with authorities in highly dramatic, unpredictable, and individual encounters.

Atomized action resembles weapons of the weak in that it uses individualistic action to thwart the aims of the powerful (Scott 1985). However, unlike weapons of the weak, there is a clear organizational element: groups coach citizens on the timing, tactics, and proper execution of contention. This collective coaching is hidden behind a façade of individual contention, thereby constituting a type of "disguised collective action" (Fu 2017a). Moreover, in contrast to the hidden, quiet nature of the weapons of the weak, the success of atomized action hinges on the loud and public communication of credible threats. These atomized contentious performances threaten to undermine social stability.

Whereas state security agents frequently target organizations that coordinate collective action, those organizations that promote the pedagogy of atomized action avoid the harshest repressive measures.

Finally, the pedagogy of discursive action is the least risky tactic because activists construct a counter-narrative of their participants as "new citizens" (*xin gongmin*) without threatening social stability directly. Making use of didactic drama, poetry, and music, activists deploy cultural mobilization to assert the identity of their participants as equal citizens. In the context of migrant workers in China, this counter-discourse is particularly important because official and popular discourses describe migrant workers as "peasant workers" whose rural household registration status does not entitle them to enjoy equal rights as urbanites. Furthermore, migrant workers are depicted as lacking in civility and in education and are thus culturally marginalized. In the face of such institutional and cultural discrimination, activists coach participants to contend by adopting a counter-discourse that affirms their status as equal citizens. Through visual art, performance pieces, essays, and other modes of artistic expression, these activists subvert dominant narratives concerning marginalized subjects and encourage migrant workers to think of themselves as entitled to the same social and political rights as their urban counterparts. In contrast to the two previous tactics, activists also attempt to influence the discourse of government officials and the wider public on migrant workers. They do so through a grammar of persuasion, rather than threatening social stability. By forging strategic partnerships with critical political insiders – government officials, journalists, and scholars – activists attempt to change the dominant discourses surrounding migrant workers and to generate debates regarding the merits of migrant workers' associations. If successfully established, these synergistic partnerships permit activists to amplify their claims for equal citizenship to the state and the broader public.

LABOR ORGANIZATIONS IN CHINA

This study is based on ethnographic research inside labor organizations in China which formed in the early 1990s and late 2000s to advocate for the rights of one of China's largest disadvantaged populations: 270 million migrant workers who inundated large metropolises in search of economic opportunities.[12] The founders were largely migrant workers with limited formal education who

[12] This study draws upon 18 months of participant observation inside labor organizations in China and 123 interviews with multiple stakeholders. As a participant observer, I accompanied workers to the sites of their confrontations with the authorities, including labor bureaus and courtrooms. This allowed me to observe first-hand worker interaction with various state actors and to analyze state actors' reactions to workers' rights claims. I attended meetings and conferences in which activists networked with sympathetic local officials. I observed the daily activities of each studied organization, including recruitment trips to nearby hospitals, legal consultations with workers, and workshops in which activists coached participants on contentious tactics.

helped other workers defend their labor rights through the legal system. Due to the difficulty of registering as a social organization, the majority of these migrant worker organizations either registered as commercial businesses or remained unregistered. Similar to what has happened to the worker centers that emerged in the 1970s in the United States to organize immigrant workers (Fine 2006; Gordon 2005), these labor organizations are based within the migrant communities where these workers live. This allowed them to reach skilled and unskilled workers employed in various factories and from diverse backgrounds. Many organizations sought to provide practical assistance to members, such as legal aid, childcare, libraries, and employment skills training. They were organizationally structured like NGOs in that they had a distinct leadership hierarchy and received their funding from foreign foundations. Moreover, they did not typically provide monetary assistance or insurance to worker-participants.

These organizations sought to address two types of injustices that migrant workers faced: labor exploitation in the form of a range of workplace abuses (Lee 2007a; Pun 2005; A. Chan 2001) as well as institutionalized discrimination in the form of the household registration system (K. W. Chan 2010; Solinger 1999; Wallace 2014). In assisting workers on issues related to exploitation – wages, contracts, work hours, industrial injuries, and managerial abuses – these organizations provided pro bono legal consultation and representation. They coached workers to navigate the official labor dispute system, which was often inefficient and failed to protect workers' rights as stipulated by the 2008 Labor Contract Law.

Labor organizations also aimed to address a second problem that migrant workers faced – the household registration system (*hukou*) which institutionally excludes those with rural registration from enjoying equal access to urban social services and public goods. This system, which has been compared to South Africa's system of apartheid (Alexander and Chan 2004), is a state institution that restricts and regulates the mobility of peasants from rural to urban China. It systematically discriminates against migrants by depriving them of the right to permanently reside in the cities. Consequently, migrant workers cannot enroll their children in urban schools, nor can they access equal opportunities for employment, healthcare, housing, and other such social services. The *hukou* system effectively relegates migrants to the status of second-class citizens and bars them from rights to the city (K. W. Chan 2010; Wallace 2014). In response, grassroots labor organizations have advocated for *hukou* reform, calling on policy-makers to revise current regulations in order to guarantee migrant workers equal access to urban social services. Such advocacy has become ever more pressing in light of an estimated additional 350 million

I also conducted 123 interviews with activists, workers, scholars, officials, lawyers, journalists, and enterprise representatives. See the Appendix for an extended discussion of data and methods.

rural residents who are expected to migrate to cities across China by 2050, which would create further migrant demands for access to urban public goods and social services.[13]

The Chinese party-state is wary of labor organizations for at least three reasons: their advocacy of labor rights; their mobilizing tactics; and their funding sources. First, labor organizations advocate for the rights of workers, an important constituency of the Chinese Communist Party. Grassroots labor organizations symbolically challenge the ACFTU monopoly on representing the proletariat. Second, while some labor organizations advocate for migrant workers' rights through legal channels – offering legal consultation and representation – others coach disgruntled workers to disrupt social stability. This is important because preserving social stability is a key pillar of the Chinese regime's legitimacy. On the surface, activists provide a range of non-threatening social services. Yet, they also surreptitiously mobilize the poor and marginalized to engage in individual action or small-scale collective action. Finally, many of these organizations' funding comes from foreign organizations, which further raises the Chinese government's suspicions that "hostile international forces" are infiltrating domestic civil society groups in order to facilitate anti-state resistance movements. For these reasons, the party-state has sought to contain the growth of labor organizations and limit their mobilization potential. Under these conditions, activists are pressed to devise tactical innovations.

BOOK PREVIEW

Part I of the book examines the broader institutional environment for mobilizing without the masses. Chapter 2 explains the structural conditions that gave rise to informal labor organizations in the broader context of China's associational revolution. It presents the distribution of informal labor organizations nationally and distinguishes between aboveground and underground sectors. It also compares the two largest clusters of labor organizations: those in Beijing and those in the Pearl River Delta. Chapter 3 examines the strategy of fragmented control deployed by local agencies to govern underground civil society. Contrary to the widely held assumption that state and underground civil society must necessarily engage in a zero-sum struggle, the Chinese party-state permits the simultaneous occurrence of both synergistic and antagonistic interactions. The outcome of these interactions is that these underground organizations engage in "censored entrepreneurialism" – a combination of self-censorship and bargaining for survival and resources. Chapter 4 turns to the strategy of competitive control deployed by local agencies to govern aboveground organizations that do not pose an immediate threat to the social stability. Competitive control encourages synergistic interactions between state and society, which conform to the logic of a competitive market.

[13] J. Woetzel et al., *Preparing for China's Urban Billion*, McKinsey Global Institute, 2009.

Part II of the book delves into the tactics of mobilizing without the masses. The preface situates these tactics in the broader theoretical framework of the relationship between repression and mobilization. Chapter 5 analyzes micro-collective action, which attempts to inspire participants to take symbolic action demonstrating their solidarity to the state and to opponents. Chapter 6 examines atomized action, a tactic that lowers the organization's risk of being repressed by the state. Chapter 7 examines the final tactical innovation, discursive action, which refrains from threatening social stability in favor of cultural mobilization and persuading state officials to permit the freedom of association. Combined, these chapters illustrate both the organizational and participant outcomes of these alternative tactics of mobilization.

The conclusion discusses whether mobilizing without the masses is a form of political compromise with the state. It argues that such a dynamic is both a product of state repression as well as a genuine form of mobilization that transgresses certain political boundaries, albeit not necessarily through direct confrontation. It also illustrates how features of this dynamic are reflected in other contentious sectors of Chinese civil society and the possibilities for discovering this dynamic in authoritarian states elsewhere. Ultimately, mobilizing without the masses demonstrates that the meeting of two weak actors – vulnerable organizations and marginalized citizens – can shape the very grammar with which citizens demand their rights from officials in authoritarian states.

Part I of this book builds upon and extends these theories by taking a disaggregated approach to examining everyday state control over civil society in China. Such a bottom-up perspective is important because very rarely does the central blueprint for state control translate into local implementation exactly as the rulers intended. This is especially true in a decentralized authoritarian state like China where central mandates are purposefully left ambiguous to allow for local states' flexible implementation (Heilmann and Perry 2011). In such a context, the analysis of the repression–mobilization nexus must take into account the diverse range of local actors – including bureaucratic agencies whose primary charge is not policing – that improvise state control. Moreover, horizontally disaggregating state actors across the same administrative level enables one to trace the origins of certain control tactics to a particular state bureau. It also helps to explain why the local state appears to be working at cross-purposes to coopt or contain or even facilitate grassroots activism. The micro-politics of repression on the ground also reveal the interactions between the actors carrying out coercion and activists in everyday settings – inside courtrooms, teahouses, and bureaucrats' offices. Although less dramatic than encounters between the riot police and protestors or between the military and demonstrators, these interactions nevertheless shape activists' perceptions of the boundaries of permissibility. This, in turn, translates into adaptive mobilization.

Chapter 2 presents the landscape of labor organizations in China, explains their emergence, and analyzes their regional variations. Chapters 3 and 4 examine the political environment in which these organizations operate. As discussed in the introductory chapter, China's party-state has adopted a strategy of flexible repression over civil society that seeks to foster the growth of obedient civil society organizations while limiting the mobilization potential of less obedient, more restive organizations. Flexible repression manifests in two strategies at the sub-regime level: competitive control over aboveground civil society and fragmented control over underground civil society. Taken together, these strategies shape the operating environment in which Chinese labor organizations learned to mobilize without the masses.

PART I

TECHNOLOGIES OF CONTROL

The transition from single-party rule to more pluralistic and open rule is among the most consequential transformations in politics (Slater and Wong 2013; Bunce and Wolchik 2011; Friedman and Wong 2008; Pei 2006; O'Donnell and Schmitter 1986). According to Tocqueville-inspired theories of civil society, the flowering of grassroots organizations in illiberal regimes is a harbinger of such democratic political change, particularly when these organizations operate autonomously from the state (Fung 2003; Tocqueville 2001; Foley and Edwards 1996; Fukuyama 1995; Putnam et al. 1993; Gold 1990; O'Donnell and Schmitter 1986:48). Yet civil society growth in many illiberal states has not ushered in formal democracy, nor has it restrained arbitrary state power. In highly repressive states, civil society remains tethered to the state and is neither able to mobilize opposition nor press for political liberalization (Dilla and Oxhorn 2002; Wiktorowicz 2000). In these polities, a strong, coercive state apparatus can dampen the potentially liberalizing effects of civil society.

However, in authoritarian states that have permitted a degree of liberalization in civil society, focusing solely on coercive power – tanks, guns, and tear gas – may cloak everyday mechanisms of social control over civil society. Part I of this book examines everyday state control of civil society in China from the perspective of local state agents and civil society activists. Analyzing state control at the local level is important because in decentralized political systems, elite directives are not always implemented by local authorities (Levitsky and Way 2010: 59–60; Earl and Soule 2006). By disaggregating state control of civil society within a single authoritarian regime, the following chapters identify state actors that design and implement control technologies at the lowest levels of the government. Even within a single local government, horizontal fragmentation across agencies can result in divergent control strategies. Exploiting these gaps between bureaus allows some civil society organizations to survive.

While existing studies have conceptualized authoritarian state control over civil society in a myriad of ways, researchers have tended to analyze the subject at the regime level. One perspective presents control as a function of the state's coercive capacity (Levitsky and Way 2010; Slater 2010; Bellin 2004; O'Donnell and Schmitter 1986). This perspective is in keeping with Max Weber's characterization of the state as possessing a monopoly on the legitimate use of violence (Weber 2004: 33). Coercion, defined as "the threat to employ brute physical force and the actual employment of such force," is central to how authoritarian states maintain power (Policzer 2009: 3). Coercion can vary in degree: high intensity coercion involves highly visible acts of violent repression such as the crackdown on Tiananmen protestors in 1989, while low-intensity coercion entails the use of surveillance, low-level harassment, and non-physical forms of repression that are largely out of the public eye (Levitsky and Way 2010: 57–8).

At the same time, coercion is not the only or necessarily the most important control tool. In soft authoritarian regimes, coercion is only one part of an "authoritarian toolkit" that includes cultivating committed supporters, enticing or blackmailing regime opponents to work with the state, managing information flows, and staging political dramas that undermine opponents' popular support (Schatz 2009a: 206–7). In Russia under Vladimir Putin, state actors rely not only on coercion but also on openness – free trade, free travel, and the free flow of information – to ensure regime survival (Krastev 2011: 12). In fact, coercion may be more difficult for open rather than closed regimes because the former must avoid excessive use of force and overt policing (Robertson 2009: 546). Under certain conditions, authoritarian rulers even make deft use of cooperation to control their would-be opposition (Koesel 2014; Gandhi 2008). Even in hard authoritarian states, authorities resort to a range of control tactics beyond coercion. In Syria, the personality cult of former President Hafiz al-Assad embodied symbolic power that induced citizens into compliance (Wedeen 1999). Similarly, while the Chinese party-state's violent repression of protestors during the Tiananmen Democracy Movement in 1989 has often been cited as an example of the state's high control capacity (Tilly 2006: 27; Levitsky and Way 2010: 57; Tilly 2006: 27), violent coercion is not necessarily the most common or important control tool used by the Chinese state. On an everyday basis, the Chinese state relies on large-scale internet censorship (King et al. 2014; Yang 2009), paying off protestors (Lee and Zhang 2013; X. Chen 2012) and putting pressure on dissidents' friends and relatives (Deng and O'Brien 2013) to keep citizens in line.

A second perspective conceptualizes state control within the framework of a "repression–mobilization nexus" (Davenport 2004). Davenport defines repression as the obstacles erected by the state or its agents to impede individual or collective action by challengers (Davenport 2004: 4). Under certain conditions repression can deter mobilization (Jeffries 2002; Jones 1988). Yet authoritarian states do not always engage in hard repression even if they have the capacity to do so. Coercion can be costly and can often backfire, triggering the radicalization of resistance (Almeida 2008; 2003; Ondetti 2006; Goldstone and Tilly 2001; White 1989). This effect is particularly likely when activists perceive the actions of the state to be disproportionately severe (O'Brien and Deng 2015; Hess and Martin 2006; Loveman 1998: 485; Opp and Roehl 1990). Other studies have shown that repression's effect on mobilization is mixed or U-shaped (Lichbach and Gurr 1981; Gurr 1970) and is affected by internalized expectations of movement success (Beissinger 2002: 383). In fact, the degree and type of repression used by the state affects the number of protests (Earl 2011; Ortiz 2007; Carey 2006; Earl and Soule 2006; Della Porta 1995; Francisco 1995) and can also impact tactical diffusion (Wood 2012: 124–5). Moreover, repression can affect the *form* of mobilization (Johnston 2012; Earl 2011: 275; Boudreau 2004), leading to different tactical innovations.

Labor Organizations in China

In China, where one official state union – the All-China Federation of Trade Unions – legally represents all workers, what explains the rise of independent grassroots labor organizations that serve migrant workers? Who were the leaders of such organizations and how did they mobilize in a repressive environment? This chapter sheds light on the landscape of grassroots labor organizations by documenting the process through which participants established organizations that advocated for labor rights under political duress. The chapter first explains the factors that contributed to the rise and expansion of grassroots labor organizations. It then presents variations in organizational characteristics along three dimensions: organizational leadership; foreign influence; and worker-participants. Two sets of comparisons are drawn: between labor organizations located in Beijing and those in the Pearl River Delta (PRD) region of South China, the two largest clusters of labor organizations; and, among the Pearl River Delta organizations, between those led by Hong Kong activists and those led by Mainland Chinese activists. Finally, this chapter analyzes the divisions between labor organizations, which prevent them from working in solidarity. Due to competition for funding, ideological differences, and the state's divide-and-conquer tactics, labor organizations have not yet formed a united front to advocate on behalf of Chinese workers.

CHINESE MIGRANT WORKERS ORGANIZING

One of the key factors that led to the rise of independent labor organizations in China was the changing demands of the country's 270 million migrant workers. Since the founding of the People's Republic of China in 1949, Chinese peasants have been migrating from the countryside to the cities (Walder 1984). In the 1950s and 1960s, rural temporary workers migrated to the cities to engage in various types of employment, including seasonal, contract, and non-contract work. Regardless of the specific category of employment, these workers remained residents of rural communes and were therefore outside of official employment rosters regulated by the state. As a result, they were not eligible for most of the benefits that permanent workers in state-owned enterprises received (Walder 1984: 28–38). For all workers, regardless of urban or rural status, the industrial workforce lacked the capacity for collective organization and was instead organized by the party-state. According to Andrew Walder:

China's new industrial workforce streamed into factories without common organization and past tradition, and was absorbed by official, party-controlled "company unions," whose function it was to distribute benefits, iron out conflicts, and prevent organized opposition. Lacking control over resources and a capacity for collective organization, workers therefore were markedly dependent on official largesse, both politically and economically.

(Walder 1984: 12)

In the early years of economic reform (starting 1979), rural migrants began flooding into cities such as Shenzhen in search of employment in newly opened special economic zones (K. W. Chan 2010; Solinger 1999). This first generation of migrant workers, often called the "floating population" (*liudong renkou*), worked in light manufacturing industries in Southern China and constituted a docile and cheap labor force (Pun 2005; Lee 1998). Unlike state workers, these migrants possessed minimal understanding of the socialist welfare system because of their exclusion from the formal work sector (Guang 2005: 482). Instead, they sought better wages and job opportunities in the urban areas in order to one day return to their villages to build homes, get married, and improve the economic circumstances of their families (Pun and Lu 2010). However, China's household registration system (*hukou*) restricted the access of migrant workers to key resources in the cities they moved to, including the same rights to housing, education, and social welfare enjoyed by urban residents. At the workplace, this first generation of migrant workers suffered egregious abuses, including forced labor and corporal punishment (A. Chan 2001).[1] In the absence of effective trade unions or labor regulators, they had few means of redress. The ACFTU functioned more like an arm of the

---

[1] Migrant workers were not the only ones to face obstacles in terms of organizing resistance. During the 2000s, when the party-state laid off masses of state-owned enterprise workers as China continued to transition out of a planned economy, there were also few formal organizations available to channel workers' protests. In the absence of effective organizations, laid-off workers made use of neighborhood networks in apartment blocks and housing projects to mobilize protests. Reliance on these "weak, informal, and spatially bounded mobilizing structures" resulted in the prevalence of intra-firm or inter-firm activism (Hurst 2009: 120). Laid-off workers also relied on individual leaders – usually elites such as enterprise leaders, former enterprise cadres, retired workers, soldiers-turned-workers, non-cadre Party members, and ordinary workers – to organize protests (Cai 2014: 109).

government rather than as a representative institution for workers (Friedman 2014; Pringle 2011).

Continued economic reform created opportunities for a second generation of migrant workers who were born in the early reform era (1970s and 1980s) to enter the labor market in the 1990s and 2000s (Pun and Lu 2010). Unlike their more passive predecessors, this new generation pressed for labor rights through a combination of legal activism and collective action (Friedman 2014; Pun and Lu 2010: 510; Gallagher 2007; Lee 2007b). First, with the passage of the 2008 Labor Contract Law, the party-state has increasingly channeled workers into addressing their grievances through the formal legal channel of the labor dispute system. In particular, after a series of legal reforms, which included the 2008 Labor Contract Law and the 2008 Labor Dispute Mediation and Arbitration Law, workers were emboldened to claim their labor rights through the legal system (Gallagher 2014). Thus, the party-state's campaign to increase both workers' knowledge of labor laws and the availability of legal aid opportunities contributed to the growth of workers' legal activism (Gallagher 2014). An aggressive labor law education campaign combined with positive propaganda sought to channel workers into individualized forms of legal activism and away from collective action (Stockmann and Gallagher 2011).

However, this system – which is comprised of a three-step process of mediation, arbitration, and litigation – has been notoriously difficult to navigate and remains inadequate in redressing workers' grievances. When individual legal action failed, workers also resorted to collective action without an organizational basis. This often took limited forms of factory-based resistance that targeted local authorities but did not challenge the fundamental political legitimacy of the party-state (Lee 2007b). In a pattern that has been described as "cellular activism" (Lee 2007b), migrant workers exploited the communicative channels made available by shared dormitory spaces to organize collective action such as strikes and protests. Their organizational resources came not from a formal union but from the informal networks created and facilitated by their common living spaces.

Among their claims for wages and better treatment, this second generation of migrant workers also demanded fairer representation in the state-run ACFTU. Two prominent labor incidents in 2010 drew public attention to this longstanding demand. The first was a strike wave that broke out in Honda factories across Guangdong Province, which diverged from the traditional pattern of single factory strikes in that it was cross-factory and was "offensive" in its demand for higher wages and representation (Elfstrom and Kuruvilla 2014). However, like other strikes in China, they were spontaneous in nature and lacked coordination of a strike committee and involvement from labor activists (Chan and Siu 2012). In May 2010, 1,900 workers at a Honda transmission factory in the Nanhai district of Guangdong Province went on strike for higher wages and for free elections in the local branch of the official trade union.[2]

2 K. Bradsher, A Labor Movement Stirs in China, June 10, 2010, *New York Times*.

Their action reverberated through the province, and another group of Honda workers in the city of Zhongshan soon went on strike for higher wages. During the original Nanhai strike, union officials and workers became embroiled in verbal and physical altercations.[3] After nearly two weeks of striking between May 17 and June 1, 2010, the workers succeeded in gaining wage increases as well as the right to elect their own union representatives in the enterprise. In fact, Kong Xiaohong, the leader of the official Guangdong Federation of Trade Unions, declared the Nanhai Honda factory to be a pilot site for free annual elections of the enterprise union chair.[4] In response to the Honda strikes, Prime Minister Wen Jiabao called on local governments to improve the living conditions of migrant workers.[5] Yet despite these initial commitments, as of 2015 workers at the Nanhai Honda plant were still unable to directly elect their union chairman.[6]

A few months after the Honda strikes, a series of worker suicides in factories run by Foxconn, a mammoth electronics supplier that produces for leading world brands including Apple, once again brought the issue of worker representation to the foreground. In response to worker suicides, several prominent Chinese scholars wrote an open letter to the government, claiming that Foxconn employees did not perceive the official union to be fulfilling its responsibility to represent their interests.[7] Following the Honda strikes and the Foxconn suicides, workers across the country continued to demand democratic elections in official unions. In May 2012, workers at the Omron electronics factory near Shenzhen secured democratic elections for a new trade union chairman to replace the non-elected incumbent.[8] These incidents showed that workers became increasingly vociferous in pressing not just for increased wages but also for a voice in choosing their union representatives.

The 2010 strike wave and consecutive suicides took place in the context of the workers' longstanding struggle for fair wages and decent work conditions in the absence of effective organizational vehicles. Despite their strength in numbers, workers have struggled to mount collective action outside of

---

[3] The union later released an open letter to the workers apologizing. See Nanhaiqu zonggonghui, shishanzheng zonggonghui zhi bentian yuangong de gongkaixin [Open Letter from Nanhai District Union and Shishan Township Union to Honda Workers]. June 3, 2010. *Business Sohu.*

[4] The Nanhai Honda Strike and the Union, July 18, 2010, *China Labor New Translations.*

[5] D. Barboza, New Strike Threat at a Honda Parts Plant, June 14, 2010, *New York Times.*

[6] As of 2015, Nanhai workers can vote for the leader of their own working group which represents 20–30 workers. This group, in turn, elects union delegates who would cast the votes for the union chairman. *China Labour Bulletin,* Five Years On, Nanhai Honda Workers Want More from Their Trade Unions, May 20, 2015.

[7] See Jiu ming shehuixuezhe fa gongkaixin; dujue fushikang beiju [Nine Sociologists Publish Open Letter, Put a Stop to the Foxconn Tragedy], May 19, 2010, *Sina News.*

[8] D. Han, A Chance to Help Build Grassroots Democracy in China, July 5, 2012, *China Labour Bulletin.*

state-sanctioned channels, failing to develop a long-term or programmatic labor movement (Gallagher 2014: 90–1). Some scholars have described Chinese workers' resistance as a "class struggle without class organization" (C. Chan 2010). Others have characterized these strikes as leading to an emergent interest-based form of protest that demands collective rights but falls short of the formation of class consciousness (Chan and Siu 2012: 91). To date, Chinese labor activism is not a full-fledged social movement but rather an "insurgency" characterized by episodic and fragmented resistance (Friedman 2014: 19).

THE RISE OF GRASSROOTS LABOR ORGANIZATIONS

In an era beset by intensifying labor conflict and inadequate labor representation (Friedman 2014; Gallagher 2005: 78), grassroots labor organizations sought to meet migrant workers' needs for protection against labor rights abuses. One of the most important factors that contributed to their rise was the associational revolution.[9] In 1986, China had only 400 registered civil society organizations nationwide. Exposure to international civil society inspired a plethora of social organizations to emerge. By 2012, there were an estimated 3.75 million non-governmental organizations.[10] These organizations focused on a wide range of issues, including the environment, HIV/AIDS, women's rights, and homeowners' rights.

It was in the midst of this associational revolution that the latest wave of grassroots labor organizations emerged in the mid-1990s.[11] The founders included migrant workers, former journalists, scholars, and former government officials. In Beijing, the earliest labor organization – The Migrant Women's Home (*Dagongmei Zhijia*) – was established by a former Women's Federation official.[12] The organization later inspired ex-journalists and migrant workers alike to found additional organizations in Beijing with support from foreign donors. In the Pearl River Delta, one group of founders were migrant workers who had accrued experience with the formal labor dispute system through

---

[9] I use the term "grassroots" to refer to all the labor organizations featured in this study which are not part of the state-run ACFTU. They include labor organizations that are registered as well as unregistered.

[10] See F. Minzhengbu, Nian Shehui Fuwu Fazhan Tongji Gongbao [Ministry of Civil Affairs Publishes the 2011 Statistical Report on Social Service Development], June 21, 2012, Ministry of Civil Affairs of the People's Republic of China.

[11] Prior to this wave, there had been workers' organizations elsewhere in China, including Zhejiang Province (Howell 2008: 186–9) and the Crane Workers' Union in South China (Pringle and Clarke 2011: 64).

[12] The All-China Women's Federation is a mass organization (also known as a government-affiliated non-governmental organization), which represents the interests of all Chinese women. Although it is termed a non-governmental organization, it is actually an appendage of the party-state.

their own legal battles and were motivated to assist other migrant workers to claim their rights. Another group of founders included Hong Kong-based activists and scholars who not only established their own network of labor organizations, but also assisted local migrant leaders in founding their own labor organizations in the PRD (Interview, activist, 2010).

By the 2010s, dozens of new organizations had formed across China. Due to the fact that many of these organizations were later disbanded by authorities and those which are still active often have minimal online presence, there is no definitive estimate of how many currently exist.[13] My research identified 72 organizations across China in 2011, with the densest cluster of organizations in Beijing (15) and in the Pearl River Delta (PRD) in Southern China (43).[14] This distribution is related to regional political economy, as Beijing is a hub for migrant workers in the construction and services industries whereas the Pearl River Delta is China's manufacturing heartland. The rest were distributed across the country, typically in large cities with high concentrations of migrant workers (see Table 2.1).[15]

These grassroots labor organizations functioned as NGOs in a political context where independent unionizing was banned and therefore had precarious legal standing. Only a few exceptional organizations were able to register with the Bureau of Civil Affairs – the proper legal channel for social organizations wishing to gain legal status. The vast majority operated in legal gray zones, with some registered as commercial businesses with the Bureau of Industry and Commerce and others remaining completely unregistered.[16] Similar to the worker centers that emerged in the United States in the 1970s to serve immigrant laborers (Fine 2006; Gordon 2005), these organizations were often located in migrant worker communities, which facilitated the provision of direly needed services to migrant workers. In the legal realm, activists assisted workers in disputes with employers over a range of issues including injury compensation, wage arrears, physical abuse by factory management, falsified

---

[13] For additional estimates and case studies of labor organizations, see Howell 2015; Franceschini 2014; Xu 2013; Chan and Siu 2012; Froissart 2011; Lee and Shen 2011; Spires 2011; Zhang and Smith 2009; He and Huang 2008; Huang 2006.

[14] This estimate is based on a compilation of organizations identified from my fieldwork in 2009–11 and those identified by other scholars. See Lee and Shen 2011; Zhang and Smith 2009; He and Huang 2008; Huang 2006.

[15] Organizations with more than one branch were counted as one organization in the city of their origin. This estimate is based on a compilation of organizations identified from my fieldwork in 2009–11 and those identified by other scholars. See Lee and Shen 2011; Zhang and Smith 2009; He and Huang 2008; Huang 2006. More recent estimates indicate up to 100 labor NGOs across China, including 55 in the Pearl River Delta and 18 in Beijing (Li 2016: 83). The Appendix explains how organizations were identified.

[16] A 2016 study of eighty-one labor NGOs across China found that 41 percent registered as commercial businesses; 30 percent as non-profits; and 21 percent remained unregistered (Li 2016: 88).

TABLE 2.1 *National distribution of labor organizations*

City	Count	Percent
Beijing	15	21
Changsha	1	1
Chongqing	1	1
Dongguan	6	8
Guangzhou	11	15
Hangzhou	1	1
Nanjing	1	1
Qingdao	1	1
Shenzhen	26	36
Shiyan, Hebei	1	1
Suzhou	3	4
Tianjing	1	1
Wuhan	1	1
Xiamen	1	1
Xian	1	1
Yongkang, Zhejiang	1	1
Regions		
Beijing	15	21
Pearl River Delta	43	60
Other	14	19
Total	72	100

labor contracts, social security, and illegally blacklisting workers.[17] On a daily basis, activists also provided free legal counsel to workers through telephone hotlines and in-person consultation. Organizations held regular legal education workshops where activists encouraged workers to demand that employers respect their legal rights and offered pro bono legal aid. These legal services met the needs of workers, many of whom had limited knowledge of labor rights and were daunted by the arduous labor dispute resolution process.

In addition to legal services, labor organizations also provided social services such as employment skills training, childcare, and cultural activities. These services filled an important void, as local governments typically did not consider migrant workers to be their constituents and therefore did not provide such services to them. In addition, holding cultural and social events were part of the organizations' mission to forge a collective identity among workers from different factories and regions across China. Social activities provided a space for workers to exchange information about labor conditions in their workplaces

---

[17] A common dispute that activists assisted in was claiming injury compensation, which is perhaps the most complicated and lengthy type of labor dispute in China. Many founders and activists were themselves formerly injured factory workers.

and to strengthen ties with other workers who they otherwise would not have encountered.

Beyond service provision, these labor organizations also promoted worker solidarity by creating volunteer networks and training future activists. Fostering a volunteer network allowed organizations to signal to the party-state that they did not aspire to become an independent union with formal members. Volunteers were usually former worker-participants who had benefited from the organization's work and were committed to its ideals. They assisted activists in recruitment, labor workshops, and other cultural and social activities. Volunteers also encouraged workers to attend the court hearings of other workers to show moral support.[18] This volunteer network served the dual purposes of expanding the organizations' influence in worker communities and training future labor activists.

Despite their relatively modest goals and limited size, grassroots labor organizations posed a threat to the party-state. First, the very existence of these labor organizations was symbolically threatening. Many of its founders, leaders, and participants were members of China's largest and arguably most restive social group: China's 270 million migrant workers. By claiming to empower migrant workers, grassroots labor organizations symbolically challenged the ACFTU monopoly on the representation of Chinese workers. Although their size and influence was limited, the fact that these organizations were advocating for the rights of migrant workers independent of the ACFTU threatened the party-state's claim to represent the interests of all Chinese workers.

Second, migrant worker organizations were threatening because of their mobilizing strategies. While some provided only social services, others engaged in more confrontational mobilizing tactics by encouraging workers to press for their rights outside of the formal labor dispute system. Because social stability is a key pillar of the party-state's legitimacy (Shue 2004), these organizations effectively challenged state officials charged with maintaining social stability.[19] Finally, many of these organizations' funding came from foreign organizations, which further raised the Chinese government's suspicions that hostile international forces were supporting domestic civil society groups in order to foster anti-regime movements. For these reasons, migrant worker associations were among the least tolerated by the state (K. W. Chan 2005: 20–41). According to a 1999 notice issued jointly by the Chinese Communist Party Central Committee and the State Council, illegal migrant associations posed a direct threat to social stability given their potential to organize some

[18] These were sometimes contentious events, as court authorities felt pressured by the presence of workers inside the courtroom, fearing that they may trigger social instability should the ruling be unfavorable (Participant observation, 2010).

[19] This is particularly the case for labor organizations in the Pearl River Delta, which adopted more radical tactics than their Beijing counterparts. See Part II of this book for extended analyses.

of China's most disaffected citizens. Yet not only did these labor organizations continue to spring up, they continued to survive well into the new millennium.

ORGANIZATIONAL VARIATION

While grassroots labor organizations were relatively homogenous in the range of social services they provided migrant workers, they differed significantly along three dimensions: leadership; clientele; and their relationship with the state. The differences are starkest when comparing organizations in Beijing to those in the Pearl River Delta. Beijing organizations were largely founded by white-collar professionals and migrant workers. The first migrant labor organization in China – The Migrant Women's Home (*Dagongmei Zhijia*) – was founded by Xie Lihua, a retired official from the state-run ACWF (Fu 2009). Xie had served as an associate editor for the state-run publication, *China Women's News*. She initially set up the Migrant Women's Home as a project of the editorial office of the magazine, Rural Women Knowing It All. Inspired by the 1995 UN Women's Conference in Beijing, Xie convinced authorities at several domestic worker intermediary companies to send two sets of letters: one to migrant women domestic workers, informing them that the organization was "a home where they will find equality," and another to employers, telling them that their domestic workers needed the opportunity to interact with the outside world beyond their isolated workplaces (Interview, founder, 2005). The Migrant Women's Home also provided a range of legal and social services to female migrant workers employed in various sectors and inspired the founding of other labor organizations in Beijing.

Several of Beijing's other labor organizations were also founded by white-collar professionals. Former journalists, Li Tao and Li Zhen, established Facilitator (*Xie Zuozhe*) (Interview, director, 2009 and 2011). Perhaps China's most prominent labor organization – the Beijing Zhicheng Legal Aid Station for Migrant Workers (*Beijing Zhicheng Nonmingong Falu Yuanzhu Yu Yanjiu Zhongxin*) – was founded by Tong Lihua, a public interest lawyer in Beijing (Interview, staff member, 2010). Tong has been widely hailed by the state media as one of China's most accomplished public interest lawyers. The organization became officially registered as a non-profit organization with the Beijing Municipal Bureau of Civil Affairs in 2009 and opened branches in twenty other localities across China.

In addition to white-collar professionals, a second category of founders was composed of entrepreneurial migrant workers. Little Birds (*Xiao Xiao Niao*) was founded by Wei Wei, a migrant worker who had worked odd jobs in the construction and restaurant industry before he started operating a migrant workers' hotline in Beijing in 2005 (Interview, staff member, 2009). Similarly, Fanrao Hotline (*XiaoChen Fanrao Rexian*) was founded by a migrant worker with elementary schooling who provided informal advice and counseling from a landline phone installed in a shack in a temporary migrant encampment in Beijing. Workers' Home (*Gongyou Zhijia*) was also founded by a migrant worker, Sun Heng, who was able to leverage his superior educational level to collaborate with multiple stakeholders.

In terms of clientele, Beijing organizations largely served migrant workers employed in the construction and services industries. As a center of industrial and commercial development, Beijing is home to large communities of migrant workers who work on construction sites. Besides long, grueling hours and inadequate safety measures, migrant workers also faced the problem of wage arrears. It was common for the contractor who served as a middleman between workers and hiring companies to run off before dispensing wages to workers. In response, a number of labor organizations emerged to service construction workers, including one founded by university students called Safety Hat (*Anquan Mao*). Another major group of clients included service industry workers such as waiters and waitresses, security guards, and domestic workers who faced maltreatment or sexual harassment in the workplace. In comparison with factory workers in South China, service sector workers in Beijing had less experience in organizing collective action such as strikes.

Finally, Beijing organizations shared a more symbiotic relationship with the state than their Pearl River Delta counterparts. For example, the director of Little Birds established a "people's mediation committee" (*Renmin Tiaojie Wenhuanhui*) as part of the Justice Bureau's program to protect migrant worker's rights (Interview with director, 2009). This committee handled mediation between workers and bosses, a function which served the purposes of both the Justice Bureau and that of Little Birds. The organization eventually registered as a business with a District Bureau of Industry and Commerce in Beijing and opened offices in the cities of Shenzhen and Shenyang. Another grassroots labor organization called Beijing On Action International Cultural Center (*Beijing Zai Xingdong Guoji Wenhua Zhongxin*) opened up branches in the cities of Suzhou and Wuhan (Interview, 2009). Like its counterparts, On Action provided pro bono legal aid to migrant workers as well as social services such as psychological counseling, cultural activities, and skills training, among others. Partnering with state agencies conferred a degree of legitimacy upon organizations and made it easier for many organizations in Beijing to register either as social organizations with the Bureau of Civil Affairs or as commercial enterprises with the Bureau of Industry and Commerce.

In the Pearl River Delta – the heartland of China's manufacturing sector – organizations could be subdivided into Mainland and Hong Kong networks of activists. These divisions were based on the origins of the founders. Mainland organizations were founded by disenchanted male migrant workers in their twenties to their forties. These men had endured the hardships of factory work, fought numerous labor battles, and won reputations as "black lawyers" (*heilushi*), or informal legal representatives, for other migrant workers.[20] Their ability to personally identify with their clients was their greatest asset for recruiting participants for their organizations. Although they had limited formal education, they possessed a wealth of accumulated experience in dealing with factory bosses and confronting labor bureau officials. These personal experiences, both with injustice and with navigating the labor dispute system, equipped these leaders to give practical advice to their clients. These migrant leaders saw themselves as social entrepreneurs who wished to "right injustices in society" (*da baobuping*).[21]

A critical motivating factor for Mainland migrant leaders was a deep sense of collective injustice. A prominent migrant worker leader explained a turning point in his life that prompted him to engage in labor activism:

> While I was working at a shoe factory in 1993 in Dongguan ... There was a worker [in my factory] who peed on the wall after he got drunk. He got into a fight with a security guard who started yelling at him ... the guard told the boss who said, "Which worker dares to create chaos in my factory?" The guard beat the worker to death ... his family only got 50,000 RMB in compensation ... [This made me realize that] workers have no value in the eyes of government and enterprise.
>
> (Interview, activist, 2010)

Personal experience with tragedy and injustice inspired many to found their own organizations. One of the first was the Shenzhen Chunfeng Labor Disputes Services Center (*Shenzhen Chunfeng Laodong Zhenyi Fuwubu*), which was founded in 2004 by Zhang Zhiru. Like Zhang, many other leaders in the Mainland network of organizations closely identified with their clients, and this self-identification as a migrant worker was a valuable asset for recruiting participants. However, their social status as migrant workers also meant limited access to government officials and connections to elites who could act as protectors or advocates for the organization. This was true for most organizations in the Pearl River Delta cluster founded by migrant workers.

A second category of founders included seasoned labor activists from Hong Kong who assisted the founding of the earliest labor organizations in Guangdong Province. The Hong Kong Christian Industrial Committee (CIC), founded in 1967, played a leading role during the Hong Kong labor movement of the 1960s. It also cultivated the growth of independent labor organizations in the PRD. After the Zhili Handicraft factory fire in 1993, which killed eighty-seven young migrant women in Shenzhen,[22] CIC staff

---

[20] See Liu and Halliday 2016 for a discussion of activist lawyers who "believe it is their duty to facilitate and empower victims who often organize in networks and incipient organizations" (85).
[21] This characterization is a generalization. One exception is the well-known Institute of Contemporary Observation founded by a scholar, Liu Kaiming.
[22] *China Labour Bulletin*, Victims of the 1993 Zhili Fire, December 31, 1999.

turned their attention towards funding and providing ideological guidance for labor organizations in Mainland China. CIC staff members visited survivors of the fire, an experience which inspired one severely injured migrant woman to set up her own organization serving disabled workers (Interview, founder, 2010). In the early 2000s, labor activists from CIC also visited lawyers, legal workers, and others engaged in labor activism in Mainland China who they had identified from news articles on migrant workers and labor disputes. CIC not only liaised between foreign donors and Mainland labor organizations; they also aided the latter in capacity building. According to a CIC staff member:

We visited people in the Mainland whose names appeared many times in the newspapers. After the initial assessment, we considered what kind of input they needed. We had our own political calculations, so we were cautious. At the time, there weren't many organizations with more than one individual and they were doing something illegal (providing legal services) so the donor needed to go through CIC to find organizations ... We provided these organizations with funding, a platform for discussion and networking with other NGOs, discussions on organizational building, etc. But CIC was only one of the supporters.

(Interview, former CIC staff, 2010)

This early and active intervention by Hong Kong labor activists shaped the organization trajectories of labor organizations in the Pearl River Delta.

In addition to assisting activists in the Mainland to set up organizations, Hong Kong activists also founded their own organizations in the Pearl River Delta as part of the Hong Kong network. Their main objective was to empower workers by coaching them to advocate for core labor rights such as collective bargaining and the freedom of association. They did this through educating workers on the practice of collective bargaining and encouraging workers to go on strike. Unlike the majority of organizations led by Mainland activists, many Hong Kong activists did not shirk from mobilizing workers to undertake confrontational collective action, even at the expense of organizational survival. According to a former staff member who worked for an organization in this network:

They [activists] are focused on consciousness-raising, on teaching workers that they should be empowered to do things for themselves instead of waiting to be legally represented by somebody else. They try to teach workers the tactics of collective bargaining. For instance, if a group of workers comes directly to them complaining about their factory, they'd teach them how to select worker leaders, prepare them for simulation bargaining ... They tell them that in the process of bargaining, a lot of your own compatriots may back out on you and you may get fired.

(Interview, former staff member, 2009)

Moreover, leaders of the Hong Kong network viewed labor advocacy as part of a broader and radical agenda of pressing for the right to associate in China:

If workers are empowered themselves, they don't need to rely on the trade union to negotiate. They can directly bypass the official trade union. We want workers to represent themselves; not to be represented by the ACFTU. Workers don't know what trade unions are like, for them [the] union is of the government. They have a blurry vision of collective bargaining. Their organizing vehicle should be able to challenge ACFTU. They should be able to exert pressure on the enterprise.

(Interview, director, 2011)

The main clientele of Pearl River Delta labor organizations were factory workers who assembled electronics, clothes, or toys for some of the world's leading brands. Unlike construction and service workers in Beijing, many factory workers in the PRD had experience in going on strike and had a greater awareness of their labor rights. As the hub of global manufacturing, the Pearl River Delta has long been a hotbed for labor activism (Lee 2007b). Accordingly, activists – especially those in the Hong Kong network – adopted risky organizing tactics such as sneaking into factories to record labor violations and alerting local officials. While their Mainland counterparts were more cautious, Mainland activists nevertheless also adopted mobilization tactics that threatened local social stability.

Adopting such contentious mobilization tactics meant that Pearl River Delta organizations were vulnerable to changing political tides in which periods of relative liberalization were followed by periods of government repression. During periodic crackdowns against unregistered labor organizations, leaders were detained and their organizations were disbanded. Although many organizations were resurrected, their relationships with the local state were fraught. A scholar who used to work as a program officer of an international organization aptly characterized the Beijing cluster as nails and the PRD cluster as explosives:

Nails are organizations like X [in Beijing] who play it cautious and wait to drive [into state policy] at the right moment, but others like Y [in the PRD] are explosive organizations that grab people's attention by getting their hands dirty. Organizations that explode will have even more power when resurrected [after state repression] because they will have impressed their members.

(Interview, former program officer, 2010)

The explosive nature of Pearl River Delta organizations contrasted sharply to Beijing organizations that largely refrained from contentious mobilization.

ORGANIZATIONAL EXPANSION: THE INCUBATOR EFFECT

One of the most important factors for the growth in the number of labor organizations in Beijing was the formation of a pioneering organization, The Migrant Women's Home, that served as an informal incubator for other organizations and as a prototype for other labor organizations. The Home aimed to empower migrant women by teaching them how to engage in rights activism, while simultaneously providing social services, including a help hotline, lectures, social gatherings, and a modest personal emergency fund for the organization's clients. In addition, it published research reports that attempted to influence government policy related to labor rights, including the rights of domestic workers. Although the organization empowered its workers by raising their awareness of legal rights, it also limited their rhetoric to the officially sanctioned discourse on workers sacrificing for the nation's economic development (Fu 2009). Despite its limitations, the organization exposed many of its participants to the idea and practices of a nongovernmental organization.

The first organization that the Migrant Home incubated was Workers' Friends' Home (*Gongyou Zhijia*), founded in 2002 by Sun Heng. This organization claimed to be even more grassroots than its predecessor because its leader and the staff members were all migrant workers. The second offshoot organization was Facilitator (*Xie Zuozhe*) whose approach was to treat migrant workers holistically as individuals and not as workers whose class consciousness needed to be awakened. Disagreeing with the ideology of more progressive labor organizations in the Pearl River Delta, the leaders sought to foster migrant workers' capabilities in all areas of social life. As the director explained: "Why can't migrants be on stage? We put them on stage. Why can't migrants teach? We give them the opportunity. Why can't they be volunteers? We train them to be volunteers" (Interview, director, 2009).

The Home also incubated Ma Xiaoduo's Same Hope Home (*Tongxin Xiwang Jiayuan*), an organization which served women and children in a migrant community of 30,000 on the outskirts of Beijing. Prior to its founding, Chinese media had hailed Ma as one of the most successful female migrant workers. Ma studied English by herself and was eventually invited to participate in an exchange program in the United States after receiving a grant from the Chinese Mutual Aid International Network in New York City. Upon her return, Ma founded Same Hope Home where she hoped migrant women would not be labeled "working girls" (*dagongmei*), a term she considered derogatory (Interview, director, 2005). Because Same Hope Home was nested in a migrant community on the outskirts of Beijing, Ma believed that it was able to target the neediest migrants. According to Ma, "We serve migrants who are worse off than those in [the more urban] Haidian district, where Same Hope Home is located. Our clients are the construction workers and domestic workers from the poorest provinces" (Interview, director, 2009). Same Hope Home also operated a modest elementary school for migrant children and a second-hand shop that sold used goods to migrants in the neighborhood.

The organization maintained an ambivalent relationship with the local neighborhood committee.[23] At times, the committee ignored the organization

---

[23] Neighborhood committees are autonomous grassroots mass organizations at the lowest levels of government in urban districts. Among the committees' major tasks are maintaining public

and tacitly tolerated its existence. At other times, it attempted to co-opt the organization's projects as the committee's own achievements. As Ma explained:

We were fortunate. At the time [of founding Same Hope Home], the local neighborhood committee had just received orders from their bosses at the street level that they should make more effort to manage the local migrant population. The neighborhood committee didn't know how to do it so when we offered to set up an office, they rented to us a small 12 square-meter room next door. They initially discouraged our activities when we wanted to open the supermarket, but after we got it started, they put up a plaque saying that this was the neighborhood committee's work.

(Interview, director, 2009)

However, Ma's most vexing challenge was not the local state but rather local migrant workers who did not trust a grassroots organization to advocate for their interests:

My biggest obstacle is educating the ignorant masses (*yumin jiaoyu*). Common folk only trust the state. They don't know what to make of NGOs. Initially when I came to this community, the migrants here were deeply suspicious of my intentions … Some people thought I was part of the Falun Gong sect. Others thought I was part of a marketing scam like Amway … When I talk about the need to make their voices heard, they think I'm going to create trouble and that I'm anti-government. So I tell them this analogy: if a robber is coming to take away your possessions, wouldn't you defend yourself? That's exactly what's happening with the developers who want to bulldoze the community.

(Interview, director, 2009)

Ma's experience reflected the difficulty of gaining migrant workers' trust in grassroots organizations. In fact, convincing migrant workers to seek the services of organizations was a common challenge for activists across Beijing and the Pearl River Delta. Migrant workers rarely had contact with social organizations in their daily lives and typically harbored deep suspicions towards organizations that offered services free of charge, fearing that they were scams. As a result, one of the major barriers for labor activists in both regions was to gain legitimacy in the eyes of potential clients by explaining their philanthropic missions.

The incubator effect was also an important factor in the growth of labor organizations within the Pearl River Delta. In this region, the Guangdong Panyu Migrant Worker Center (*Guangdong Panyu Dagongzu Fuwubu*) served as a critical incubator organization.[24] Liao Xiaofeng, a migrant worker and self-trained lawyer, founded it in 1998 to provide legal advice to migrant

security and safeguarding the rights and interests of residents. It is important for grassroots civil society organizations to maintain good relationships with these committees. If the committee sees the organization as a threat to the community's security, it may report the organization to the police.

[24] Huang 2012 also uses the term "incubator" (*fuhuaqi*) to describe the network expansion of labor organizations in the Pearl River Delta.

workers and represent their claims in labor arbitration and litigation proceedings. Because he was not certified as a professional lawyer, the local Bureau of Industry and Commerce only gave him a permit to operate a documentation center, a permit which stipulated that the organization was allowed to prepare legal documents for its clients but could not represent them in court.[25] Despite such legal restrictions, Liao continued to represent workers in court as a citizens' legal agent.[26] In order to sustain the organization's operational budget, he charged his clients a nominal fee when they won compensation. However, workers who received compensation sometimes fled to their own villages in order to dodge payment to the organization. Under financial strains, Liao left the organization a year after the organization's founding (Zhang and Smith 2009).

After Liao's departure, a young, idealistic law graduate named Zeng Feiyang became the director of the Panyu Center. With only a 6,000 yuan (950 US dollars) operational budget in hand, Zeng soon encountered difficulties. Just a year after the organization's founding, the local Bureau of Justice revoked the organization's permit on the basis that its operations extended beyond the stipulated area of providing legal documentation. Although Zeng later managed to recover the permit, the Bureau's scrutiny of the organization made it increasingly difficult to operate (Interview, 2009). The support of Hong Kong labor activists was critical during those arduous times. From 2001 to 2004, CIC provided financial support to the organization and sent a staff member each week to assist with its operations. CIC also assisted the organization in applying for grants from foreign foundations over the following years (Interview, member of the board of directors, 2010).

The Panyu Center inspired a number of other migrant workers to found their own organizations in the Pearl River Delta (Huang 2012). Huang Zhiming, a former client and staff member at the Panyu Center, founded the Shenzhen-based Raindrops Worker Care Hotline (*Yudian Zai Xindong Laowugong Guanai Rexian*) in 2008 (Interview, 2009). In addition, Wang Wu Li, a migrant woman from Henan who used to volunteer at the Panyu Center, became the founder of the Shenzhen chapter of Little Birds in 2006 (Huang 2012). Zhu Qiang, an injured worker who later founded the Zhiqiang Service Center (*Zhiqiang Xingxi Fuwubu*) in 2004, also gained experience from volunteering at the Panyu Center (Interview, 2009).[27]

Among the organizations that the Panyu Center inspired, perhaps the most influential was the Shenzhen Chunfeng Labor Disputes Services Center. Like

---

[25] The organization was only permitted to prepare court documents for litigants. See Zhang and Smith 2009 for a descriptive case study of the Panyu Migrant Worker Documentary Center.

[26] This was colloquially known as a "black lawyer" or "*hei lushi.*"

[27] After 2011, the Panyu Center also spawned the Zhongshan Center, the Goose Flying South Worker Social Work Center (2012), the Sunflower Center (2012), and the Brother Hai Center (2014). See Li 2016: 100–12.

many of his fellow activists, Zhang's relationship with the local state was tense. In 2006, the organization earned a reputation for audacity when it organized a signature campaign on the streets of Shenzhen with the goal of supporting the abolition of labor arbitration fees, which were usually paid by workers. Zhang was promptly detained and his organization temporarily disbanded by the authorities, although he later resurrected the organization by moving it to a different locality in the same city. In 2014, Zhang made international headlines for assisting a workers' strike at the Yue Yuen shoe factory in Dongguan city of Guangdong Province.[28]

Zhang's organization was one among many in the Mainland network that was either spawned or influenced by the Panyu Center. These organizations all adopted similar organizational structures, with the leader of the organization acting as "the boss" (*laoda*) who made the major decisions, solicited funding, and hired the employees. Unlike the organizations in the Hong Kong network, Mainland organizations rarely voted on strategic decisions, and activists complained about the lack of transparency with regards to budget allocation, which was often determined by the director. Such shared characteristics reflected the incubator effect at work in the development of labor organization networks in the Pearl River Delta.

DISUNITY AND BROKERAGE

The expansion of labor organizations did not necessarily translate into the formation of strong advocacy networks among organizations. In public, labor leaders spoke of forging organizational solidarity and the importance of collaborating with one another. But in private, they accused their fellow activists of misusing funds and being co-opted by the State Security Bureau (Interview, activist 2009).[29] Leaders of organizations in both Beijing and the PRD harbored deep suspicions about each other even as they worked together on common projects and conferences.

One underlying source of tension was the competition for funding. Resource-strapped labor organizations competed fiercely for funding from a handful of Hong Kong-based and foreign donors. While certain Beijing-based organizations were able to solicit funding from the local state, Pearl River Delta organizations largely vied for external funding.[30] This competition for resources created tension among organizational leaders who struggled to raise funds and whose precarious legal status made it hard for them to approach government agencies for resources. Leaders of different networks also disagreed with one another over

---

[28] D. Sevastopulo, China Charges Labor Activist after Yue Yuen Shoe Factory Strike, April 29, 2014, *Financial Times*.

[29] Between 2009 and 2011, I attended a number of labor conferences where the leaders of labor organizations gave speeches about building a strong advocacy network.

[30] A 2016 study indicated that primary funding source of ninety labor NGOs in Mainland China came from Hong Kong (35 percent) and foreign organizations (26 percent) (C. Li 2016: 86).

ideology and mobilization tactics. The Mainland network perceived the Hong Kong network as far too radical in their tactics and goal in relation to the PRD cluster. Meanwhile, the Hong Kong network perceived the Mainland network to be undemocratic in their organizational culture and overly cautious in their interactions with the state, which in turn compromised their advocacy role.[31]

In addition, activists accused the local State Security Bureau of using divide-and-conquer strategies to fuel mistrust among labor leaders. Labor activists suspected that certain colleagues were informants for the local State Security Bureau (Interviews, activist, 2010). For example, during fieldwork I encountered an activist who felt that the leader of a fellow labor organization had betrayed him by informing the state security of his involvement in a collective action event. The activist believed that the leader had been co-opted by the state security:

> I feel that my biggest failure [as an activist] was that I didn't realize what was going on right next to me. X [name of the fellow organization] got called in by the state security and told on us. That's how they [State Security] found out which workers were involved.
>
> (Interview, activist, 2010)

This activist's perception reflected the mutual distrust among organizations, which security agents reinforced by playing organizations off of one another. Other researchers of labor organizations in China also found mistrust between the leaders of labor organizations, described as a lack of "bonding social capital" (Franceschini 2014: 489–9).

Under such conditions, domestic labor scholars became critical brokers, attempting to foster a sense of solidarity among organizations as well as liaising between state officials and activists. For example, in 2009 scholars from several Chinese universities undertook a project sponsored by a philanthropic foundation to train labor activists to use digital cameras to record the lives of migrant workers. The project convened core labor activists for major conferences in these respective cities, creating forums in which activists from different regions could network. During these conferences, labor scholars also taught migrant leaders to frame their activism using the discourse of citizenship and civil society. By advancing these concepts of civic engagement, scholars hoped to create a common vision for this motley group of migrant workers, many of whom had different ideas concerning the goals of their activism. As the director of a research center explained to a group of core activists during a workshop:

> We need to use the theory of citizenship. If we succeed in advocating for citizenship rights, that's sufficient. We can't use Marxist ideologies to do rights activism because that would only result in class struggle which necessitates forming a political party. And we're not going to form an independent party. We're all about advocating citizenship rights.
>
> (Participant observation, 2010)

Domestic scholars also brokered relationships between local state officials and labor activists. For example, a scholar who organized monthly informal

---

[31] See Chapter 7 for Hong Kong leaders' critique of Mainland organizations.

gatherings with the leaders of several labor organizations, and coached activists on how to use the media to establish relationships with state officials, stated that:

You need to pay attention to the news. The police find people through reading news clips, so if you can show them that you're actually a stabilizing agent, then that would be good for your organization. Say you managed to dissuade a group of migrants from collective petitioning, write an opinion article and submit it to the *Southern Metropolis Daily*! That would be good for your organization. Pay attention to what officials are saying in the news. Connect with Hu Xiaoyan [the token migrant worker among People's Congress representatives in Guangdong Province]. She recently mentioned in a public statement that migrant workers need their own grassroots organizations. Take advantage of this and introduce yourselves to her.

(Participant observation, 2010)

In addition to giving counsel on how to communicate with officials, this scholar also brokered relationships between officials and activists by contributing to internal policy debates. For example, the scholar invited the editor of a state-run policy magazine to dialogue with the leaders of several labor organizations about the necessity of addressing migrant workers' issues. He also contributed an opinion article to an internal policy magazine circulated to Party cadres advocating for government tolerance of grassroots labor organizations, arguing that cracking down on these organizations would only drive them underground. He wrote that by working with these organizations, the state could halt the rising tide of labor unrest and ensure social stability. By acting as brokers between the government and worker activists, domestic scholars attempt to liaise between state and society in the hope that local state authorities permit grassroots labor organizations to operate with more legitimacy in the eyes of the state.

CONCLUSION

This chapter presented the landscape of China's grassroots labor organizations. Drawing upon original interviews and participant observation, it identified the factors that influenced the rise of independent labor organizations. Although these labor organizations share some characteristics, there was significant variation between the two largest clusters in Beijing and the PRD with respect to their clientele, leadership, and relationships with the local state. Moreover, within the PRD cluster, there were considerable differences between organizations led by activists from Mainland China and those led by activists from Hong Kong. Whether the leaders came from Hong Kong or Mainland China influenced their ideologies and shaped their organizational goals. Whereas Hong Kong activists pressed for worker solidarity and genuine representation outside of the ACFTU, Mainland activists were engaged in a more modest, immediate struggle for labor rights under the continued rule of the Communist Party. Differences in leaders' social status – white-collar professionals versus migrant workers – also influenced the relationship between organizations and local states. Whereas white-collar leaders in Beijing forged synergistic partnerships with the local state, migrant worker leaders in the Pearl River Delta had fewer opportunities to partner with the state. Instead, they relied on domestic scholars to broker ties with the authorities.

These differences indicate that grassroots labor organizations in contemporary China are not unified in their aims. They compete for funding from foreign donors, for influence among workers, and they are divided in terms of ideology and mobilization tactics. As a result, these organizations do not constitute a unified network that can mobilize migrant workers. Many of the labor organizations featured in this study have been banned by the party-state and forced by the authorities to close down. Yet against these odds, many of these organizations managed to resurrect themselves and some have also managed to expand their operations into multiple cities. Documenting and analyzing their organizational process and their micro-level interactions with the state are critical to understanding how weak citizens organize under state repression.

Despite their ability to threaten local social stability, it is important to recognize the ambitions and influence of these labor organizations. Unlike civil society groups that emerged in the 2000s to challenge authoritarian incumbents across Eastern Europe (Bunce and Wolchik 2011: 58), these labor organizations are not part of an active underground movement seeking to bring down the Chinese Communist Party. Also, unlike leftist terrorist organizations and militant groups in Italy (Della Porta 1995), underground labor groups in China do not engage in anti-state violence. Moreover, they also differ from underground student organizations in Burma that attempted to mobilize against the state surreptitiously leading up to the 1988 pro-democracy uprising (Boudreau 2004) because even unregistered organizations were not fully surreptitious in their activities. Instead, these labor groups are weak and scattered, and because collective, large-scale resistance is swiftly crushed, they are unable to engage in sustained acts of resistance against the state. The smattering of pro-democracy human rights groups and underground religious organizations in China primarily aim to *survive* rather than to *resist* the state. Nevertheless, because labor groups potentially threaten social stability – a key pillar of the Chinese regime's legitimacy (Shue 2004) – they provide a unique opportunity to examine state control and contention in an authoritarian regime.

As the following chapters show, the rise of grassroots labor organizations reveals an alternative channel through which ordinary workers, who may not be able or willing to participate in strikes, can organize contention. Under certain conditions, weak civil society organizations, such as grassroots labor groups, can serve as unconventional mobilizing structures. These organizations, acting under the radar, play a critical role in mobilizing workers to undertake individualized action beyond atomized legal action. This type of disguised organizing takes place alongside the more observable collective action of their counterparts. Although mobilizing without the masses lacks the dramatic resonance that spontaneous strikes and demonstrations may have, it nevertheless evidences that there exist active mobilizing structures that have been overlooked in the analyses of overt collective action.

3

Fragmented Control

In the midst of China's associational revolution, cauldrons of social instability present new challenges to state domination. How does the Chinese state attempt to control underground labor organizations, and how does this sector of civil society contend with the state? This chapter pries open the black box of China's coercive apparatus to reveal patterns of interaction between different local state agencies and "underground" civil society organizations. The labor organizations examined in this chapter can be considered "underground" in the sense that the vast majority of them are not registered with any government bureau and also deploy contentious mobilizing strategies that threaten social stability. In analyzing their interactions to various bureaus within the local state in Guangzhou Province, this chapter theorizes the horizontal fragmentation of state control and its effects on under-the-radar mobilization.[1]

When Chinese civil society organizations coordinate collective challenges such as demonstrations or public signature campaigns, government agencies attempt to work together to "fight an integrated battle" aimed at demobilizing these organizations (Lee and Zhang 2013). However, on an everyday basis, local agencies do not necessarily coordinate repression. In the absence of emergency mass incidents such as strikes or demonstrations, local state agencies deployed "fragmented control" – a diverse array of strategies including soft repression, co-optation, and even neglect – to govern underground labor organizations. In contrast to competitive control in which state agencies use the market to stimulate competition among organizations (Chapter 4), fragmented control encompasses an array of control strategies across local agencies. Central mandates were refracted through individual agencies' incentives and bureaucratic missions, resulting in divergent and sometimes opposing control tactics (see Figure 3.1).

---

[1] Parts of this chapter draw from an earlier article in *Governance* (Fu 2017b).

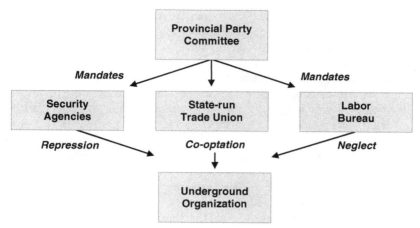

FIGURE 3.1 Fragmented control in Guangdong Province (2009–11)

Fragmented control contained, but did not completely demobilize, underground labor organizations. The diversity of control tactics created opportunities for activists to mobilize as "censored entrepreneurs." As they learned to self-censor, these groups also exploited the opportunities created by horizontal fissures between local state agencies to mobilize. Thus, instead of state repression backfiring on the state as suggested in the work of other social movement scholars (Earl and Soule 2010; Almeida 2008; Hess and Martin 2006; Goldstone and Tilly 2001), fragmented control changed the *form* of mobilization.

HORIZONTALLY DISAGGREGATING THE CHINESE STATE

In theorizing state control, this chapter horizontally disaggregates the Chinese state across different agencies within Guangdong Province. The Chinese political system is one of the most decentralized in the world (Birney 2014; Landry 2008) and the central state's policies are prone to being reshaped through a process of "bureaucratic bargaining" by local governments with parochial political goals (Lieberthal and Lampton 1992). This tension between the central state and local governments in China has long been the focus of scholarly analysis (Birney 2014; Mertha 2009; Landry 2008; O'Brien and Li 2006; Lieberthal and Lampton 1992). The divergence between the central and local states has become even more pronounced with economic reforms and fiscal decentralization (Oi 1992). Likewise, it has also affected the state's coercive capacity, as the policing institution in China appears to be highly ordered at the top but can "dissipate long before it reaches the street" (Scoggins and O'Brien 2016: 228).

While such vertical fragmentation has created governance problems for the state, it has also yielded opportunities for popular protestors who regularly exploit the divisions between higher and lower level officials to press their claims (Chen 2012: 165; Cai 2010: 9; O'Brien and Li 2006). So long as they avoid sensitive political issues and the scope of their mobilization remains localized, protestors benefit from the central state's incentive to permit some degree of unrest, which in turn allows the central state to collect information on local government malfeasance (Lorentzen 2013). Likewise, civil society organizations also leverage central–local divisions to partner with local governments (Hsu and Hasmath 2014; Teets 2014; Hildebrandt 2013), which shoulder the burden of executing the center's mandates. Even ostensibly illegal civil society organizations have taken advantage of local officials' incentives to accrue political credit with superiors by encouraging a kind of "contingent symbiosis" with the local state – a partnership that is contingent upon civil society staying within certain political boundaries (Spires 2011).

While recognizing the pivotal role of central–local tensions, this chapter seeks to *horizontally* disaggregate the local state, an analytical focus that has been previously eclipsed by vertical disaggregation. Horizontally disaggregating the state sheds light on the diverse forms of control that local agents have deployed in implementing the center's mandate of maintaining social stability. Local states in China have considerable latitude to operationalize and implement central policies (Heilmann and Perry 2013: 14). In putting these policies into practice, local officials have devised a range of creative strategies such as bargaining, bureaucratic absorption, and patron-clientelism (Lee and Zhang 2013; Su and He 2010). Like many of their peer street-level bureaucrats, local police in China are burdened by unfunded mandates (Scoggins and O'Brien 2016: 239–40). As a result, they have had to devise creative control tactics including "relational repression" – putting pressure on the family and social networks of known activists – to demobilize protestors (Deng and O'Brien 2013) and relying on ordinary citizens to do surveillance and policing in neighborhoods (Tanner 2000). Local officials have also made extensive use of informal coercion such as the hiring of thugs to rein in boundary pushers, a practice that has become more prevalent with the commodification of informal policing (X. Chen 2017) and which may undermine regime legitimacy (Ong 2015). Finally, local officials sometimes practice "blind-eye governance" in which they purposely ignore certain illegal activities so long as they do not cross a certain line (Weller 2012). This diverse toolkit of control at the grassroots level evidences the need to horizontally disaggregate the local state in order to understand exactly *which* local agencies are at work and *how* different agencies work together or at cross-purposes to rein in grassroots activism.

CENTRAL MANDATE: REPRESS UNDERGROUND ORGANIZATIONS

The central state has always faced a dilemma when governing civil society because it needs to foster aboveground organizations while simultaneously keeping underground organizations contained. Keenly aware of the role that civil society played in instigating the Color Revolutions in Eastern Europe, the Chinese party-state has remained vigilant against civil society organizations that could potentially mobilize the citizenry outside of the Party's control. Prior to the emergence of the most recent wave of labor organizations, the party-state had attempted to suppress the emergence of independent labor organizing. For example, the ACFTU deemed the Migrant Workers' Association in Zhejiang Province to be illegal despite its support from the local bureau of civil affairs (Howell 2008: 186–89). It also coopted crane operators in South China by turning their demands to set up an independent trade union into an opportunity to set up an official trade union (Pringle and Clarke 2011: 64). In the late 1990s, the Jiang Zemin administration declared the growth of illegal organizations (including migrant associations) to be anti-Party and unequivocally ordered the repression of unofficial civil society. On the brink of the Color Revolutions in Eastern Europe, the CCP Central Committee and the State Council issued the 1999 "Notice on the Work of Strengthening Management of Grassroots Organizations," declaring the growth of illegal organizations to be a direct threat to the party-state.[2] Migrant workers' associations were flagged as one type of illegal organization that harbored an anti-state agenda:

These illegal organizations' activities are concealed and are extremely destructive. Some ... utilize the sensitive, unsolved problems created by the state's reforms to plot the establishment of "laid-off workers associations," "veterans' associations," and "*migrant workers associations*" [emphasis added], creating disturbances. Some organizations employ a tactic of registering outside of the border while carrying out activities within the borders in their struggle against us.[3]

Having characterized illegal grassroots organizations as enemies of the state, the party-state commanded its various local agencies to repress illegal grassroots organizing:

We must devote our efforts to combating antagonistic illegal grassroots organizations; those that oppose the four cardinal principles pose a hidden threat to the country's political stability and are extremely harmful. The struggle against them is a serious political struggle that is related to the Party's fate, the success and failure of socialism, and the fundamental interests of the people.[4]

Thus, even before Hu Jintao's administration, the central state's mandate was clearly to repress these threatening organizations.

---

[2] Zhonggong Zhongyang Bangongting, Guowuyuan Bangongting Guanyu jinyibu jiaqiang minjian zuzhi guanli gongzuode tongzhi [General Office of the Central Committee of the CPC, State Council General Office's Notice on the Work of Strengthening Management of Grassroots Organizations], November 1, 1999.
[3] Ibid.
[4] Ibid.

Under Hu Jintao (2002–12), the control of threatening organization was part of a broader agenda of social management that promoted Hu's key idea of a "harmonious society" (*hexie shehui*). Maintaining social stability became a key priority of the national agenda and an important criterion in local Party cadres' performance evaluations (Lee and Zhang 2013). The "one veto rule" stipulated that any outbreak of mass incidents such as collective protests, strikes, or petitions would negatively impact the career trajectory of the officials in charge of that locality (Sun et al. 2010; Edin 2003). Accordingly, the administration strengthened the internal security apparatus while reforming the regulatory framework to permit more organizations to formally register. In 2011, the central state approved an internal security budget of 624 million yuan (95 billion dollars), which surpassed the military budget for a second consecutive year.[5] This truncheon investment in internal security reflected the regime's paranoia that domestic enemies might instigate social unrest. At the same time, the security apparatus has come to include a wider array of party-state and social institutions engaged in maintaining social stability (Wang and Minzner 2015: 356–7). District governments were allocated a "stability maintenance fund" which could be used to demobilize protestors through buying off individuals or groups who stage collective action with cash payments (Lee and Zhang 2013).

LOCAL FRAGMENTATION: MIXED CONTROL TACTICS

Yet while this repressive posture toward civil society organizations that challenged social stability filtered down to lower levels of the government, it was implemented and interpreted in different ways by various local government actors. The case of Guangdong Province illustrates the way in which these central government directives were differentially interpreted at the local level. At the provincial level, this central mandate to maintain social stability was echoed by the powerful Guangdong Committee on Politics and Law. In 2009, the Committee launched a province-wide investigation into labor activism and unofficial legal agents, the latter identified as "an illegal, for profit organization or person, who, acting in their capacity as a citizen, specializes in representing clients in litigation or non-litigation activities."[6] Accordingly, these agents "disguise [themselves] with a legal cloak," use "deception" to solicit worker clients, and use "radical actions to complement their 'agency' work" including "luring them [clients] to petition rowdily and doggedly or collectively blocking traffic, creating mass incidents." The report ordered local agencies across the province to repress these disruptive groups.

[5] C. Buckley, China Internal Security Spending Jumps Past Army Budget, 2011, Reuters, www.reuters.com/article/us-china-unrest-idUSTRE7222RA20110305.

[6] The full citation of the report has been omitted for the purposes of protecting the anonymity of individuals and organizations.

However, this central mandate was interpreted and implemented in different ways across different agencies in Guangdong. As the following examples show, the diverse strategies adopted by local agencies stemmed from their differing bureaucratic missions, the existence of informal mandates, and the kinds of information available to each bureau. Working at cross-purposes, various agencies working within a single local government pursued contradictory control strategies. Activists and the worker-participants of underground labor organizations came into contact with eight different government agencies in Guangdong Province (Table 3.1). On a regular basis, worker-participants interacted with the Bureau of Labor[7] and the courts which processed their rights claims, while activists contacted the Bureaus of Civil Affairs and the Bureau of Commerce in order to obtain registration for their organizations. In addition, the State Security and Public Security Bureau intermittently monitored the operations of these organizations and occasionally disbanded those that they believed threatened social stability. Finally, activists also occasionally allied with the local chapters of the state-run ACFTU, which at times supported their work.

Security Bureau: Hard and Soft Repression

The security bureaus of Guangdong Province (the Bureau of Public Security and Bureau of State Security) employed a toolkit that combined the deft use of hard repression to pre-empt the outbreak of mass incidents as well as everyday soft repression to contain the scope and expansion of underground labor organizations. Hard repression entailed forcing organizations to close, confiscating material and resources, as well as detaining activists. This was sometimes done through the security agencies' recruiting of third parties including thugs, bureaucratic actors, and landlords to exert high pressure on the organization. In contrast, soft repression included infiltration inside these groups, verbal warnings, and informal interrogation. Local authorities are veteran participants in exerting soft control, routinely "buying out" protestors with cash concessions (Chen 2012; Cai 2010; Su and He 2010) and putting pressure on the friends and relatives of activists in order to demobilize protests (Deng and O'Brien 2013).

In dealing with any mass incidents that occur as a direct result of civil society involvement, the state security agencies were at the helm of a team of local agencies that "fight an integrated battle" (Lee and Zhang 2013: 1495–9). When labor organizations crossed the line of acceptable behavior and attempted to organize collective action, the state security agencies were unequivocally harsh in their response. For example, in an incident that has been told and re-told among labor activists in Guangdong Province, a labor activist organized a

---

[7] The official name is the Bureau of Human Resources and Social Security.

TABLE 3.1 *Local agencies interacting with underground labor organizations in Guangdong*

Government agency	Interaction frequency	Interaction content
Courts	Frequent	Processes labor-related civil lawsuits; deals with collective worker "sit-ins" at court hearings.
Human Resources and Social Security Bureau (Labor Bureau)	Frequent	Overlooks underground organizations; deals with worker-participants' rights claims.
State-run Trade Union (ACFTU)	Infrequent	Partners with labor activists to co-opt and learn from them.
State Security Bureau	Intermittent	Gathers intelligence and issues warnings when taking activists to "tea" (informal interrogation); infiltrates and monitors groups.
Public Security Bureau	Intermittent	Executes closures of organizations and detains activists; mobilizes other agencies to harass activists.
Civil Affairs Bureau	Intermittent	Controls registration permits for social organizations.
Industry and Commerce Bureau	Intermittent	Conducts annual inspections of organizations; revokes or suspends registration permits for NGOs registered as enterprises.
Street/Sub-district Committees	Intermittent	Tacitly permits organizations to rent properties, so long as they do not cause social disturbances.

public signature campaign to rally support for a proposed amendment to the labor contract law. Taking to the streets, he called on pedestrians to sign a red banner in support of the cause. After gaining a purported 10,000 signatures, he and a colleague attempted to sneak the banner into the local people's congress meeting. They were immediately caught and later detained by the police, who confiscated the banner. After the lead activist's release, he attempted to stage a similar collective action again. This time, local agencies intercepted his attempt and coordinated a raid of this organization. According to the activist, this joint action involved plain-clothed policemen who stormed into his office and confiscated materials and equipment (Interview, activists, 2010). The security bureaus similarly targeted another labor organization in Guangdong Province, which had organized events that attracted up to 100 workers. According to a key activist who witnessed the closure of this organization, the state security mobilized thugs and a team of other bureaucratic agencies to harass the organization:

That gangster told us that he was the landlord's nephew. He said if you don't move out I'll smash all your stuff! Afterwards, we found out that the gangster and the local police were in it together; they came together to pressure the landlord not to lease to us. It was July or August; they shut our front doors but we continued working in the office. Then the fire department, the housing Association, utilities department, and the police – ten of them total – cut our water and electricity and went through all of our documents. We had no choice but to move to district X.

(Interview, activist, 2010)

During emergency cases, the state security agencies took charge of coordinating hard repression in the form of raids, detention, and forced closure of the trouble-making organization. In these times, the state agencies appeared quite coordinated across the same administrative level as they acted in concert to stymie social unrest.

Yet, the horizontal fissures between agencies re-emerged outside of these periods of coordinated bureaucratic action. Between 2009 and 2011, the state security agencies primarily used soft repression to control labor organizations on an everyday basis. According to activists' accounts, this included infiltrating organizations under the guise of a worker needing the organization's assistance. Many activists also reported that state security agents had "invited them to tea" (*qing wo hecha*), an informal method of interrogation regularly used by state agents to gather information and issue warnings to activists. During "tea," security agents inquired about the activities of an organization and warned activists about the consequences of inciting collective action. These meetings also offered opportunities to recruit activists as informants. I observed first-hand as two organizations that had collaborated to stage a flash demonstration in front of a district court-house came to harbor deep mistrust for each other. The main activist of one group believed that the leader of their partner organization had been co-opted by State Security:

I feel that my biggest failure [as an activist] was that I didn't realize what was going on right next to me. [The partner organization] got called in by the State Security and told on us. That's how they [State Security] found out which workers were involved [in the flash demonstration].

(Interview, activist, 2010)

This activist's perception reflected the mutual distrust that many labor organizations had for each other, suspicions security agents reinforced by deploying a "divide and conquer" strategy through the recruitment of informers.

State surveillance also extended to the sites of activism, as the security apparatus dispatched agents to monitor the activities of civil society organizations. Activists reported that plainclothes agents would sometimes disguise themselves as migrant workers seeking assistance (Interview, activist, 2010), while workers who had been engaged in contentious activity also reported being followed by agents (Interview, worker-participant, 2010). These measures reminded activists that their organizations were under constant surveillance by the state. Finally, security agencies sought to drive organizations into other jurisdictions, making them a problem for other local authorities. One tactic involved pressuring landlords to terminate the leases held by activists and dispatching health and safety teams to "inspect" the offices of civil society organizations for violations (Participant observation, 2010). While such actions did not reduce the total number of underground organizations, local officials who were in charge of particular jurisdictions had incentives to compel activists to move to neighboring localities (Field notes, 2011).

The goal of this soft repression was to contain these organizations rather than to eliminate them altogether. Despite the high coercive capacity of the security apparatus, local government officials opted for "low-intensity repression" (Way 2015) because it carried lower political risks. If any part of a coercive operation went awry, superiors in the local government would hold security officials responsible. In addition, heavy-handed efforts to eradicate organizations could radicalize the affected activists. Recognizing that coercion might set off a vicious cycle of social instability, security agencies preferred a repertoire of soft repression with the goal of containing these organizations.

Labor Union: Co-optation

In contrast to local security bureaus, a local chapter of the labor union sought to maintain social stability through an entirely different control strategy. Unlike the security agencies, whose primary mission was to preserve social stability, the ACFTU's nominal mandate was to represent the interests of China's workers. This mission allowed them to engage with, and even attempt to co-opt, underground labor organizations. In 2007, the Shenzhen municipal-level union experimented with forging partnerships with underground labor organizations. According to union officials, this decision was made in response to an informal mandate – a handwritten note on a policy document (*pishi*) – issued by the then-Party Secretary of Guangdong, Zhang Dejiang (2002–7). Zhang was concerned that the official union was losing legitimacy in the eyes of its primary constituency: ordinary workers. Accordingly, Zhang issued hand-written instructions to the union to learn from underground activists' strategies of serving workers. Such a note from a superior can take precedence over formal state mandates, as closely monitoring the ambiguous and shifting signals from one's superiors (*chayan guanse*) is a common practice in Chinese politics. Zhang's note thus served to inform union officials that they were not fulfilling their mission of responding to workers' interests. This informal mandate was echoed by an article in an internally circulated policy brief urging the union to learn from underground labor organizations (Interview, scholar, 2010).

Because Zhang did not dictate a specific course of action, this mandate left room for interpretation by lower-level officials (Interview, scholar, 2010). For example, Kong Xianghong, vice-chair of the Guangdong Federation of Trade Unions (a subsidiary branch of the ACFTU) publicly stated that people informally representing workers should not be labeled black lawyers and should instead be incorporated into the state's official labor union. The vice-chair of the Shenzhen Federation of Trade Unions (another ACFTU subsidiary), Wang Tongxing, stated that based on preliminary investigations, the union "should actively engage with them [independent labor organizations] and explore how to incorporate them into the labor unions' rights protection system in an orderly manner" (Interview, scholar, 2010).

The Shenzhen municipal trade union translated this informal mandate into action by attempting to co-opt labor activists into its "street-level rights protection service centers" (*jiedao weiquan fuwu zhongxin*).[8] In order to learn from underground labor activists how to better serve migrant workers, the union selectively invited activists to speak with them. Through interviews with these activists, union officials categorized them into three groups: political career-oriented actors; apolitical profit-driven actors; and mixed-goal actors with both political and economic motives (Interview, union official, 2011). In January 2008, the union held a joint conference with an influential leader of a grassroots labor organization to explore possible avenues of collaboration. According to a union official involved in the initiative, the union's experiment was an answer to the Party Secretary's informal mandate:

In 2006 or 2007, *Xinhua* published an internal policy brief introducing these organizations. Also, provincial level leaders [Zhang Dejiang] instructed us to investigate these organizations ... At the time, Zhang Dejiang said that these rights activists were making an impact. In the People's Congress meeting, he discussed whether workers would follow the ACFTU, whether the union had any draw among workers.

(Interview, union official, 2011)

The union's invitation created an unusual political opportunity for underground groups to forge synergistic relations with the local government in the midst of repression by the security agencies. The partnership promised to benefit both parties: it could provide an exit option for activist groups caught in a cycle of repression while the official union could learn how to win the support of workers. At the conference hosted by the union, underground activists who normally avoided contact with officials spoke directly to union representatives.

However, the interests of these two parties were not wholly aligned. While labor activists sought an equal partnership, the union sought to bring labor organizations under its own leadership. Eventually, the Shenzhen municipal-level union aborted its experiment due to the political riskiness of such a state-grassroots partnership and the perceived low personal and educational quality

---

[8] These centers dealt with labor disputes before they could erupt into mass incidents.

(*suzhi*) of the activists. According to a union official who was involved in the co-optation effort:

Overall, I give them [illegal labor organizations] a positive rating, but we discovered that most of them are profit-driven, the good and the bad mixed together. Their *suzhi* (personal quality) is also not high. They were all once engaged in labor disputes themselves. The union would have difficulty partnering with them. Their educational levels are insufficient to meet society's needs ... their [quality of] speech is very low, and they mostly do things [rights activism] for the money.

(Interview, trade union official, 2011)

This union official's assessment of the "low quality" of grassroots activists was publicly echoed by the vice-chair of the Shenzhen trade union, who stated, "The members in these *minjian* (grassroots) organizations do not have very high *suzhi* (quality) or strong moral character."[9] In reality, a personnel shift in provincial leadership also contributed to the union's decision to abandon efforts at state-civil society collaboration. According to the director of a prominent law firm that employed a network of labor rights lawyers, it was unclear at the time whether newly appointed Guangdong Party Secretary Wang Yang would share this tolerant disposition toward underground labor organizing. The union therefore abandoned the experiment after Zhang Dejiang's departure from provincial politics (Interview, lawyer, 2011).

Such fears about the new Party Secretary were unfounded. In 2012, the union not only revived its experiment but also brought its partnership with the underground labor organization to new heights under Wang Yang's leadership. This time, it was not the municipal-level union but the provincial-level union that invited labor activists to establish a Federation of Social Service Organizations for Guangdong Workers (Howell 2015: 715; Xu 2013: 255). The Federation sought to foster the development of the labor organizations' capacity and to facilitate their delivery of core social and legal services to migrant workers. The provincial union's political objectives were similar to the previous attempt at co-optation by the Shenzhen municipal-level union; it felt competitive pressure from underground labor organizations to demonstrate its responsiveness to workers, particularly after a wave of worker strikes in 2010 (Howell 2015: 715).

This experimentation took place in the context of fragmented control strategies. The 2012 co-optation initiative by the provincial trade union occurred in the same year as a crackdown that disbanded at least five underground labor organizations in Guangdong Province (Xu 2013: 255). Beyond taking a different approach to governing labor organizations, the union also acted as the protector of these civil society organizations by occasionally coming to the rescue of activists who had been detained by the security services (Interview, activist,

[9] C. Xu, *Zhusanjiao laogong weiquan NGO jubu weikun* [Pearl River Delta Labor Weiquan NGO Faces Difficulty Each Step of the Way], February 21, 2008.

2010). Driven by its own bureaucratic interests and informal mandates, it pursued an entirely different strategy of control from that of the security apparatus.

Labor Bureaus: Neglect

Unlike the ACFTU and the security apparatus, local Labor Bureaus neither actively repressed nor partnered with underground labor organizations and instead largely neglected them. This was done for two reasons: a lack of information on their activities and the need of the Labor Bureaus to focus on their primary bureaucratic mission of processing labor disputes and demobilizing worker protestors. Local labor officials were mainly concerned about workers disrupting social stability. In the words of district-level labor officials:

The number of strikes, collective petitions, traffic blockages, jumping off buildings and other such emergency incidents have increased, especially the number of mass incidents. Migrant workers' rights consciousness is low, and they are not willing to use legal means to resolve problems. They are prone to the wrong rationale that "the bigger commotion they cause, the more likely their problem is to be resolved and if they don't cause a commotion, then their problems won't be resolved at all."

(Interview, district-level officials, 2010)

These bureaucrats lacked information about which protests and strikes were staged by underground groups and which were organized autonomously by workers themselves: "it is hard to distinguish if black [illegal] lawyers are behind [mass incidents] since it is always the workers who are in the front" (Interview, city-level Labor Bureau officials, 2010). The Labor Bureau was therefore largely ignorant of the roles that organizations played in facilitating contention. This was also due to the fact that activists typically refrained from accompanying workers to Labor Bureaus where complaints were filed, and when they did, they introduced themselves as friends or relatives of the aggrieved workers. At other times, Labor Bureau officials sometimes mistook the activists for profiteering illegal lawyers. In interviews, Labor Bureau officials complained: "These [black lawyers] are outwardly protecting rights but actually are not a harmonious force. Their aim is profit and sometimes they forestall the resolution of disputes" (Interview, city-level officials, 2010). In reality, many of these leaders were motivated by ideological goals and earned little for the assistance they offered migrant workers.

These findings show that even within a single province, governance over civil society can be highly fragmented. The provincial committee report cited "the lack of coordination among state agencies" as an obstacle to controlling these groups: "the supervision of the citizens' legal agents' activities is in a vacuum, with no department able to deliver adequate scrutiny."[10] The horizontal disaggregation of the local state presented in this chapter revealed

---

[10] The full citation has been omitted in order to protect the anonymity of organizations and individuals.

TABLE 3.2 *Censored entrepreneurialism*

Self-censoring	Minimize involvement in contentious collective action
	Refrain from appearing in foreign and domestic media
	Reduce activities during major public holidays and events
	Minimize presence at the sites of confrontation between workers and authorities
Entrepreneurial	Disperse the organization across multiple sites and jurisdictions
	Relocate to new jurisdictions
	Seek protectors in the government
	Develop volunteer networks in lieu of formal membership

the contradictory control strategies adopted by various local state agencies. The mandate to maintain social stability was executed by different local government actors according to divergent bureaucratic missions, the presence of informal mandates, and the level of information each had about underground labor activism. These drivers help explain the origins of the "mixed signals" (Stern and O'Brien 2012) that local governments send to contentious social actors. While State Security and Public Security carried out their mandate by deploying a mix of soft and hard repression, the labor union attempted to co-opt labor activists. In contrast, the Labor Bureau overlooked underground labor activism due to its unique bureaucratic mission and a lack of information about which individual workers who took part in contentious activities had been coached by labor organizations and which were self-motivated. Thus, state control of labor organizations was the cumulative effect of the combined activities of local state agencies with competing goals, pulling underground organizations in different directions.

GRASSROOTS MOBILIZATION UNDER FRAGMENTED CONTROL

In response to these divergent pressures from the state, underground labor activists engaged in "censored entrepreneurialism" – a combination of self-censoring and entrepreneurial behaviors that allowed them to reduce political risk to themselves and their organizations while capitalizing on unexpected political opportunities. Instead of completely demobilizing underground activism, fragmented control created considerable opportunities for activists to ensure the survival of their organizations and even engage in limited forms of mobilization. Through soliciting the assistance of sympathetic actors within the state and society, underground groups were able to barter for their own survival despite being labeled by the state as threats to social stability. Their self-censoring and entrepreneurial behaviors appear in Table 3.2.

These behavioral responses depend on whether activists interpreted state signals as threats or as opportunities. Despite the state's apparent ubiquity

TABLE 3.3 *State to society signals*

Signal	Example
Verbal warnings	Cautioning activists to "lay low" for a certain period during formal interrogation or "tea chat" (he cha)
Indirect coercion	Harassment by thugs or mafia
Indirect pressure	Pressured by landlords to move offices, or notices of violations from bureau in charge of health and safety
Detainment	Detained for reasons other than being implicated in activism, such as for a traffic violation
Ignoring	Officials turning a blind eye to an organization's jurisdiction hopping

in the lives of Chinese citizens, the internal workings of the Chinese state apparatus can often appear to take place in a black box. Scholars have long noted the special role of signaling in Chinese politics (Walder 2009a: 14; Cai 2008; X. Chen 2008; O'Brien and Li 2006: ch. 2; Perry 2002b) but have only recently examined it as a central feature of China's political system (Zhi and Pearson 2016; Stern and O'Brien 2012: 74–98). When different state bureaus send divergent signals to activists, they amplify political uncertainty for those activists who must learn to interpret them. My fieldwork identified the following classes of signals that the local state regularly sent to underground activists (see Table 3.3).

In each of these cases, activists have to interpret the particular signal: does forcing the landlord to terminate leases with an organization mean that State Security is staging a crackdown on all illegal groups, or does it simply mean that the street-level government wants to minimize the potential for disturbances to public order in this specific neighborhood? Does being arrested and jailed for driving without a license signal that the police are singling an activist out for punishment because they direct a prominent labor organization, or are they just unfortunate to have encountered the traffic police?[11] These types of interpretive decisions inform activists' strategic decisions on a daily basis.

Like other boundary pushers such as journalists and rights lawyers, labor activists are aware of state domination and of their own fragility:

This [the activist makes gesture of a gun with his hand] is in [the state's] hands; even if I let you [grassroots organizations] jump, can you jump to the sky? No matter how large the organization is, what can it do? The state can shut it down at its whim ... Would a powerful state apparatus be afraid of a tiny grassroots organization? The only thing it's afraid of is multiplication. Imagine if every city had ten grassroots organizations ... that would be truly scary [for the state].

(Interview, activist, 2010)

---

[11] Personal diary of a detained activist, *Wo bei juliu de rizi* [The Days of My Detainment].

As the weaker player, activists adopted a range of self-censoring tactics that circumvented overt confrontation with the state. This included keeping a low profile by limiting their contact with the foreign media and refraining from organizing visible events during important national holidays. In order to avoid being labeled an independent union, they also called their participants "volunteers" rather than "members." When interacting with officials or the state-run media, they called their organizations "institutions" (*jigou*) rather than NGOs, which has a foreign implication. In taking these precautions, activists signaled to the local government that they understood the political limits placed upon them and did not intend to breach them.

However, their self-censoring behaviors did not translate into demobilization. On the contrary, they capitalized on unexpected political opportunities created by horizontal fragmentation across bureaucratic agencies. Many shared the perception that even an authoritarian state like China could not completely obliterate popular organizations as such coercion would backfire on the state by driving organizations further underground. They believed that the local state was constrained by the threat of organizations multiplying in a clandestine fashion:

The more they repress, the more we spring up. You can't repress; humans will resist. Anyways, they're afraid to repress too hard because they don't want to tear their faces completely [completely destroy relations with the labor organization] ... If they repress too hard and we might expand from four to eight or nine offices; then they'd be in real trouble.

(Interview, activist, 2010)

In response to repression by local governments, activists engaged in location hopping – moving to different jurisdictions in order to avoid arrest or the shuttering of their organizations. In 2007, the same year that the Shenzhen municipal trade union made an overture to underground labor organizations, authorities cracked down on one of the most prominent organizations in the Pearl River Delta. The authorities used red tape to make an "X" on the doors of the organization's main activity center (located in a migrant workers' residential community) and suggested that foreign groups were using the organization as a puppet to advance their own agendas. They pressured activists to move the organization out of the district and offered to help them find alternative employment (Interview, activist, 2010).

However, this crackdown did not lead to the organization's demise. Instead, activists moved five times and eventually reopened their main office in the same city and started additional branches in neighboring cities. The activists reasoned that local officials were first and foremost interested in protecting their own positions (*wusha mao*) and therefore sought to expel the organization to another locality. As one activist reasoned:

Because State Security is organized city by city, if we get kicked out of one city, we can set up shop in another city. Our primary office is in one district and none of the other offices are in this city, so they're not in the same system.

(Interview, activist, 2010)

In short, fragmented control deployed by different local agencies contained but did not demobilize underground activism altogether. While activists' self-censorship limited the scope of their organizing, these groups continued to test the boundaries of political acceptability.

CONCLUSION

Drawing upon interviews and participant observation inside underground labor organizations and government offices in Guangdong Province, this chapter evidenced that everyday state control was fragmented across different agencies. While State Security and Public Security carried out central state mandates by deploying a mix of soft and hard repression, the official state labor union attempted to co-opt labor activists. At the same time, the Labor Bureau overlooked underground labor activism due to their unique bureaucratic mission and a lack of information about which workers engaged in contentious activity due to coaching by labor organizations and which were self-motivated. State control thus emerged through the combined activities of local state agencies with competing goals that pulled underground organizations in different directions. This fragmentation was driven by three factors: divergent bureaucratic missions; the presence of informal mandates; and the level of information about underground activism each agency possessed. Combined, these factors help to explain the origins of mixed signals (Stern and O'Brien 2012) that the state sent to activists.

Fragmented control contained but did not demobilize underground organizing altogether. Activists censored their behavior while also exploiting horizontal fissures between local agencies in order to ensure organizational survival and even pursue organizational expansion. In the case of underground labor organizations, state control neither demobilized activists nor radicalized them, as scholarship on other social movements might have predicted (O'Brien and Deng 2015; Ondetti 2006; Almeida 2003; Jeffries 2002; Goldstone and Tilly 2001; Jones 1988). Instead, state control changed the form of mobilization. In a highly uncertain political environment where the state deliberately kept the "rules of the game" ambiguous, activists adapted their behavior to minimize political risk while simultaneously capitalizing on unexpected political opportunities in order to ensure the survival of their organizations. Having examined how the state controls underground organizations, the next chapter analyzes state control over aboveground groups using a different strategy: "competitive control."

4

Competitive Control

How does an authoritarian state foster civil society growth while keeping unruly organizations in line? Such governance dilemmas may emerge when authoritarian states seek to reap the benefits of civil society growth while simultaneously limiting the potential of civil society to mobilize citizens against the state. Engineering state control over a pluralistic civil society requires the state to experiment with new methods of repression and identify best practices of governance. Authoritarian rulers know all too well that an unbridled civil society can challenge state power. The resurrection of civil society in Eastern Europe, Latin America, and elsewhere proved fatal to the respective authoritarian governments of these regions (Alagappa 2004: 16; Ekiert and Kubik 2001; O'Donnell and Schmitter 1986: ch. 5). Single-party states that seek to prolong their reign must carefully balance the need for civil society with the threat that civil society poses to authoritarian power.

While the previous chapter examined state control over underground organizations, this chapter analyzes a second strategy that I term "competitive control" which is used to govern aboveground organizations, those that were officially registered in some capacity and operated in full view of the state. This control strategy sought to channel civil society organizations into assisting the state with social services delivery. It involved establishing a market for government contracting that encouraged organizations to compete with one another for opportunities to collaborate with local state agencies on a range of social service projects. Such partnerships enabled organizations to gain political legitimacy and to accrue scarce resources from the state such as financial support, office space, and even opportunities to consult on and shape public policy. And because the market for contracts was controlled by the state, these partnerships allowed the state to marginalize organizations whose missions did not align with the state's agenda.

By deploying this strategy, the party-state exploited civil society organizations' expertise in social services delivery and participatory development in order to improve the quality of authoritarian governance. An important political objective under the Hu Jintao administration was to reduce the scope of government activity by encouraging non-state organizations to participate in service delivery, a goal captured in the political slogan "small government, big society" (*xiaozhengfu, dashehui*) (Ma 2006). In response, an "aboveground" civil society sector emerged with the blessing of the state (Teets 2014; Lu 2009; Shieh 2009; Howell 2003). This sector was composed of relatively apolitical organizations that could assist the state in improving governance without challenging state power. These organizations – typically registered as businesses either with the Bureau of Civil Affairs or with the Bureau of Industry and Commerce – worked "within the system" to assist the party-state in transforming itself into a more responsive authoritarian government.

Local states sought opportunities to partner with this aboveground sector because it could assist in dealing with the challenges created by China's massive and ongoing internal migration. By 2050, an additional 350 million rural residents are expected to migrate to China's cities, creating unprecedented demand for public services.[1] Migration of this epic scale poses a dire challenge for the party-state in terms of developing institutions of social service provision to the migrants who have inundated the cities. Failure to deliver these goods and services may lead to the growth of urban slums and trigger social unrest, as migrants continue to demand access to housing, schooling, and other social services that they have historically been excluded from by the household registration system.

In response, a number of local states have turned to civil society organizations to provide key social services while also delivering valuable feedback from the grassroots. This effort is in keeping with a broader trend across the developing world, where states lacking capacity or resources have sought to partner with non-state actors to provide public goods (Tsai 2011; Posner 2003). When bureaucracies are embedded in "a concrete set of social ties that bind the state to society," they can improve their capacities to deliver critical goods and services (Evans 1995: 12).[2] In China, where local states are burdened with unfunded mandates to provide public services and laden with debt (Frazier 2010), officials facing pressures from above and challenges from below have begun to seek willing partners in civil society to assist with governance.

At the same time, these state-society partnerships do not signify a loosening of state control over new NGOs. In fact, local states adopt "competitive control" which enables them to exercise effective disciplinary power

---

[1] J. Woetzel et al., *Preparing for China's Urban Billion*, McKinsey Global Institute, 2009.

[2] While such state-civil society partnerships can bolster public goods provision, Mattingly (2016) evidenced that local elites' embeddedness in civil society can also result in "elite capture" of local politics and enable official malfeasance.

over social organizations. Modern states invest enormous resources in making their populations more "legible" by measuring, mapping, and collecting information about them (Scott 2009, 1998). By ordering and categorizing organizations engaged in the competitive process of awarding government contracts, China's party-state effectively renders civil society more "legible" and thus more governable. In order to gain political legitimacy and increase their chances of winning government contracts, aboveground organizations also censor both their rhetoric and their behavior. Civil society leaders know that in order to secure state resources and official recognition, they have to refrain from engaging in confrontational rights advocacy work, mimic the state's discourse on social development, and align their organizations' missions with the state's agenda.

Nevertheless, this strategy does not render civil society organizations entirely passive; state-civil society partnerships also create fortuitous opportunities for non-state actors to participate in policy consultation. In fact, the degree of willingness to experiment on the part of government agencies influences whether a synergistic partnership with civil society organizations is forged. When local governments exhibit openness to policy experimentation, synergistic partnerships are possible. These political opportunities allow civil society actors to act as consultants on a range of local policies, including ones on governing civil society groups. In contrast, where the local state is less open to policy experimentation, civil society actors remain tasked with delivering services. They are viewed as "substitutive" social services providers. As a result, while competitive control increases the state's disciplinary power over civil society, under the right conditions it also creates new channels of participation within an authoritarian political environment.

After describing the state's efforts to embrace civil society through competitive control, this chapter examines the interaction between this control system and a migrant labor organization that harbors ambitions for organizational expansion and public policy influence. With careful political maneuvering, the organization achieved an impressive expansion into migrant worker communities in three major cities. However, it did so within the confines of competitive control. In each city, it aligned with the policy objectives of local officials and agencies that permitted them to operate in the community. Officially promoted themes of "harmony" and "stability" were prominently woven into the organization's discourse, and the mediation of conflicts was prioritized over the defense of worker rights.

The priorities of local governments also shaped the extent to which the group could realize its policy goals. In Beijing, authorities were empowered to experiment with new models of civil society governance, and even allowed certain NGOs to participate in these policy-making initiatives. Their evident trust in it was part of the "legitimacy cascade" that facilitated the organization's expansion into new cities. However, authorities in the other two cities viewed the organization with more ambivalence. While they outsourced some social services to the organization, they did not allow for participation in the policy-making process.

FROM CORPORATISM TO COMPETITIVE CONTROL

Under the leadership of the Chinese Communist Party, state corporatism has been the dominant mode of state control over civil society. An ideal-type of corporatism is defined as "a system of interest representation in which the constituent units are organized into a limited number of singular, compulsory, non-competitive, hierarchically ordered and functionally differentiated categories, recognized or licensed (if not created) by the state and granted a deliberate representational monopoly within their respective categories in exchange for observing certain controls on their selection of leaders and articulation of demands and supports" (Schmitter 1974: 93–4). China's regulatory framework for social organizations prior to the 2000s reflected strong corporatist elements. The *1998 Regulations on Registration and Management of Social Organization* put in place a two-tiered registration system which required civil society organizations to find an official sponsoring agency (*guakao danwei*), colloquially known as a "mother-in-law" (*popo*). Sponsors had to ensure that organizations' missions did not overlap with those of other similar organizations, that its members were professionally competent, and that its activities were law-abiding (Saich 2000: 129–30). It also stipulated that similar organizations could not legally co-exist, ensuring that mass organizations enjoyed monopoly representation of a particular constituency (Saich 2000: 131). Organizations were also required to register with the appropriate Civil Affairs Department from the county level upward, a requirement which limited the horizontal spread of grassroots organizations (Saich 2000: 132).

However, beginning in the 2000s, a vast transformation in state-civil society relations unfolded: the party-state began to transition away from strict corporatism and to permit civil society organizations to operate with varying degrees of autonomy (Lu 2009; Wang 2006). In keeping with the tradition of "guerrilla policy-making" (Heilmann and Perry 2011), the party-state encouraged local governments to experiment with relaxing the registration requirements for certain types of organizations (Simon 2013: 316). As of 2011, at least four cities – Beijing, Changsha, Foshan, and Guangzhou – had spearheaded reforms aimed at the "one-stop registration" of civil society organizations (Simon 2013: 316). In 2016, the charity law was passed, which removed the requirement to find a supervisory unit before registering and also permitted more than one social organization to operate in a given sector.[3] These reforms evidenced a gradual loosening of corporatist regulatory structures to allow for the growth of operationally autonomous organizations.

[3] For a detailed analysis, see S. Shieh, Charity Law Facts, March 29, 2016, NGOs in China Blog.

Under this new control system, civil society played an increasingly important role in local governance as well as policy consultation (Teets 2014; He
and Warren 2011; Mertha 2008). Aboveground organizations collaborated
with local states to provide critical social services to marginalized populations
(Hsu and Hasmath 2014; Simon 2013; Lu 2009; Zhang and Baum 2004) and
assisted in disaster relief during national emergencies (Teets 2012, 2009). Some
religious organizations such as Protestant churches also collaborated with
local states in exchange for protection (Koesel 2014; Cao 2010). In other cases,
organizations also participated in the policy-making process as a deliberative
actor (He and Warren 2011). In a model that has been termed "consultative
authoritarianism," collaborations between state actors and civil society organizations, as well as their observing of state-civil society partnerships elsewhere,
resulted in a process of mutual policy learning (Teets 2014: 3). For example,
environmental groups have acted as "policy entrepreneurs" by aligning themselves with sympathetic local state agencies and the media to push for broad
policy changes (Mertha 2008).

These state-civil society partnerships have empowered both sets of actors.
On one side, these partnerships benefited local states, which were debt-laden
and burdened by unfunded mandates from the central government (Frazier
2010). Collaboration with civil society organizations not only attracted international funding but also provided valuable opportunities for the state to learn
about innovative service models and participatory governance (Teets 2014).
On the other side, civil society organizations could obtain coveted resources
and extended political legitimacy by partnering with the government. Some
groups "beg[ged] to be co-opted" by the state (Foster 2001). The spread of
new collaborative models gave rise to new synergies between the state and civil
society groups.

These new forms of state-society collaboration did not signify the end of
state efforts to control civil society. The party-state adopted "graduated control," using different tactics to deal with organizations that posed varying levels
of threat to the state (Kang and Han 2008). The state continued to set the rules
for collaboration, resulting in "co-dependent state-society relations" characterized by power asymmetries (Hildebrandt 2013). In this context, aboveground
organizations could not establish truly equal partnerships with the state, as the
state dictated the terms and content of their collaboration. Under such "contingent symbiosis" (Spires 2011), civil society organizations had to tread carefully
in order to avoid direct state repression.

This chapter argues that this new form of governance entailed a type
of "competitive control" that, in addition to assisting in local governance,
used the economic relationships created by government contracts to discipline aboveground civil society organizations. The creation of markets to
offer public services allowed the state to move away from rules and regulations to discipline civil society and instead embrace a new mechanism of
control: economic opportunities that channeled potentially contentious civil

society organizations into the delivery of social services. In doing so, the state could shape the agenda of civil society organizations by controlling access to resources and political legitimacy for organizations interested in collaborating with the state. Vying for coveted collaborations with local governments induced organizations to provide information about themselves and to self-censor their rhetoric and activities. In the process, they consented to the party-state's governing ideology which insisted upon the importance of maintaining social stability and the need to effect social change within existing Party-led political institutions. The following section examines the development of this control strategy within the broader political context of China under the Hu Jintao administration.

EXPERIMENTING WITH COMPETITIVE CONTROL

Competitive control emerged under the party-state's broad policy agenda of "social management" (*shehui guanli*), an agenda which created favorable conditions for state partnerships with civil society. Whereas previous development agendas had placed economic growth, usually measured by gross domestic product, as the top goal for state administrators, the Hu Jintao administration emphasized improving the health of society, with "human-centered development" (*yiren weiben*) as a core objective. According to President Hu, social management was about building "a socialist management system with Chinese characteristics, aiming to safeguard people's rights and interests, promote social justice, and sustain sound social order."[4] In other words, state officials were to devote their attention to improving the welfare of the masses and not simply focus on stimulating economic growth.

"Social management" involved new initiatives in social services delivery. The 12th Five-Year Plan on Economic and Social Development (2011–15) called for social organizations to play a larger role in helping the state shoulder the burden of providing social services.[5] The Plan outlined a dual strategy of governing civil society by both fostering the development of social organizations and tightening state supervision over them. On the one hand, state agencies were encouraged to nurture certain types of social organizations by lowering registration barriers, "releasing public resources to social organizations, and extending the scope of tax deductions."[6] On the other hand, the Plan also called for tightening supervision by establishing a multi-stakeholder oversight

[4] *Xinhua News*, Chinese President Urges Improved Social Management for Greater Harmony, Stability, February 19, 2011.

[5] *Guomin jingji he shehui fazhan dishierge wunian guihua gangyao* 2011–2015 (The 12th Five-Year Plan on Economic and Social Development, 2011–2015).

[6] The Plan advocated for nurturing the following types of social organizations: economic, philanthropic, non-profit, and urban/rural community organizations (12th Five Year Plan, Chapter 9, Section 39, Clause 1).

system composed of actors in the legal system, the government, society, and the organization itself.[7]

One element of the Plan was the creation of markets in which NGOs competed for opportunities to deliver social services. Markets for such contracting were initially explored through a series of pilot projects at the local level. Shenzhen pioneered the government contracting model, delegating 80 percent of its administrative management and services to social organizations in 2010.[8] Other cities, including Shanghai and Beijing, followed thereafter. In March of 2011, Li Liguo, the Minister of Civil Affairs, declared that the Shenzhen and Beijing models should be gradually replicated across the country: "I hope that the Shenzhen municipal social management innovation experience can be exported nationally, that diverse actors would pay attention to it and borrow from the model."[9]

At the same time, top cadres repeatedly articulated the need to maintain the Communist Party's dominance over civil society. Their views were expressed in a series of publications in the state-run media and the official magazine, *Qiushi*.[10] Zhou Yongkang, the former head of the Party's Political and Legislative Affairs Commission and a Politburo Standing Committee member, argued for continued Party leadership over civil society:

Our [country's] mass organizations such as the All-China Federation of Trade Unions, the All-China Youth Federation, the All-China Women's Federation are the transmission belts and bridges between the party-state and the people. They reach every aspect of politics, economics, culture, and society, which is different from non-governmental organizations in other countries ... the most important difference being that our country's organizations work under the leadership of the Chinese Communist Party. These intrinsic differences determine that reforming our social management system must start from our country's realities, [which means] upholding the Party's leadership, forging our own path.

Zhou claimed that social management with Chinese characteristics meant that the party-state must continue to steer the ship of society. Specifically referencing social organizations, he called on provincial and ministerial-level Party officials to innovate models for managing social organizations by categorizing them, establishing a comprehensive registration system, boosting coordination and clarifying the division of labor among agencies, and improving the annual inspection system.[11] These sentiments were echoed by Zhou Benshun, Secretary

---

[7] 12th Five Year Plan, Chapter 9, Section 39, Clause 2.
[8] S. Wang, Minzhengbu cheng san lei shehui zuzhi you wang yunxu zhijie dengji [The Ministry of Civil Affairs Declares Three Types of Social Organizations May Be Permitted to Directly Register], November 24, 2011, *Caixin*.
[9] Ibid.
[10] Y. Zhou, Jiaqiang he chuangxin shehuiguanli, Jianli jianquan zhongguo tese shehuizhuyi shehui guanli tixi [Strengthen and Innovate Social Management, Fully Establish Social Management System with Chinese Socialist Characteristics], 2011, *Qiushi*, 9.
[11] Ibid.

General of the CPC Central Commission of Politics and Law. Writing in the following issue of *Qiushi*, Zhou Benshu warned fellow Party members and officials that they should not be deceived by the "civil society trap" that certain Western countries have devised for China:

> We must not mistakenly believe, mistakenly transmit or fall into the "civil society" trap that some Western countries have designed for us. We must reinforce and innovate social management, not giving the state's work over to society but ensuring that the social management and public service of the Party and government are on the mark ... Instead, we must increase standardization, provide guidance, and incorporate social organizations into the party-state's social management system. This way, we ensure their healthy development into a supplemental force for social management and services.[12]

Zhou Benshun was unequivocal about the need for all types of social organizations to be brought under the party-state's leadership. Nevertheless, he suggested that social organizations should become a "supplemental force" for social management and service. Competitive control thus evolved in the context of beliefs that the Party must maintain its dominance and leadership over all social organizations.

Civil society organizations' partnerships with the state benefited local governments in two ways. First, organizations compensated for local governments' lack of expertise and capacity in delivering public goods to marginalized groups such as migrant workers. In some cases, organizations also brought in funding from foreign donors for projects that debt-laden local governments could not undertake on their own (Teets 2014: 23). In addition, civil society organizations contributed to maintaining social stability at the grassroots level. This benefited local states which had been charged with responding to social conflicts at the lowest administrative levels (Lee and Zhang 2013; Sun et al. 2010). In the realm of labor, aboveground organizations assisted the local state in providing social services such as education, healthcare, and legal aid to migrant workers who did not enjoy equal access to these public goods and were seen as a source of social unrest. Embedded in communities and equipped with professional expertise on conflict resolution, civil society organizations attempted to defuse social discontent at the local level by extending social services and encouraging participatory development.

One way in which aboveground civil society organizations assisted the local state was by training cadres in the methods of professional social work. This was in response to a call by the party-state to foster a nationwide network of volunteers and local-level state workers drawn from the ranks of the state and society to mediate conflicts at the micro-levels of the *jiedao* (street) and *shequ* (community).[13] These agents included neighborhood retirees who donned red

---

[12] B. Zhou, Zou Zhongguo tese shehui guanli chuangxin zhilu [Take the Path of Innovative Social Management with Chinese Characteristics], 2011, *Qiushi*, 10.

[13] W. Luo, Ministry Encourages Increase in Social Workers, Community-Based Services, November 22, 2015, *China Daily*.

"volunteer" arm bands, neighborhood committee members, and street (sub-district) level officials. In the past, this motley group of local community actors sought to resolve social conflict through informal mediation. As the state sought to professionalize these agents in the methods of social work, social organizations were precisely the instruments needed for the task.

CASE STUDY: SOCIAL ENGINEERING

The experiences of the aboveground labor group Social Engineering illustrate how competitive control worked in practice.[14] As one of China's most dynamic labor-related organizations, Social Engineering illustrates several aspects of state-civil society partnerships. First, it shows the effect of the state's disciplinary power on making civil society more "legible" and thus more governable. Organizations such as Social Engineering also play a role in rendering themselves more legible to the state by mimicking the state's rhetoric and aligning their mission with state policies. Second, the case of Social Engineering demonstrates the cascade effect of political legitimacy: once an organization forges a partnership with a state agency in one locality, it signals to agencies in other areas that the organization is a "safe" partner, making it easier to expand operations to other jurisdictions. Third, the case evidences that competitive control was not deployed in the same way across local governments, nor that it completely transformed aboveground civil society into passive social service providers. On the contrary, organizations were able to participate in the policy-making process only under certain conditions. Where local governments actively experimented with competitive control and "innovative governance" (*zhengfu chuangxin*), state-society partnerships extended into the realm of policy consultation. Where local governments only had a moderate willingness to experiment, partnerships gave rise to creative tripartite arrangements between the state, private enterprises, and organizations – agreements which provided substitutive social services but did not provide a channel for organizations to take part in policy consultation. Where local agencies were least interested in policy experimentation, partnerships remained in the realm of substitutive social services delivery. The case of Social Engineering demonstrates the wide variety of state-civil society partnerships, even within a single organization. Table 4.1 illustrates the different partnerships that Social Engineering formed with three local governments, each of which gave rise to different possibilities for policy consultation.

Social Engineering was founded in 2003 by white-collar professionals. It was grassroots both in the sense that none of its leaders or staff members held official positions in the state, and because the organization had full operational autonomy in terms of its decision making and agenda-setting powers. Less than a decade later, the organization developed into one of the most prominent

---

[14] In order to protect informants' identities, I use the pseudonym Social Engineering in lieu of the organization's name.

TABLE 4.1 *Social engineering's partnerships with local governments*

Branch	Registration	Clientele	State openness	Partnership type
City A	Non-profit, supportive organization	Service workers; construction workers; migrants' children	High	Policy consultation; substitutive social services
City B	Non-profit	Construction workers; street vendors; migrants' children	Low	Substitutive social services
City C	Non-profit	Factory workers	Medium	Substitutive social services (tripartite)

civil society franchises in China with legally registered branches in three major metropolises.[15] Moreover, the Beijing Municipal Civil Affairs Bureau promoted Social Engineering to the special status of a "supportive organization" (*zhichixing zuzhi*). This gave the organization coveted access to opportunities for policy consultation, including the opportunity to assist the Civil Affairs Bureau in designing a new regulatory framework for registering civil society organizations.

One of the key factors that propelled Social Engineering into the spotlight was its leadership's adeptness at mimicking official discourse. If you walked into any one of the three branches of Social Engineering, its staff members recited the organization's mission like a high school student would recite passages from a textbook:

Our mission is to promote social well-being, to contribute to the development and innovation of social service organizations and to the social work profession. We do this through innovating new models of social work services; researching and advocating for policy changes related to social work; professionalizing the construction of social service organizations, and advocating for social philanthropy.

(Participant observation, 2011)

This mission of promoting social work echoed the Ministry of Civil Affairs' language on innovating models of social management:

It [constructing a national corps of social workers] is also an effective strategy for maintaining a secure and safe society, and it safeguards the construction of a harmonious

---

[15] The main branch was registered as a non-profit with the Beijing Bureau of Civil Affairs (City A). The second branch is registered in a different city as a non-profit organization with a district Bureau of Civil Affairs, and the third branch is registered in another city as a non-profit with the City Bureau of Civil Affairs. For the purposes of anonymity, the cities where the subsidiary branches are located are named City B and City C.

culture as well as a trusting, friendly, and good societal atmosphere. It is an innovative method for the Party to do mass work, and is a pressing requirement for strengthening our work in local provision of basic services.[16]

Moreover, Social Engineering's publications highlighted its accomplishments using official language that mimicked state agency reports:

In 2005, Social Engineering completed its first strategic development plan, creating a model of social services which combines social work services innovation and social policy education with advocacy. It was named an "advanced work unit promoting the innovative education of youth social services" by the Beijing municipal government ... It has successfully probed the "volunteer cultivation and organization expansion" model.[17]

This strategic mimicry enabled the organization to establish partnerships with state agencies.

The organization also strategically aligned its mission with the state's goals. Unlike other labor organizations that emphasized worker empowerment, Social Engineering marketed itself as an innovator of models of social work and participatory development. Instead of embracing "rights advocacy" (*weiquan*), the organization championed harmonious labor relations which prioritized mediation and consultation over collective bargaining. Although Social Engineering branded itself primarily as a grassroots organization serving and empowering migrant workers, a significant aspect of its work consisted of training local cadres in the principles and practices of social work. This was in keeping with the state's agenda of social management, which entailed professionalizing local cadres in order to maintain social stability. Since local cadres increasingly shouldered the burden of stability maintenance (Lee and Zhang 2013), they stood to gain from learning new methods of resolving social conflict at the community level. Social Engineering capitalized on such opportunities to collaborate with the local government with the goal of introducing the principles of social work to local cadres.

Secondly, the organization's expansion trajectory illustrated the cascade effect of political legitimacy. Since its creation in 2003, Social Engineering has forged a dense network of state-society collaborations in three different municipalities. In June 2010 the main Beijing branch, which initially operated illegally as a commercial entity, became the first non-profit organization registered directly under the Municipal Bureau of Civil Affairs, which boosted its political legitimacy. Since then, various local state agencies have

---

[16] Minzhengbu guanyu kaizhan shehuigongzuo rencai duiwu jianshe shidian gongzuo de tongzhi [Notice from the Ministry of Civil Affairs Regarding Setting Up Experimental Sites for the Construction of a Corps of Social Workers], February 15, 2007, *Ministry of Civil Affairs of the People's Republic of China*.

[17] Organization calendar, 2011.

contracted the organization to provide social services such as after-school care for migrant children, community theater programs, legal consultation, and skills-building workshops for migrants. In addition to providing social services, the Beijing branch also consulted for the municipal Ministry of Civil Affairs on civil society regulation and the methods of professional social work.

In May 2007, Social Engineering opened a second branch upon the invitation of a local Bureau of Civil Affairs in another province (City B). This fortuitous partnership was formed after local officials visited the Beijing branch and decided that the organization was politically safe to work with. It had already partnered with the Beijing Bureau of Civil Affairs and the Ministry of Civil Affairs.[18] The new branch in City B provided community-based social services to a migrant clientele of construction workers, street vendors, and their children. Social Engineering then opened a third branch in City C which entailed an innovative partnership between the organization, the local government, and a large local enterprise. In 2009, the head of the global corporate social responsibility (CSR) division of one of the largest electronics manufacturers in China invited Social Engineering to establish a community service center for workers in its industrial complex in City C. This initiative first encountered resistance from officials in the Municipal Bureau of Civil Affairs. Officials considered it politically risky to partner with a civil society organization in a region characterized by high levels of labor conflict. However, the turning point came when the leadership of the Bureau of Civil Affairs visited the Beijing branch of Social Engineering and recognized that the organization had political legitimacy in the eyes of both Beijing and central officials. Upon receiving this political signal, they permitted Social Engineering to register as a non-profit with the City C Bureau of Civil Affairs. This organizational trajectory evidenced that political signaling mattered: approval by one influential set of political actors could trigger a "cascade" of legitimacy that facilitated expansion to other jurisdictions.

Nevertheless, legitimacy did not translate into the same types of partnerships in every jurisdiction. In Beijing, where the municipal Bureau of Civil Affairs was actively engaged in innovative governance, Social Engineering both gained access to policy consultation and provided social services. In contrast, in City B, the organization was unable to consult for local policy-makers and instead primarily served as a substitutive social services provider. It addressed social services provision needs that the local government struggled to satisfy, but it had little input on government policy-making. In City C, Social Engineering's partnership with the state was balanced against its collaboration with an enterprise that sought the organization's assistance in reducing worker turnover rates. Thus, the organization was also not able to participate in policy-making and also compromised its advocacy of workers' rights.

---

[18] Ibid.

The nature of state-civil society partnerships depended in part on the degree of the local state's openness towards experimentation. The Beijing Municipal Bureau of Civil Affairs was one of the leading agencies to experiment with partnering with civil society organizations to improve governance and to set up a system for government outsourcing to organizations. In the process of this experimentation, the Bureau was keen to solicit input from civil society organizations. Social Engineering took advantage of this opportunity to directly participate as a policy consultant. According to one of its directors, the Beijing branch directly advocated for changes on several policy measures related to migrant worker rights. In 2004, Social Engineering provided policy recommendations to the Municipal Bureau of Civil Affairs on how to respond to industrial occupational diseases, recommendations which were incorporated into an internal policy brief circulated to government officials. In 2009, the organization wrote a report on how to use social work to resolve the livelihood problems of migrant workers, which it submitted to the Bureau.[19] The organization made the case that migrant workers could be empowered to resolve their own problems and that the development of social work was closely related to the development of civil society. As the project manager of Social Engineering explained, the Bureau of Civil Affairs needed to solicit input from grassroots actors who had direct experience in serving migrant workers:

At the time [of the project], we were still registered as a commercial business with the Bureau of Industry and Commerce. We wrote a report for the Bureau of Civil Affairs with specific policy recommendations. They wanted to see how social work could serve different groups, especially migrant workers. Civil Affairs is supposed to advance social work but they are not sure how to serve migrant workers, nor do they know how to do professional social work. They don't have a roadmap for "small government, big society."

(Interview, project manager, 2011)

In 2010, the Municipal Bureau of Civil Affairs solicited policy recommendations from Social Engineering for streamlining the registration process of social organizations (Interview, director of Social Engineering, 2011). Eventually, the Beijing Municipal Bureau of Civil Affairs elevated Social Engineering to the special status of a "Supportive Organization" (*Zhichixing Zuzhi*), a formal designation which created opportunities for the organization to play a role in policy-making. Specifically, it played an important role in the Beijing Government Purchasing Social Services Resources Fair in 2010. It served as an independent evaluator of the approximately 400 civil society organizations competing for state funding. It also provided 100 young volunteers from its organization to work at the fair. After the municipal government purchased services from some organizations that attended the fair, it contracted with

[19] Shehui gongzuo rencai fuwu nonmingong wenti yanjiu [The Challenges of Social Work Professionals Service Provision for Migrant Workers].

Social Engineering to send their volunteers to these organizations to train their members.

The Beijing branch of Social Engineering also influenced local governance by training local officials on the theories and methods of social work. Transforming state employees into social work professionals was a critical component of the party-state's agenda to maintain social stability. During the 6th Plenum of the 16th Party Congress, Party officials called for agencies to foster a harmonious society through promoting social work (Leung and Xu 2015: ch. 2). In 2008, the Ministry of Civil Affairs initiated the first national qualifying exams for social workers and assistants, a measure that encouraged social service organizations to proliferate across the country.[20] University graduates majoring in social work were funneled into internships at organizations with legal status, including Social Engineering. The party-state also pushed for its own state workers at various administrative levels to adopt professional methods of social work in order to resolve social conflicts. However, because in China "social work" was both a novel concept and a new profession, the Ministry of Civil Affairs needed the assistance of organizations like Social Engineering to set up training programs for local cadres. Previously these officials had relied largely on informal methods of mediation to resolve social conflicts, and the training program aimed to upgrade and professionalize that skillset.

To this end, Social Engineering furnished local states with a corps of professional social workers who served as the state's handmaidens in managing society in neighborhoods and communities. At the district level, the Beijing chapter of Social Engineering worked closely with both the district Bureau of Civil Affairs as well as the Social Work Committee to establish a social work association. The association was in charge of training the district's grassroots officials, including neighborhood committee members, into professional social workers and for establishing a more centralized management system of state workers. At the street and neighborhood level, Social Engineering trained local cadres in the methods of professional social work and the language of community development and participatory governance. During a training workshop, the director of Social Engineering addressed a group of neighborhood committee members on the merits of participatory governance:

Oftentimes, when we have a project, it is initiated from above [authorities above the neighborhood committee level]. So we jump from project planning to project implementation immediately, without regard for how to incorporate residents' opinions into it. Then we wonder why it is hard to mobilize residents to join the project even though we put so much effort into it … the residents are not appreciative. We should instead think about how to bring people into the project planning stages, hearing their opinions on what the community needs.

(Participant observation, 2011)

---

[20] W. Hui, Government Procurement Promotes Social Work Agencies, February 7, 2010, *China Development Brief.*

The goal of this training was to persuade neighborhood committee members – who occupied the lowest ranks of the state apparatus – that support for projects could be mobilized from the bottom up by soliciting the input of community members. In doing so, the organization hoped to create a pathway to shape local governance by advocating for more participatory approaches to local decision making.

In addition to participating in policy-making, Social Engineering also provided substitutive social services for migrant workers in all three municipalities in which it operated. These services benefited local government partners because they allowed officials to claim "political credit" (*zhengji*) for the organization's work. In exchange, Social Engineering was permitted to operate with minimal interference from the authorities. For example, the Beijing branch partnered with street level government actors to establish a migrant workers' population planning association, which provided after-school care for migrant children. The organization also partnered with the Communist Youth League and the Beijing Municipal Party Committee to establish a street-level community youth association in 2007. In total, the Beijing branch established collaborations with both government and Party agencies at four different administrative levels. By strategically mimicking state discourse on models of social management, and by collaborating with multiple levels of the local state, Social Engineering gained resources, political legitimacy, and increased access to opportunities for policy consultation.

In contrast, in City B, where the Bureau of Civil Affairs was more reluctant to experiment with competitive control, Social Engineering provided substitutive social services in a tripartite arrangement that involved the local government and a private enterprise but did not fulfill its aspiration to engage in policy consultation as its Beijing counterpart had done. In contrast to other labor organizations that encouraged workers to adopt confrontational tactics when making demands of their employers, Social Engineering consented to the state's goal of maintaining social stability above all else.

Operating just outside the factory compound of its partner enterprise, this branch of Social Engineering provided migrant workers with psychological counseling, workplace dispute meditation services, and recreational activities. Through this tripartite partnership, the local government won the cooperation of Social Engineering in maintaining social stability in exchange for permitting it to operate openly in City B. This was a bargain that the leader of the organization was aware of and consented to, as in his view one of the primary missions of the organization was to assist the government in stabilizing society by fostering harmonious labor relations:

Our job is to facilitate their [the state's] work, helping them to invest more into grassroots organizations. We have to work together with the government rather than against it. I often say that not all migrant workers are right, not all bosses are bad, and not all governments are bad ... It's too easy to incite people's emotions, but that doesn't solve any problems.

(Interview, director, 2011)

Of the three branches of Social Engineering, this branch faced the most formidable challenge in promoting harmonious relations because it dealt most directly with factory workers who could go on strike. A promotional pamphlet from Social Engineering in City B defined its efforts to foster peaceful labor relations as such:

In order to help private enterprise employers to establish harmonious relationships with their employees, [our organization] is cultivating individuals to engage in professional social work in private enterprises. Through this work, [our organization] enriches employees' cultural life and encourages private enterprises to use social work methods to promote harmonious labor relations as well as to realize their corporate social responsibility.

(Organization pamphlet, 2011)

In practice, promoting harmonious labor relations meant that the organization recommended workers to use non-violent, non-confrontational means to resolve labor disputes and avoid direct confrontation with factory management and state officials. To this end, staff members coached migrant worker-participants to adopt this discourse of harmonious labor relations. The following is a transcript from my interview with a worker-participant who had been handpicked by the branch director to respond to my questions in her presence. In this exchange, the branch director attempted to guide the worker's narrative in order to highlight how the organization facilitated his communication with management to achieve harmonious labor relations.

WORKER: At this plant, I work on an assembly line making MP4 players. In June of 2010 [after less than a year of working at the plant], I got fired because I often fell asleep on night shifts. According to the rules, if a worker gets four points out of six points subtracted [for bad performance at the workplace], then he can be fired. Afterwards, I went to ask the human resources manager why I got fired. He was very touched because he said it was the first time a worker had approached him directly. I told him that I fell asleep often because of a medical condition. That way, I feel I left with a clear conscience.

DIRECTOR: You didn't talk in detail about how you resolved the problem. I remember you came to us after you were fired and said a phrase which left a very deep impression on me. Do you remember? You said you had a clear conscience upon leaving the plant. You haven't narrated your experience in detail.

WORKER: Oh, the human resources manager went to investigate [after I asked him why I was fired]. [Besides sleeping on the job], I also had personal conflicts with the assembly line leader. One time, when he [the line leader] yelled at me, I couldn't take it anymore and I threw the PCB (printed circuit board) on the floor. Then, I went to confess my actions to the head manager. He said I should be fired, so I signed the slip. Afterwards [after being fired], I went to Social Engineering and they encouraged me to find the human resources manager [to explain that I fell asleep often due to a medical problem]. Then I felt I had left with a clear conscience.

(Interview, worker, 2011)

Establishing harmonious labor relations also benefited the enterprise by reducing worker turnover rates.[21] In the words of the director of the global corporate social responsibility office, the partnership with Social Engineering was also expected to reduce the rate of worker suicide:

Through our research, we foresaw issues that confronted all of us last year; all this suicide [at Foxconn]. We did our own demographic research. We knew the demographic was changing, the supply [of labor is] shrinking, and [workers'] aspirations are changing … the younger generation have different needs and aspirations. They want to make something out of their lives but don't know what; don't know how. They feel they have no way out. There's a vicious cycle of problems so we see a need for professionals to help them discover themselves and then develop a suitable plan to reach their goals; discover their own self-worth.

(Interview, head of global CSR, 2011)

To this end, the organization trained its staff members in psychological counseling and maintained a hotline for workers to call when they encountered problems on the job. By keeping workers content, the organization aided the enterprise in reducing the high employment turnover rate, which had become a problem due to labor shortages across China. According to the branch director, "We hope they [workers] become a part of the community, not just a part of an enterprise. This way, we would also reduce worker turnover. We encourage our workers to use rational means to resolve labor disputes" (Interview, branch director, 2011).

In terms of its collaboration with the state, the organization's services offered the local Bureau of Civil Affairs opportunities to claim political credit for innovating new ways of delivering public services. According to both staff members at Social Engineering's City B branch as well as representatives from the enterprise:

They [the local Bureau of Civil Affairs] have not done anything but claim credit. They paid 5,000 US dollars to Social Engineering to purchase services to train government officials. The official involved got a promotion out of it. [The organization's branch in City B] is not widely supported by the entire city government; [the support was] confined to the Civil Affairs Bureau. [I know this] because another colleague of mine was hosting a visit by a city official from the People's Liberation Army and [this official] visited Social Engineering. A female official called the Security Bureau to investigate Social Engineering. [She] saw on their brochure they were receiving funding from foreign sources.

(Interview, enterprise representative, 2011)

---

[21] Foxconn, a major electronics manufacturer in South China, made international headlines in the spring of 2010 with a string of consecutive worker suicides.

In spite of these concerns, Social Engineering gained access to resources from the enterprise as well as political legitimacy in the eyes of the state. In 2011, the State Council Research Committee visited the organization's City B branch and endorsed its operating model, upholding it as a prototype for other civil society organizations operating across China. In fact, the head of the Committee's research team, and vice director of the local chapter of the ACFTU, declared:

As a grassroots organization, [Social Engineering] is well positioned to experiment with local service delivery, bringing together multiple resources in this industrial complex in order to build community. It has enriched Chinese social organizations as well as the connotations of social work ... This model should be promoted in other regions in order to inspire the development of the nation's social philanthropy.[22]

Responding to opportunities to partner with the state, Social Engineering in City B had formed a state-civil society partnership that resulted in an innovative tripartite arrangement benefiting all three parties – the local government, the enterprise, and the social organization. However, this came at the cost of consenting to assist the local state in maintaining social stability. Moreover, the local government's limited willingness to experiment with social management created few pathways for Social Engineering in City B to take part in policy consultation.

The third branch of Social Engineering was located in City C, a municipality where local state agencies were similarly ambivalent about partnering with a labor group and therefore wary of experimenting with the innovative governance models seen in Beijing. As a result, the state-civil society partnership in City C between Social Engineering and the local state resulted solely in substitutive service provision. Initially many local officials harbored doubts about Social Engineering's intentions, fearing that civil society organizations were equivalent to anti-government forces. Despite their skepticism, in 2007 a liberal-minded district leader permitted the organization to establish a branch in the same office building as the neighborhood committee. A district official explained the role that social organizations should play:

From a bottom-up perspective, residents now have an organization. From the top-down perspective, public administration has found a social organization to hand over assignments to. The advantage of social organizations is their objectivity, low cost, and social legitimacy ... The government needs to let society decide on some policies ... grassroots democracy starts from little decisions. What kind of flowers should we [the community] plant? How many hallway windows should be open? Grassroots democracy is all about mediation and compromise. For instance, if the government is drafting an environmental policy, it should consult environmental NGOs. Right now, we listen to whoever's title is bigger, louder, and more powerful.

(Interview, district official, 2011)

---

[22] In the interest of anonymity, the source article has been omitted.

Social Engineering assisted the district level government with an immediate problem: how to manage the influx of migrant workers into their communities. To serve marginalized migrant workers denied access to basic public goods such as access to public schools for their children, the organization coordinated a range of community service projects, including summer camps for migrant children and skills-building workshops for migrant workers. Its staff also regularly visited and organized activities for migrant children in nearby communities who relocated every time their homes were demolished for real estate development. For its services, the branch received considerable financial and political support from the district government, which commissioned approximately 100,000 yuan (15,600 US dollars) worth of projects from the organization and provided it with an office. The organization also received 1,000 yuan (156 US dollars) per month for its collaboration on a migrant youth project with the street-level Party committee.

Yet such assistance came at the price of district and municipal state officials in City C claiming political credit for the work done by Social Engineering. When upper-level officials visited the sub-district government's office, the Party committee demonstrated its achievements, which were prominently displayed on plaques that were commendations for their innovative social work. As one state official explained:

Social Engineering expresses a lot of its needs indirectly. For instance, during their annual galas, they express that the street-level government should let them use more of their public resources. Although the city government hasn't formally been authorized to purchase services from social organizations, it has already done so informally, and Social Engineering won 20,000 yuan.

(Interview, district official, 2011)

Through this partnership, officials came to view social organizations as valuable assets in local governance. A district-level official in City C who worked with Social Engineering expressed the need for more social organizations to provide substitutive social services:

It's time for the government to provide fish with water. The government needs political credit and innovation. This is true of both upper and lower administrative levels. But I feel that quality is of utmost importance ... If the government gives its own projects over to social organizations, the hope is that these organizations would possess several qualities: maturity, independence, competence ... The government is not omnipotent. We need to combine service delivery with social management.

(Interview, district official, 2011)

Through the provision of social services to migrant workers, Social Engineering effectively assisted the local government in bolstering local social stability. However, its partnership with a more politically cautious local state did not create pathways for the organization to engage in policy consultation.

As the case of Social Engineering demonstrated, competitive control was implemented differently by agencies in different cities and resulted in different opportunities for the organization to take part in policy consultations. Only when a local state agency was actively experimenting with new models of governance could a civil society organization become a policy consultant. By training local officials to become professional social workers, Social Engineering introduced new ideas of participatory governance to local government actors (though the long-term effects of this policy advocacy remain to be seen). In contrast, in cases where the local government was mainly interested in soliciting substitutive social services, civil society organizations had a minimal impact on policy-making. Nevertheless, even in these cases, this did not mean that civil society remained passive or was simply co-opted by the state. Through their daily interactions with state officials and private enterprises, even competitive control left room for civil society organizations to influence the attitude of the local government towards civil society under certain conditions.

CONCLUSION

This chapter evidenced that the party-state deployed a strategy of competitive control to discipline aboveground civil society organizations. Under the broad policy agenda of social management, the central state provided the conditions for local governments to experiment with innovative models of state-civil society partnerships. Through the creation of a system for government contracting, the state attempted to channel the activities of the aboveground civil society sector into substitutive social services delivery. In doing so, it secured the consent of partnering organizations to maintain social stability in lieu of confrontational rights advocacy.

As the case of Social Engineering showed, the specific nature of the partnership varied depending on the local government agency's openness to experimenting with innovative governance. In Beijing, where there was a high degree of openness, these partnerships created pathways for policy consultation on issues ranging from participatory governance to reforming the regulations governing civil society. In City B, where there was a low degree of openness, the partnership took the form of a tripartite arrangement between the social organization, the local government, and a private enterprise. Finally, in City C, where the degree of openness was moderate, the partnership was limited solely to substitutive social service provision. This case demonstrated that even in a single organization, there was significant variation in the nature of partnership with various local governments and that the effect of competitive control on civil society organizations depended on specific arrangements with local government agencies.[23]

---

[23] Benjamin Read's study of homeowners' associations in China also argues for the need to identify micro-level factors that contribute to the successes and failures of civic organizations (Read 2008: 1260).

Social Engineering was not the only labor organization to have provided substitutive social services, although it was arguably one of the most successful ones to do so. Many other organizations both in Beijing and Guangdong Province also offered a range of services to migrants whose needs were unmet by their local governments since they were not considered a core constituency. Generally, labor organizations in Guangdong Province focused more squarely on legal aid and education while also providing social outings and staging plays by workers for workers. Their Beijing counterparts were focused less on legal advocacy and were more active in providing substitutive social services such as childcare, basic skills courses, leisure activities, and the provision of cheap consumer goods. At least two organizations in Beijing owned co-op stores that provided used clothing and household goods to workers at a discounted price. This essentially provided a substitutive market that allowed workers to purchase consumer goods that were otherwise prohibitively expensive. One of these organizations also provided substitutive educational services in the form of a migrant elementary school and a worker's college (see Chapter 7). Providing a wide range of substitutive services was only possible for well-resourced and sufficiently staffed organizations. This meant that labor organizations competed with one another for state resources in a managed process that allowed the party-state to exploit rivalry within civil society.

The party-state sought to achieve three goals through the strategy of competitive control. First, it aimed to improve the quality of authoritarian governance without requiring the Party to relinquish political control. Aboveground civil society organizations channeled critical information about the needs of the masses while also facilitating knowledge transfers from civil society to the state. Because these partnerships were unequal – state agencies maintained control over the agenda and funding of these partnerships, as well as oversight of their execution – the local government effectively maintained political control over civil society organizations while reaping the rewards. Second, through competitive control, the party-state exercised disciplinary power over civil society. The market for government contracts rewarded obedient civil society organizations with financial resources and political legitimacy. And third, competitive control entailed a process of ordering and categorizing organizations that rendered the aboveground civil society sector, in the words of James Scott, more "legible" to the state (Scott 1998).

This chapter presented a case study of how one relatively successful labor organization and its various local state partners mutually adapted to one another. On the one hand, Social Engineering adapted to the political climate by mimicking official discourse and reframing their missions to align with the social management agenda of the party-state. On the other hand, certain local governments also adapted their governance models to become more participatory and inclusive of non-state actors. Yet this strategy had limited effectiveness for controlling threatening organizations, many of which refused to partner with local governments or were excluded from the market for policy consulting. By simultaneously deploying both fragmented and competitive control, the party-state was able to stave off restive forces of the underground sector while exploiting the benefits of an expanded aboveground civil society sector.

PART II

COACHING CONTENTION

Part I of this book examined how the Chinese party-state deployed flexible repression to control civil society. This mode of control created an operating environment in which it was highly risky for civil society organizations to coordinate collective action. In order to ensure their survival, aboveground organizations forged mutually beneficial partnerships with local states. In contrast, underground organizations engaged in censored entrepreneurialism, restraining contentious activities while exploiting opportunities to grow. In such an environment, how do organizations mobilize citizens to press the state to guarantee their rights? In liberal democracies, civil society groups have the right to circulate petitions, lobby the government, and organize protests. But in states where organized collective action is legally forbidden or practically constrained, civil society groups must devise innovative tactics in an effort to circumvent state repression.

Part II of this book examines the tactical innovations that Chinese organizations have devised in response to flexible repression. Ethnographic case studies of labor organizations reveal three tactical innovations that fall under the broader dynamic of mobilizing without the masses: the pedagogy of micro-collective action; the pedagogy of atomized action; and the pedagogy of discursive action. The term "pedagogy" captures the process of teaching in which activists instill in participants a commitment to make rights claims and provide them with the necessary moral and strategic resources to do so. These pedagogies depart from the dynamics of contention model presented in classic social movement literature (McAdam et al. 2001). In the work of earlier social movement theorists, each link in the mobilizing process builds towards tactical innovation – an iterative exchange between challengers and opponents that disrupts status quo politics and which signals turning points in the development of social movements (McAdam 1983: 735). Tactical innovations are typically collective in nature: the bus boycotts, lunch-counter sit-ins, freedom rides, and urban riots of the civil rights movement all involved mobilizing large numbers of individuals to partake in collective action (McAdam 1983).

The tactical innovations examined in the following chapters are therefore unconventional; they do not involve large numbers of participants. Because they are limited in scale, these contentious performances do not aim to mount collective challenges to the party-state, nor do they have the power to do so. The goal of such tactical innovations is to strike a middle ground between rights advocacy and organizational survival. The innovation lies in devising novel, self-limiting tactics that organizations can use to win tangible rights for their constituents without staging the kind of mass incidents that the party-state fears. Although these tactics represent a form of political compromise with the state, they nevertheless seek to disrupt status quo politics through the creation of frames, or shared understandings of a problem and solution (Benford and Snow 2000).

These strategies can be placed on a continuum of the risk posed to the civil society organization (see Table 11.1). The riskiest tactic is micro-collective action, which organizes small groups of citizens to engage in brief demonstrations. The main differences between micro-collective action and other forms of popular protest in China are its symbolic demonstration of worker solidarity and its coordination by a civil society organization. Worker-activists engaged in micro-collective action demonstrate to both the state and onlookers that workers across different factories can act in solidarity to demand labor rights. A second and more moderate tactical innovation is atomized action, which disguises the involvement of a civil society group behind a façade of individual contention. Activists coach participants to threaten authorities as individuals rather than collectives, thereby transferring risk from the organization to the individual. Individuals are coached to mount verbal and performance threats that disrupt local social stability and incentivize officials to respond to their demands. Finally, the least risky tactic is discursive action, in which activists refrain from directly threatening social stability and instead engage in cultural mobilization. Discursive action entails producing and disseminating didactic theater, poetry, music, and other forms of visual and performance arts in order to construct a common identity of workers as citizens.

Each tactical innovation emerged from activists' experimentation with different means of mobilizing that did not necessitate large-scale collective action. The pedagogical process which takes place in the organization entails legal workshops, discussion groups, and social events. It is through this process that activists construct and disseminate diagnostic, prognostic, and motivational frames (Snow and Benford 1988) which shape the nature of labor activism. Because these frames present labor rights as part of a broader struggle for equal citizenship, they lead to a transformation in consciousness that is perhaps the most significant outcome of mobilizing without the masses. These frames couch the struggle for labor rights in terms of a broader struggle for equal citizenship. Migrant workers from rural China who are treated by both

TABLE II.I *Variants of mobilizing without the masses*

Pedagogy	Micro-collective action	Atomized action	Discursive action
Frames	*Diagnostic* State and capital are colluding to exploit workers	*Diagnostic* Local state fails to implement labor laws	*Diagnostic* Migrants are treated as second-class citizens
	Prognostic Unite in solidarity	*Prognostic* Devise illegal tactics	*Prognostic* Demand equal citizenship
	Motivational Employers have united; workers should also unite	*Motivational* Power comes from threatening authorities	*Motivational* Migrants are citizens
Action	Flash protests, collective sit-ins, signature campaigns	Suicide shows, stalking officials, sabotage, individual sit-ins, contacting journalists	Performance, visual, and written arts, partnership with state agencies
Organization Outcomes	High risk	Medium risk	Low risk
Participant Outcomes	Collective consciousness	Collective consciousness	Collective consciousness
	Practice in collective action	Individual concessions	State-civil society learning

the state and society as second-class citizens are taught by labor organizations to think of themselves as equal citizens bearing the same rights as their urban counterparts. In this sense, civil society organizations play an instrumental role in constructing a new grammar of contention.

5

Micro-Collective Action

In the spring of 2010, a dozen workers in a major South China metropolis staged a flash demonstration in front of the district court-house. Wearing sanitary face masks to disguise their identities, the workers lined up in two rows as if to take a group photo on the steps of the courthouse. Each worker held up a large Chinese character pasted on cardboard that, strung together, formed the phrase: "Workers against blacklisting." Across the street, a fellow worker-activist was filming the protest. Their flash demonstration ended in less than a minute when the court security guards came to disperse them.

Although they were employees or former employees of twenty different factories, these workers shared a common grievance: the manufacturers' association had allegedly blacklisted hundreds of workers who they deemed as trouble-makers. These workers had filed complaints with the Labor Bureau against their employers for failing to pay overtime wages and provide social insurance. In retribution, their employers dismissed them and placed their names and personal information on a blacklist that was circulated to other employers. Blacklisted workers found it nearly impossible to find new employment in the district. In response, four defiant workers filed joint lawsuits against their employers as well as against the association. Simultaneous with their pursuit of legal action, they also engaged in flash demonstrations to amplify this issue and to demonstrate worker solidarity.

To the casual observer, the flash demonstration may have appeared as a spontaneous event, coordinated by a small handful of disgruntled workers. Yet behind this event was a protracted and semi-covert process of mobilization. These workers were disciples of an underground labor organization that had trained them to frame individual grievances as a larger collective problem. Emphasizing terms like "solidarity" (*tuanjie*) and "collective" (*jiti*), activists coached workers to articulate their grievances and to attribute their problems to structural factors such as collusion between the local state and business interests. This pedagogical process inspired workers to stage such micro-collective action.

MICRO-COLLECTIVE ACTION

In contemporary China, it is politically risky for organizations to coordinate protests, petitions, and demonstrations. Those that act as "the invisible black hands" (*muhou heishou*) behind contention may find themselves targets of state repression. Due to these risks, the vast majority of popular protesters in China have deliberately avoided coordinating through formal organizations (Reny and Hurst 2013; X. Chen 2012: 8–10; Cai 2010: 16; Zhou 1993). For the most part, protesting groups are "temporary communities without an organizational basis" (Cai 2010: 16). In the realm of labor activism, workers have largely taken matters into their own hands by organizing strikes without the support of a union (Friedman 2014; Hurst 2009; Lee 2007b). In the absence of a formal mobilizing structure that can bind the aggrieved together in a sustained manner, protestors typically disband when they receive concessions (Lee and Zhang 2013; X. Chen 2012; Cai 2010: 16).

However, as the above case illustrated, some labor organizations have been able to coordinate micro-collective action. Compared with other forms of popular protests in China, the scale of such action is considerably smaller, involving only a dozen or so participants that are committed disciples of the organization. This limited scale is a common feature of organization-based activism. In addition, the symbolic nature of micro-collective action distinguishes it from other types of economic-based popular protest. Instead of solely extracting economic concessions from the state or business interests, participants engage in micro-collective action as a display of solidarity with each other and with those who share similar grievances. Inspired by the organization's call for solidarity among participants, their goal is to amplify their grievances and to make claims for broader political change. Whereas many protestors are pacified by financial concessions by the state (Lee and Zhang 2013; X. Chen 2012; Cai 2010), workers deploying micro-collective action aim to inspire others to follow suit despite state repression. These worker activists felt "the pleasure of agency" – the sense that they were making history by asserting their rights and identities (E. Wood 2003: 18). This call for bystanders to become adherents is inevitably challenging to a party-state that fears social instability.

CASE STUDY: SOLIDARITY IN ACTION

The case of an underground labor organization, Solidarity in Action, illustrates the pedagogy of micro-collective action.[1] Hong Kong activists founded the

---

[1] This is a pseudonym for the organization in order to protect informants' identities. Even though this was set up as a temporary platform for training workers to become activists, its staff

organization in 2009 as a parachuting mission to facilitate grassroots labor activism in China. The organization was unregistered and had no pamphlets and no official motto. It served as a platform for cultivating worker leaders who could identify labor exploitation in their factories and disseminate legal knowledge on labor rights to other workers. Its parent organization considered it an enabling platform for mobilizing workers rather than as a social organization. The director of the Hong Kong-based parent organization explained its founding in these terms:

> It [Solidarity in Action] is a permanent worker base [for gathering information on] worker discontent, workers know which problems need to be solved … We didn't want to do an NGO … it's a parachuting [mission] since we have to find some active workers first. How to find these active workers? We have to use a platform like a resource center to do some worker activities every once in a while to do discussions as fact-finding missions.
>
> (Interview, director, 2011)

The organization sought to provide leadership and material and cognitive resources to migrant workers in a local industry. Located in a non-descript ground-level apartment that opened to the street, the organization was easily accessible to nearby workers. Like other organizations in the Pearl River Delta, it provided workers with pro bono legal consultation and services, including referrals to an affiliated labor rights lawyer. Workers in the nearby industrial district would gather in the apartment for weekly discussions, seminars, films, and other activities. Because the organization had no formal membership, there was no definitive count of worker involvement. During fieldwork in 2010, I observed no more than twenty workers that met for regular discussions at the organization. The reason for this low number (more than twice as many would turn up to legal workshops at other organizations) was that the focus of these workshops was not just to answer workers' questions about the labor dispute system but also to train them to become committed activists who would act as leaders in their respective factories.

Unlike other labor organizations that provided social services or sought the implementation of existing labor laws, Solidarity in Action advocated for a broader, more radical right to collective bargaining (*jiti tanpan*). This demand was a significant departure from the state-sanctioned collective consultation (*jiti xieshang*),[2] which did not give workers leverage over employers because union officials were not freely elected and therefore failed to truly represent workers' interests. Such state-led consultation was predicated upon a non-confrontational relationship between the state, capital, and workers, an

---

members and core participants often referred to it as an "organization" or "institution" (*zuzhi* or *jigou*). Other labor organizations also referred to it by the name of its parent organization. In keeping with these conventions, Solidarity in Action is analyzed as an organization.

[2] *Economist*, Out, Brothers, Out: Guangdong Province Pioneers a New Approach to Keeping Workers Happy, January 31, 2015.

arrangement that the party-state promoted through the ACFTU (Chan and Hui 2014; Liu 2010).[3]

The organization's leadership felt that the ambitious goal of collective bargaining was not out of reach, particularly since the May 2010 Honda strikes had reignited discussions within the Guangdong government regarding workers' participation in collective consultation, leading to "collective bargaining by riot" (Chan and Hui 2014).[4] Seizing upon this opportunity, the leadership of Solidarity in Action, along with other labor organizations in the area, pushed for independent collective bargaining in which representatives of the bargaining team would be typically elected by workers. According to the director of its Hong Hong-based parent organization:

We want to strengthen workers' collective power, increase their collective negotiation capacity so that there would be a trade-based collective bargaining power. If the masses aren't there, collective bargaining will be eaten by the trade union so workers wouldn't be represented. [Therefore], we want to empower workers' organizing capacity. We want them to understand what rights are through bargaining with enterprises ... The step before collective action is how to be a collective, how to bargain collectively.

(Interview, director, 2011)

Accordingly, the organization sought to teach workers the differences between collective consultation and collective bargaining through discussions and workshops.[5] The leadership hoped that such awareness raising would inspire workers to demand genuine collective bargaining in their workplaces.

In the long term, the leadership of Solidarity in Action aspired to the even more radical goal of promoting worker solidarity and the right to represent themselves outside of the state-run union. The director of its parent organization articulated this broad goal:

We want workers to represent themselves, not to be represented by the ACFTU [All-China Federation of Trade Unions]. Workers don't know what a trade union is like. For them, the trade union belongs to the government. They have a blurry vision of collective

[3] For an analysis of different types of union organizing and collective bargaining in China, see Liu 2010.
[4] In August 2010, the governments of Guangdong Province and Shenzhen Municipality revived discussions over the controversial draft *Regulations on the Democratic Management of Enterprises* and the draft *Collective Consultation Ordinance*, respectively. These proposed measures promised workers a greater role in collective consultation (Chan and Hui 2014). See also *China Labour Bulletin*, Guangdong's New Labor Regulations Open the Door to Worker Participation in Collective Bargaining, July 26, 2010.
[5] In September of 2014, three years after Solidarity in Action was forced to close, the Guangdong Provincial government passed the *Regulation on Enterprise Collective Consultations and Collective Contracts* in an effort to reduce the number of labor strikes across the province. The new regulations gave workers the right to collectively negotiate over wages, benefits and working hours, with the support of half of all employees. However, in addition to removing the right to strike (which had appeared in an earlier draft law), the regulations also required worker representatives to be selected by the state-run unions.

bargaining. Their organizing vehicle should be able to challenge ACFTU. They should be able to exert pressure on enterprises.

(Interview, director, 2011)

This would directly challenge the monopoly of the state-run ACFTU and is a particularly threatening political prospect to the party-state because it calls to mind the Solidarity Trade Union which instigated the overthrow of the Communist government in Poland (Bernhard 1993). During the Tiananmen Democracy Movement in China, autonomous workers' organizations were also among the many civil society organizations that emerged to advocate for political liberalization (Gold 1990). Post-1989, few organizations in China, outside of those in the Hong Kong network, fought for independent labor organizing in China. Even among organizations such as Solidarity in Action, such radical goals were rarely mentioned openly as the leadership directed workers' attention to more immediate and attainable goals such as the right to collective bargaining.

THE PEDAGOGICAL PROCESS: FRAME CONSTRUCTION AND DISSEMINATION

The first step towards achieving these goals was to raise workers' collective consciousness of themselves as citizens and to construct collective action frames. This was challenging for the leaders due to the fragmentation of migrant workers. During my fieldwork, activists and participants alike often described workers as a "pile of loose sand" (*yi pan san sha*). This perception accorded with previous studies suggesting that Chinese workers tend to engage in "cellular activism" – workplace-based rights activism confined to individual enterprises (Lee 2007b: 121). According to Ching Kwan Lee, this pattern of cellular activism cannot be attributed solely to "myopic workers' consciousness" or to state repression. Instead, it is a consequence of structural factors such as the state's decentralized economic decision making, which creates "localized communities of interests and responsibilities" amongst workers. As a result, the working class has been fragmented into disparate interest groups and channeled into limited activism (Lee 2007b: 121).

Thus, organizations such as Solidarity in Action faced the formidable challenge of mobilizing a diverse group of skilled and unskilled workers employed at different factories to collectively advocate for labor rights. In the face of such fragmentation, frames were critical to facilitating collective action. In the case of Solidarity in Action, activists constructed and disseminated diagnostic, prognostic, and motivational frames to worker-participants through a pedagogical process. This process of frame construction entailed dialogue between activists and participants as well as among participants over the meaning of their grievances and possible tactics. Diagnostic frames consisted of analyzing workers' particular grievances within the context of larger structural issues related to an unfair legal system and their lack of a legal right to independently organize. Worker-participants learned to attribute blame to local officials who sought to attract investment at the expense of protecting workers' rights, as well as profit-driven bosses seeking to keep wages low and workers fragmented. Prognostic frames offered possible solutions, including actions that demonstrated worker solidarity such as flash demonstrations. Motivational frames provided a rationale for action, which entailed educating workers that the reason they ought to act in solidarity was because their employers had united to exploit workers.

Throughout 2010, Solidarity in Action activists and worker-participants met on a bi-weekly basis to exchange information about their workplaces, share grievances, and support one another during the arduous process of labor dispute resolution. During these meetings, one to two dozen workers would assemble in the apartment that served as the office of Solidarity in Action. An aluminum sliding door opened to the criss-crossing streets of the local community. Activists and workers alike suspected that the men loitering outside their apartment were plainclothes policemen. To minimize the attention of these authorities, activists pulled down the aluminum sliding door at the beginning of the meetings.

During the meetings, seasoned labor activists from Hong Kong asked workers to articulate what types of exploitation they faced at work and how these issues related to broader patterns of labor exploitation in China and elsewhere. During one such discussion, activists instructed workers to analyze the larger economic and political factors contributing to wage inequality in China. The facilitator, a Hong Kong labor activist and labor researcher, distributed several newspaper articles announcing minimum wage increases in Guangdong Province. He asked the workers to discuss whether or not local businesses would abide by the new wage regulations and if the local state would enforce it. A debate ensued among worker-participants, as recorded in my field notes during participant observation:

The group of workers disagreed. Some argued that enterprises would not abide by the minimum wage standards because they would lower their profit margins; others thought that enterprises would comply if workers exerted pressure on management. Still, a lone dissenter believed that his boss would surely adhere to the new standards because he was a law-abiding businessman.

(Participant observation, 2010)

The activist then used this discussion about wage increases to discuss the broader, more politically sensitive issue of collective bargaining. Specifically, he sought to convey to the workers that they were not at the mercy of their employers and that they should engage in collective bargaining whenever possible. The facilitator distributed an article on collective consultation to the participants and explained the difference between bargaining and consultation to the participants as such:

Collective consultation is a softer term for collective bargaining that the government uses. I bet you didn't know that there is actually a regulation on collective wage consultation, which was passed in October of 2000.

(Participant observation, 2010)[6]

He then directed workers to a copy of the collective consultation regulation, drawing their attention to the stipulation that if a factory did not have union representatives, workers should be allowed to democratically elect representatives for the purpose of collective consultation. Thus, by starting with an interest very close to the workers – the increase in minimum wages across the province – the activist was able to introduce them to collective bargaining. The activist then asked workers to diagnose the broader structural causes for labor exploitation, including why the labor dispute system failed to protect worker rights. He also attempted to convey that inequality was not restricted to China; it was a pervasive global phenomenon present throughout capitalist economies. During one meeting, the lead activist showed documentaries about the opulent lives of wealthy businessmen in developed Asian countries. These documentaries made visible the inequitable distribution of wealth under capitalism and suggested that under such a system, workers did not receive their fair share of the economic pie.

Meanwhile, activists also constructed prognostic frames that provided possible solutions to this problem. In particular, they attempted to persuade workers that they needed to act in solidarity with each other in order to contend with the powerful business alliance represented by the local manufacturers' association. After leading the workers in a reading of the collective consultation regulation, the facilitator invited them to share their experiences in taking collective action:

FACILITATOR: When have you ever engaged in collective bargaining?
WORKERS: Never. Collective bargaining doesn't exist in practice!
FACILITATOR: But you have! How many of you have gone on strikes before? That's a type of collective bargaining!

(Participant observation, 2010)

The facilitator then asked each worker if he or she had participated in a strike before. Four of the ten workers present had participated in a successful strike in the past. They became animated and began to share stories of their experiences:

WORKER A: There were fifty, sixty of us in total, including four or five leader representatives who collectively bargained with the boss. At first, we would keep it secret so that it would come as a surprise to management. We discussed among the leaders that we must trust one another and maintain an influential standing among the masses.

---

[6] The activist was referring to Gongzi jiti xieshang shixing banta [The Implementation of Collective Wage Mediation], Ministry of Human Resources and Social Security, 2000.

We recruited leaders who have a lot of workers under them who had the ability to mobilize [others].

WORKER B: You have to get a leader who is not afraid to chop [literally and figuratively]. Once, I chased a guy who ran away from a strike with a hatchet and threatened to kill him. I had organized a strike that was factory-wide and forced the factory boss to pay for medical treatment for a worker who had been beaten by the factory guards. Also, if you want to leave a factory, don't resign. You've got to fire your boss! Write up a letter to end your labor relations and then go through the arbitration system!

(Participant observation, 2010)

Sharing previous experiences with strike action showed other workers that, despite the potential risks and disunity among workers, it was possible to take part in collective action.

During a heated discussion, the facilitator asked workers why their bargaining position remained weak despite labor shortages across the Pearl River Delta.[7] After the initial discussion, he explained that the main reason was that business interests had united while the workers had not. As noted above, the district manufacturers' association had blacklisted hundreds of workers, putting their names on an internal, secret list that identified them as trouble-makers. These workers had distributed pamphlets on labor rights or had spoken to co-workers to inform them of their rights. Blacklisted workers could not find employment in the same district, and factories that belonged to the association would not hire them. In doing so, employers sought to squelch labor activism by making it almost impossible for blacklisted workers to find employment. The association's actions also served as a warning to other potential worker-activists that their dissemination of labor rights knowledge would come at the price of future employment in the district.

Having explained this, the activist then called for worker solidarity as a counter-tactic to the measures adopted by the manufacturers' association:

Why haven't workers been able to successfully bargain for their wages despite the current labor shortage? Because the bosses have united. They have formed a manufacturers' association which meets once a month, and through discussions, they have agreed to keep wages low, to keep workers scattered, and to blacklist certain workers. So what strategies can you use to unite?

(Participant observation, 2010)

His call to action quietened the room as the participants began to reflect upon how they could work collectively in the struggle for labor rights.

---

[7] Beginning in 2009, there began to be a shortage of migrant laborers in coastal cities because of a decline in the growth rate of the migrant worker population and because many migrant workers chose to seek employment in China's interior provinces.

FROM FRAMES TO ACTION

While activists deliberately constructed diagnostic and prognostic frames to influence workers' interpretation of labor exploitation, they did not provide a blueprint of action because the organization's primary mission was to raise workers' awareness of labor rights and to inspire them to work together to devise specific forms of collective action. The construction of these frames inspired some of the participants to experiment with micro-collective action. Thus, when Solidarity in Action's workers ultimately decided to stage a flash demonstration in front of the court-house to protest the blacklisting of worker-activists by the manufacturers' association, they did so because they had been inspired by the organization's pedagogy.

The lead activist of the flash demonstrations was Jay,[8] a skilled worker in his mid-twenties who had been working in the industry for over a decade. As a committed participant of Solidarity in Action, Jay emerged as a leader in the micro-collective action taken against the manufacturers' association. He had been employed as a department leader with a team of twenty workers under him. While employed, he noticed that the factory management was pressuring workers to quit before the end of their contract terms by reducing their hours and falsely accusing them of violating factory codes. The management would hire cheap replacements in the form of temporary interns who were paid less. In addition, the factory failed to pay overtime wages and did not purchase social insurance for its workers even though this was stipulated in the labor contracts workers had signed.

After Jay and three other department leaders reported these violations to the local Labor Bureau, they were fired without compensation. When they attempted to find employment in other factories, potential employers told them that they had been put on the association's blacklist. Jay and his colleagues set out to collect evidence in preparation for civil lawsuits. They obtained a copy of the blacklist and covertly recorded a hiring manager who told Jay that he had been blacklisted and that no enterprise belonging to the association would hire him. With this evidence in hand, Jay and two other worker-partici-pants of Solidarity in Action filed a civil lawsuit with the district court against their employers for putting their names on the blacklist of "trouble-making" employees. They also filed a separate lawsuit against the association, which eventually made its way to the Municipal Intermediate People's Court.

On the day of the district court's hearing, nearly two dozen workers from across the industry crowded into the courtroom to show support. It was hoped that such a demonstration of solidarity would pressure the judge to hold a fair trial for Jay and his fellow plaintiffs. Initially, court officials attempted to prevent workers from entering the courtroom as observers. The workers subsequently entered into a verbal dispute with court authorities, insisting that they

---

[8] Pseudonym.

had the right as stipulated by Chinese law to observe a public hearing. In the end, court officials permitted a limited number of workers to audit the case and ordered the rest to wait outside (Participant observation, 2010).

The court hearing ended without significant disruption. However, just before the workers filed out of the courthouse, they distributed sanitary masks and poster-sized pieces of cardboard to one another. On the steps of the courthouse, they lined up on the steps in two rows as if to take a group photo. At that moment, they thrust a camera into the hands of an accompanying journalist while another activist was filming them across the street. Arranged in two lines, the workers flipped over their cardboard signs, each bearing a Chinese character that when strung together read: "Workers against blacklisting." Before they could attract the attention of bystanders, security guards came to disperse the workers and ordered the journalist to delete any photos that had been taken. The workers responded that they were only taking a group photo and were not violating any laws. The guards threatened to call the police. At this point, Jay signaled for participants to scatter. They boarded a public bus to an industrial district where the man-ufacturers' association was located. Standing in two rows in front of the association's building, they again raised the same signs. This time, they were able to take a few photos of their flash demonstration before it began to rain and the workers dispersed (Participant observation, 2010). Workers were aware that their actions were risky, but they aspired to set a precedent for other workers to follow suit. Jay viewed the lawsuit as a symbolic form of collective action that he hoped would inspire hundreds of other blacklisted workers to also take action. He thus framed his actions in the language of setting an example for others:

At the time of the lawsuit, 90 percent of the workers who we talked to supported us [in private], saying it was right for us to sue them, but they did not support us openly. When we lost [the lawsuit at the district level], everybody was shocked. We wanted this to be the first case that won. Once the others see this, they would also sue the association. Most workers who found out they were blacklisted concocted all sorts of ways to get around it like using a fake identification card. I also thought of using these methods, but I somehow thought they wouldn't work. Besides, I really thought the legal route was the way to go. I believed in the law but now I'm not so sure that the legal process is a just one.

(Interview, worker-activist, 2010)

Inspired by the teachings of Solidarity in Action, Jay sought to mobilize other workers to act in solidarity instead of leaving them to resolve their problems individually.

ORGANIZATIONAL AND PARTICIPANT OUTCOMES

Micro-collective action ultimately imposed significant costs on the organization and its participants. Following the flash demonstrations outside the courthouse and the association's headquarters, the authorities shut down Solidarity in Action's office. As a mobilizing structure, the organization had provided cognitive and material resources that inspired workers to stage a symbolic kind of collective action, one with the goal of uniting workers from different factories to press for labor rights. This form of action, although small in scale, contrasted sharply with larger-scale worker action in terms of its *nature*. While strikes were much larger in scale than micro-collective action, they did not tend to elicit the same levels of state repression because they represented forms of "cellular activism" that were facilitated by informal networks (Lee 2007b). In contrast, micro-collective action was inspired by a civil society organization that, from the perspective of the party-state, acted as an "invisible black hand" conspiring to incite workers to disrupt social stability. Thus, although the scale and duration of micro-collective action was negligible compared to worker strikes across the province, the fact that it was inspired by a civil society organization was deeply threatening to the state. Moreover, whereas factory-based strikes for higher wages and benefits were primarily economic in nature, these flash demonstrations were viewed by the state as more explicitly political because they signaled the presence of an organizational backbone. Thus, it was not surprising that Solidarity in Action would have suffered such dire and immediate consequences in the form of organizational closure.

After being forced to close its operations, the leadership of its Hong Kong-based parent organization aspired to build a more sustainable informal workers' network in the same district. Specifically, they planned to train key workers in the industry to disseminate labor law knowledge through pamphleteering as well as by serving as informal liaisons between workers in different factories. These worker-activists would also document labor violations, visit workers in their homes, organize workers' gatherings, and distribute informal questionnaires on labor conditions in factories. The leadership hoped that by creating such a network of worker-activists, they could lay the foundations for a future labor organization (Interview, director, 2011).[9]

Engaging in micro-collective action also carried consequences for worker-activists. Plainclothes security agents followed and monitored Jay's activities in the aftermath of the flash demonstrations. In addition, authorities informally interrogated the organization's affiliated lawyer and threatened to withdraw his legal license if he continued to involve himself in workers' collective action. The director of the Hong Kong parent organization explained the consequences for worker-activists:

They [the workers] didn't know what to do; they needed to form a workers' network to support them. So what they did was to create a scene. But from now on, the government

---

[9] As of the spring of 2010, this informal workers' network was still in the initial planning stages and had not yet materialized.

follows and harasses them so that it makes it difficult for them to expand the workers' network.

(Interview, director, 2011)

According to a key activist who was involved in the flash demonstrations, the workers' attempt to stage micro-collective action was premature. They needed to build a wider support base:

> I was thinking how to unite the workers together, [so that] they would know about [Solidarity in Action]. The mistake was we don't have anything … we don't have capital. We don't have anything to show to the government, we don't have any power. So why would they care or listen? The capital we need is to establish a permanent workers' base so that if anything happens, we could call and hundreds would answer.

(Interview, lead activist, 2010)

Ultimately, the series of micro-collective actions – flash demonstrations, observing court trials, and collective lawsuits – failed to pressure the courts to rule in the workers' favor. The Intermediate People's Court ruled that there was insufficient evidence to support the existence of an illegal blacklist.

Despite this outcome, Solidarity in Action nevertheless instilled collective consciousness in its core worker-participants and inspired them to experiment with symbolic forms of micro-collective action. This was a significant achievement in light of the fact that the modus operandi of workers seeking to gain concessions from their employers across China remained factory-based strikes centered on economic grievances. In contrast, these workers sought to use micro-collective action to rally others to the cause of worker solidarity. Their actions expressed the collective consciousness that the organization had instilled through the pedagogical process that shaped workers' interpretation of labor exploitation and of possible solutions. Thus, unlike workers who participated in strikes or other routine forms of contention with narrow and immediate economic goals, these workers harbored broader political goals.

CONCLUSION

This chapter analyzed the pedagogy of micro-collective action, the first tactical innovation in the broader dynamic of mobilizing without the masses. Two characteristics of micro-collective action distinguished it from more conventional forms of popular contention such as strikes, protests, and petitions. The first was a civil society organization's direct involvement in the framing process, which shapes the way workers understand labor exploitation as well as their own agency. Unlike episodic protests, which typically involved "temporary protest communities" (Cai 2010), this tactic traced its origins back to an organization. Although on the surface the contentious episode – flash demonstrations in front of a courthouse and a business association – appeared to be spontaneous, it was in fact inspired by the organization's pedagogy which emphasized the importance of worker solidarity. Through constructing a diagnostic frame that attributed labor exploitation to the disunity of the working class, the activists inspired participants to undertake action for a broader cause on behalf of all workers blacklisted by the manufacturers' association.

The second difference from more ordinary contention was the use of micro-collective action as a symbolic form of contention. In this case, workers' goals were not solely economic because had they only sought to increase their chances of re-employment, they could have pursued wholly individualistic solutions such as obtaining fake personal identification cards. This would have allowed blacklisted workers to circumvent restrictions by falsifying their identities when applying for jobs in other factories. However, because they had been coached by the organization to frame their individual grievances as part of a broader struggle for worker rights, they aspired to take symbolic collective action on behalf of all workers who had been treated unfairly by the association due to their activism. Thus, the case of Solidarity in Action suggested that even in a repressive environment, it was possible for an underground civil society organization to mobilize limited forms of collective action.

Solidarity in Action was somewhat typical of organizations belonging to the Hong Kong network in Guangdong Province in that its main goal was to instill a sense of collective consciousness in workers. Organizations belonging to this network all shared a similar goal of advocating for collective bargaining as a first step towards setting up independent labor representation in the future (see Chapter 2).[10] They prioritized workers' collective consciousness and solidarity above extracting immediate economic concessions from the local state. This commitment stems from the influence of Hong Kong labor activists who came from a more liberal political context and advocated for more radical forms of social change. In this sense, Solidarity in Action was typical of labor organizations in the Hong Kong network.

However, the organization may also have been atypical in deploying more radical tactics to achieve shared goals. It is unclear whether or not other organizations operating in Guangdong Province also coached workers to engage in flash demonstrations in front of government buildings. While other organizations in both the Hong Kong and the Mainland network shared similar tactics including providing pro bono legal aid, offering discussion groups, organizing cultural activities, and training workers to become volunteers, those in the Mainland network tended to avoid direct, small-group confrontation such as flash demonstrations. Instead, they preferred to coach workers to threaten local officials individually in order to incentivize them to pressure employers to give monetary concessions such as wage arrears or injury compensation.

---

[10] After 2011, a few leading organizations in the Mainland network also advocated for collective bargaining and played an active, behind-the-scenes role in facilitating worker strikes in 2015. See Chapter 8.

There are several conditions under which the pedagogy of micro-collective action may be successful in forging workers' collective consciousness. First, it is easier to construct a sense of solidarity if participants occupy similar social positions and hold common grievances. For example, the workers at Solidarity in Action were all employed in the same industry and shared the common grievance of being targeted by their employers for trouble-making behaviors such as reporting labor violations. This made it easier for them to establish affinity with one another despite coming from different factories. Second, an organization has more latitude in adopting tactics when their funding is not directly tied to their ability to deliver financial compensation to participants. If leaders are under pressure to give "deliverables" in terms of how many workers they serve and how many legal cases they win, then they are less likely to engage in risky symbolic tactics such as micro-collective action.

Finally, even if micro-collective action is a successful strategy for fostering worker solidarity, not all organizations are expected to adopt it. Leaders have different risk profiles; those that are more risk averse are less likely to adopt micro-collective action because it attracts undue attention to the organization. As this chapter demonstrates, micro-collective action could, in the worst case, result in organizational closure. The riskiness of such a strategy explains why other organizations chose instead to adopt the pedagogy of atomized action or discursive action. In order to circumvent the risks associated with coordinating collective contention, other labor activists devised the alternative pedagogy of atomized action, the second tactical innovation of mobilizing without the masses. The next chapter illustrates this tactic in action, unveiling yet another pathway for organization-based contention.

6

Atomized Action

This chapter examines a second tactic of mobilizing without the masses: the pedagogy of atomized action. Activists devised this tactic after having directly experienced or witnessed the repression of organizations that had organized politically charged acts of collective contention. In response, activists scaled down their actions by training and sending out individuals to claim legal rights from the state by threatening social stability. Unlike the micro-collective action described in Chapter 5, which carried significant risks for activists and participants alike, this individualization of contention reduced political risks for the organization and for activists and allowed activists to strike a balance between rights advocacy and organizational survival. Moreover, compared to micro-collective action, which aimed to achieve politically symbolic goals, atomized action sought to secure practical pay-offs for worker-participants.

The pedagogy of atomized action reduced organizational risks because the scale of action was limited to a single aggrieved individual. Activists strategically coached individuals to take atomized action based on the calculation that the state and private enterprises would erroneously perceive such actions to be uncoordinated. A single aggrieved citizen who staged a sit-in at a bureaucrat's office was not likely to elicit suspicion that an organization was orchestrating this act from behind the scenes. In contrast, if citizens threatened social stability en masse, officials would classify the situation as an "emergency incident" (*tufa shijian*) or "mass incident." In response, bureaucrats would alert the bureaus of State Security and Public Security, who would repress the leaders and organizations behind the unrest. This possibility was not just hypothetical; authorities had previously closed down an underground labor organization in the same province after activists staged a collective signature campaign on the streets (Interview, activist, 2010). Learning from these experiences, activists devised the pedagogy of atomized action, which coached the individual contender to threaten social stability on a contained scale while lowering the likelihood of a state crackdown on the organization.

The pedagogy of atomized action emerged in the context of an ineffective formal labor dispute system, the official legal channel for dealing with labor conflicts.[1] Under the Hu Jintao administration, the central government continued to promote legal channels to resolve labor disputes as part of broader legal reforms aimed at bolstering state legitimacy (Gallagher 2005: 101–32). Following the implementation of the 2008 Labor Contract Law and the streamlining of labor arbitration, the number of recorded labor disputes surged (Gallagher 2014). Yet workers continued to face high barriers when seeking to defend their rights through legal channels.[2] Despite state rhetoric to the contrary, workers deploying the "weapons of the law" to resolve disputes often ended up stuck in an inefficient bureaucracy with few alternative channels of redress.

Among the many reasons for the labor dispute system's inefficiency was official disincentives to enforce labor laws. Performance of labor bureau officials was evaluated in large part based on their ability to stimulate local economic growth (Li and Zhou 2005). China's decentralized fiscal environment encouraged local governments to generate economic growth by attracting enterprises to invest in their region (*zhaoshang yinzi*) (Wong 2009). This growth mandate often ran counter to efforts to enforce labor laws as local governments were expected to deliver a steady supply of cheap labor to businesses operating in their jurisdiction. With different local governments competing to win investment and extract revenue from businesses (Lu and Landry 2014), economic interests often took precedence over labor rights, making labor law implementation a lower priority for local states. As a result, migrant workers seeking redress for a range of issues – from industrial injury compensation to wage arrears to forced lay-offs – found the official labor dispute system to be inadequate. The pedagogy of atomized action offered an alternative channel of redress.

REPERTOIRE OF ATOMIZED ACTION

The pedagogy of atomized action is characterized by a repertoire of verbal and performance threats utilized by aggrieved workers and usually carried out simultaneously alongside efforts to defend their rights through the labor dispute system (see Table 6.1). Rather than acting as substitutes for formal channels of resolving labor grievances, this repertoire of atomized action is meant to speed

[1] The labor dispute resolution system typically entails informal consultation, mediation, arbitration, and litigation. The Bureau of Human Resources and Social Security (Labor Bureau) is responsible for mediation and arbitration while the civil courts deal with labor-related lawsuits.
[2] Barriers are particularly high for workers seeking industrial injury compensation. *China Labour Bulletin*, China's Labor Dispute Resolution System, 2014.

TABLE 6.1 *Repertoire of atomized action*

Verbal threats	Performance threats
"I will take extreme action"	Staging a sit-in at a government office
"I will contact the media"	Stalking the factory boss or blocking factory doors
"I will make a scene"	Staging a suicide show

up the process through which authorities resolve labor disputes through negative inducements – "the creation of a situation that disrupts the normal functioning of a society and is antithetical to the interests of the groups' opponents" (McAdam 1983: 735). Whether verbal or performance threats, these atomized actions create negative inducements in much the same way that the various tactical innovations adopted by civil rights activists in the United States, including lunch counter sit-ins, bus boycotts, and freedom rides, forced authorities to respond to their demands (McAdam 1983: 735). Verbal threats to state authorities or employers are communicated in person (at a bureau or factory compound) or via text messaging and phone calls. Such threats typically entail utterances such as "If you don't help me solve my problem, I will take extreme actions," or "I will contact the media."

Performance threats include (but are not limited to) individual sit-ins at government offices, stalking factory bosses after work, and, in the most extreme cases, staging a "suicide show" (*tiaolou xiu*). This term, originating in China's popular media, describes an aggrieved citizen's public performance of *threatening* suicide by standing on the edge of a tall building. Such performances may be used to demand redress for perceived injustice at the hands of a state or private sector actor. In many cases, such suicides are not carried out but are only threatened to induce the relevant authorities into taking action on the citizen's behalf.

When taking atomized action, there is a tendency for individual contenders to escalate from the use of verbal threats to the use of performance threats, though the choice of one tactic over another is often ad hoc. Activists coach workers to take actions that are tailored to the specifics of an individual's case. However, activists generally advise workers to begin with verbal threats because these are less costly and easier to deliver than performance threats. When verbal threats fail, activists will then encourage workers to escalate their activities by engaging in riskier and more specific performance threats. Performance threats require more training and moral support from activists, especially in the case of suicide shows, which are emotionally costly for a worker to act out even if he or she has no intention of actually committing suicide. Even sit-ins or stalking power-holders requires perseverance and planning on the part of workers. They often need a great deal of moral support from activists in order to carry out these performance threats. These more radical actions are thus often reserved for cases in which the worker has exhausted the use of less costly verbal threats and yet still has the audacity to carry out other contentious performances.

Conceptually, the repertoire of atomized action resembles other forms of individualized contention such as "weapons of the weak" (Scott 1987), which do not require the explicit coordination of collective action. However, these atomized actions differ from weapons of the weak in two major respects. First, rather than resorting to quiet forms of resistance such as foot-dragging and false compliance (Scott 1987: xvi), atomized protestors (particularly those engaged in performance threats) purposefully attract the attention of both the media and bystanders, which amplifies the effect of their actions. And second, unlike weapons of the weak, which do not require explicit coordination, the repertoire of atomized action is an organized strategy. Activists actively coach citizens on the timing, use, and proper execution of this tactical repertoire. Through this process, activists and workers transform organically devised atomized action into strategic resources for contention.

Moreover, the pedagogy of atomized action also departs from other forms of individual contention in China and elsewhere because it makes use of an explicit organizational vehicle. Among the most successful instances of atomized contention is the non-coordinated peasant resistance that took place across rural China in the 1980s (Zhou 1996; Kelliher 1992). At the time, Chinese peasants had few viable alternative organizations to turn to apart from the Chinese Communist Party (Kelliher 1992: 22). In response, peasants across China engaged in the illegal practice of contracting production to the household (*baochan daohu*) because they witnessed their friends or neighbors doing so (Zhou 1996). Like "social non-movements" in the Middle East (Bayat 2013) or individual lawsuits in the United States, Chinese peasant contention was powerful because of the cumulative effects of atomized actions. Their atomized practices gained traction because peasants across China started engaging in them at the same time, thereby creating a bottom-up push for eventual de-collectivization.

A similar form of atomized resistance took place among peasants in Hungary in the 1950s. In his classic essay "The Advantage of Being Atomized," Istavan Rev (1987) argued that Hungarian peasants could only resist the government's efforts to centralize agricultural production through individualized means. When millions of individual peasants withheld produce from the government's delivery system in order to sell their commodities on their black market, they were effectively resisting the central state's policies, sometimes with the complicity of local state officials. More importantly, these atomized actions were advantageous because they did not need a formal organizational vehicle. Instead, Hungarian peasants in villages tacitly recognized that their actions were, in fact, carried out in concert:

And the peasants knew; they saw what the others were doing secretly. The survival of the village was exactly equivalent to the successful resistance of the individual; and the individual welfare to the welfare of other individuals. The more the peasants succeeded in hiding their produce, the higher the prices rose on the black market, the less incentive the peasants had to give over their goods. The more successful the peasants were, the more incentive they had to resist. It was the invisible hand of resistance, the micro actions, having a profound effect on the macro sphere of politics.

(Rev 1987: 348)

As a result of the aggregated impact of such atomized actions, Hungarian peasants were able to effectively challenge a state that "was not prepared for, had no technique to cope with, millions of individual acts – which were the response to centralization" (Rev 1987: 347).

This type of atomized peasant resistance emerged precisely because of the lack of trustworthy organizations available. As Daniel Kelliher argued in the China case, "Most alternative organizations were suppressed, surviving only underground or behind closed doors of private homes. Peasants were left standing alone to face the new state they had brought to power" (Kelliher 1992: 22). They explicitly avoided coordinating organized action, relying instead on spontaneous, unorganized, leaderless, non-ideological apolitical movements (Zhou 1992). In post-reform China, workers continue to lack viable organizational vehicles to press for their rights apart from the ACFTU. While they have deployed a range of atomized actions such as filing complaints, suing employers, petitioning, and threatening to take extreme actions on their own accord, these alone do not qualify as the pedagogy of atomized action. Instead, the types of actions analyzed in this chapter are atomized actions that have been coordinated or inspired by activists inside labor organizations.

WHY ATOMIZED ACTION WORKS

In terms of inducing officials' responses, the repertoire of atomized action works through two mechanisms: targeting the incentive of local governments to maintain social stability and appealing to the moral authority of local officials. Threatening social stability can be an effective way for citizens to induce local bureaucrats into responding to their grievances as any outbreaks of social unrest negatively impact local officials' performance evaluation. Under the Hu Jintao administration, maintaining social stability was a key bureaucratic mandate (Birney 2013) and a pillar of the Chinese party-state's legitimacy (Shue 2004). The performance of local officials was evaluated in part based on how well they maintained social stability. The one veto rule (*yipiao fojue*) stipulated that any outbreak of mass incidents, such as collective protests, strikes or petitions, would discount local government achievements in other areas, including economic growth (Sun et al. 2011; Liu and Tao 2007; Tsui and Wang 2004). By threatening to create a public spectacle and disrupt social stability, even atomized protestors pose a clear problem for career-minded local officials. Although the scale of disruption is limited, atomized protestors signal to authorities that their grievances must be addressed *before* the situation escalates into a mass incident. Threatening to publicly commit suicide is one method frequently adopted by atomized protesters.[3] In contemporary China, these suicide shows have credibility due to numerous cases of aggrieved citizens (especially workers) actually committing suicide without being coached by activists (Lee and Kleinman 2003).[4] Thus, when activists coach participants to stage a suicide show, they tap into a powerful tradition of using suicide as a symbolic form of protest. This tradition of suicide protests is familiar not only to the authorities but also to onlookers, whose emotions may be stirred by witnessing such an act of public self-destruction. When an atomized protestor threatens to commit suicide, he or she can stir the crowd's emotions *against* the local state. And it is the possibility of further and collective unrest triggered by this suicide show that incentivizes authorities to respond to the individual contender as a preemptive measure.

The repertoire of atomized action also challenges the moral authority of local officials. Unlike "rightful resistors" who solicit upper-level officials to pressure officials down the ranks to comply with the law (O'Brien and Li 2006), atomized protestors directly challenge local state officials, thereby shirking the need for elite assistance. Through their words and actions, atomized protestors imply that a state that cannot guarantee the basic legal rights of its citizens is not legitimate. Performance threats pose a question to bystanders, the media, and officials alike: "What kind of a state would drive its citizens to the brink of suicide in order to claim their basic legal rights?" Bystanders who "collectively witness" (Distelhorst 2013) these solo performances amplify the effect of atomized action. The combination of these two mechanisms – the threat to social stability and the appeal to moral authority – can induce officials to respond to atomized protestors. The following case study of Pay It Forward shows the disguised role that organizations play in designing and disseminating the repertoire of atomized action.

CASE STUDY: PAY IT FORWARD

Pay It Forward was an underground labor organization based in Southern China that adopted the pedagogy of atomized action as a mobilizing tactic. In 2011, the organization had eight employees including the director, a lawyer, five male migrant activists, and a secretary. It provided legal services to workers

---

[3] Suicide as a symbol of resistance is also common elsewhere. For example, in 1963 the Buddhist monk Thich Quang Duc lit himself on fire at a busy intersection in Saigon to protest the Diem regime in South Vietnam. In 2011, a Tunisian street vendor setting himself on fire to protest both the confiscation of his wares and his abuse at the hands of the police, served as the catalyst for the Tunisian revolution that began the Arab Spring.

[4] As discussed in Chapter 2, in 2010 at least thirteen workers in China's largest electronics manufacturer, Foxconn, jumped to their deaths (Barboza 2010). In addition, aggrieved Chinese citizens have also committed suicide in protest against forced demolitions, land grabs, and poor labor conditions (Chakrabortty 2013; Johnston 2013; Langfitt 2013).

grappling with a range of labor grievances, including unpaid wages, fake labor contracts, and forced dismissal. However, like many labor organizations in the region, Pay It Forward's main clientele was injured workers. Some workers had lost fingers or toes while operating machines while others had contracted illnesses from exposure to chemicals and dust in the workplace. Injured workers faced the dire possibility of becoming permanently handicapped if they did not receive medical attention,[5] and many were unable to gain compensation, or gain it in a timely manner, through the formal labor dispute system. By focusing on this group, Pay It Forward served some of the most vulnerable workers through its legal workshops, pro bono legal consultation and representation, and the provision of moral support.

Activists recruited worker-participants during their daily visits to nearby hospitals. On a typical day, a lead activist, accompanied by several worker volunteers wearing official-looking social work badges, would wander the hallways of a hospital. When the group saw an open door, they would enter the patient's room. Without introducing themselves, activists would ask a patient if they had been injured at work. Ever on guard against con artists and illegal lawyers,[6] many injured workers were automatically suspicious of the activists' intentions. Some would gaze blankly at the activists for a few seconds before turning their attention back to the hospital room's television. Occasionally, one or two patients gave an affirmative response to the activists' questions. Upon hearing this, the activists would introduce themselves as volunteers from a charity organization (*cishan jigou*) (Participant observation, 2010).

In order to establish affinity with potential recruits, some activists who were themselves injured workers would hold up their hands to show their missing fingers and narrate their personal stories of seeking injury compensation. Having established their credentials as fellow injured workers, they would begin tentative conversations.

PATIENT: When did you get injured?
ACTIVIST: A few years ago at my old factory. Factory bosses are real cunning, you know. They don't want to pay for medical bills. Is your boss paying for your bills?
PATIENT: The factory took me to the hospital. They told me to stay calm and recover.
ACTIVIST: Did the factory take away your factory ID badge? Whatever you do, don't give it to them or else you won't be able to prove that you were their employee!
PATIENT: Oh ... [looking confused, then turns his attention to the television]

---

[5] According to a 2007 China Labor Watch report, 40,000 fingers are severed every year among workers in the Pearl River Delta Region. See: *China Labor Watch*, The Long March: Survey and Case Studies of Work Injuries in the Pearl River Delta Region, 2007.
[6] Workers shared a common suspicion that activists were in fact marketers who would con participants into attending a free workshop but later pressure them to purchase products or services. Workers also assumed that activists could be illegal lawyers who would take a cut of the compensation awarded to them through the courts in exchange for providing legal consultation and representation.

ACTIVIST: You might think it's a waste of your time to know these things, but when you get screwed over by the boss, then you'll come running to us! So you'd better take precautions. Many bosses have bad hearts [lack moral conscience].

(Participant observation, hospital, 2010)

After these conversations, the activist would record the patient's basic information on a form and hand each patient a booklet explaining how to seek industrial injury compensation through the labor dispute system.[7] Activists would then invite patients to attend a free legal workshop at the organization's office. Some workers, trusting their factory's management to arrange appropriate compensation, would decline the offer. In these cases, it was difficult for activists to convince workers that they needed to make a plan for seeking compensation before leaving the hospital. However, other workers who had already encountered difficulties securing compensation would be persuaded to attend the free legal workshop.

GRIEVANCE ARTICULATION

Pay It Forward held legal workshops on a biweekly or monthly basis. The average workshop would draw thirty to fifty workers, the majority of whom were males. On the day of the legal workshop, injured workers hobbled into the room, some still wearing their striped hospital gowns. First-timers eyed the dilapidated interior of the organization's office with suspicion. Once inside the office, they were instructed to sit on stools arranged in a circle and to introduce themselves to each other. Speaking in front of a large group was an intimidating experience for many participants who at their jobs were expected to work silently on assembly lines. Many were diffident because they did not have a formal education beyond the elementary or secondary school level, and even those with a high school education had little experience with public speaking. Like migrant workers elsewhere, participants complained of having "a stomach full of words" (*yi duzi de hua*) but being unable to articulate them (Fu 2009). This was a critical barrier to making rights claims, one which the activists hoped these workshops would help the workers overcome.

Most workers spoke timidly and recounted their stories in a non-chronological fashion, making eye contact only with the activists in attendance:

WORKER: I'm from Hunan. I want to ask ... I've been out of the hospital a long time now but the factory hasn't given me any money yet. What about the money?
ACTIVIST: You want to ask for the standard compensation or the actual amount of compensation you should receive?
WORKER: The standard [amount of compensation].

(Participant observation, 2010)

---

[7] The questionnaire form asked for the following information: factory name, the date of their injury, and whether or not the worker had sought a formal assessment of the extent of their injuries.

During these legal workshops, activists encouraged workers to practice narrating their grievances as if they were speaking directly to state officials:

I have a small request. When we face the boss or the Labor Bureau official, we might be fearful. So use this as a platform for you to practice. When you stand up to speak, you should face everybody else; pretend they are the bosses and the officials.

(Participant observation, 2010)

During one of the best-attended workshops at a different branch of the organization, the staff lawyer taught workers to approach officials as rights-bearing citizens and not as supplicants:

When you go to the Labor Bureau, you should speak with a loud voice and as if you've got all the reason in the world [to claim your rights]. Workers are the ones keeping the civil servants employed; not the other way around. So don't speak like you're begging them to do a favor. The first step to rights protection (*weiquan*) is to speak up.

(Participant observation, 2009)

In this way, activists helped participants overcome the psychological and emotional barriers that stood in their way of making rights claims in front of power-holders.

The next step entailed building trust with worker-participants. In order to assure workers that the members of Pay It Forward were indeed NGO activists and not con artists, activists explained the nature of their work:

When I look around the room, I see a lot of people with suspicious, fearful looks. We are not here to cheat you. You might be thinking, if we don't charge [for our services], what do we eat and drink? How do we survive? Well, we live off of donations from a charity organization. We are also injured workers just like you. My co-workers will introduce themselves.

(Participant observation, 2010)

Activists would line up in front of the room to tell their personal stories of working in factories. They would display their injured limbs for the workers to see and describe their work accidents and the subsequent battles they had with an unjust legal system.

After gaining the trust of the participants, the organization's staff lawyer would educate workers on how to navigate the labor dispute system. The lawyer cautioned workers to refrain from using violent tactics out of frustration with the legal system. He taught workers how to collect evidence of wage arrears, mistreatment by management, or industrial accidents. In one instance, the lawyer provided a group of workers with specific advice regarding how to deal with their bosses:

First, you should mediate; you should avoid taking extreme actions like that worker Liu Hanhuang who killed his boss and ruined his own life and family in the process. You have to think: "the boss owes me money." Second, if you don't have a labor contract, you should think about what evidence you can collect to prove that you have labor relations with the boss such as your work badge and bank statements. Then, you should think about how to mediate. You must guard against being cheated by your factory's management staff and by the Labor Bureau officials. Don't just sign documents without thinking; make sure you know what the document says. These days, a lot of officials don't have a moral conscience.

(Participant observation, 2009)

The staff lawyer almost always stopped short of advocating extra-legal means of rights activism. However, Pay It Forward's other worker-activists spoke frankly about the limitations of the legal system:

The law is written for the rich ... The bosses are afraid of losing their money; we have nothing to fear ... We need to fight for our rights (*weiquan*) to the end; don't compromise ... We need to do things our own way, from our own perspective. Sometimes, we have to use forceful means ... We don't discourage using illegal methods.

(Participant observation, 2010)

This critique led to the next important step in the pedagogical process of coaching workers to wield atomized action: "telling stories."

COACHING ATOMIZED ACTION

Activists disguised their efforts to coach workers in the tactics of contention behind narratives about other workers who had deployed atomized action and successfully claimed compensation from their employers. They framed these narratives as "telling stories" (*jiang gushi*) rather than as step-by-step training in the use of contentious tactics. Through these narratives, activists indirectly taught workers that, when taking the legal route proved ineffective, they could take an alternative pathway to making rights claims. Classic narratives featured workers who deployed atomized action against factory management. One featured an injured construction worker whose 60-year-old father stalked the factory boss:

In the city where I work, there was a worker who fell while working on a construction site and was paralyzed from the waist down. He was in the hospital only a few days before his boss stopped paying his medical bills. The boss thought that since he's paralyzed, it's a waste of money to keep him in the hospital. So the worker's dad, a 60-year-old man, went around to the Labor Bureau and to the petitioning office, but of course nothing came of it. Finally, he stalked the factory boss. If the boss went to the bathroom, he followed; if the boss went out to eat, he went too. If the boss didn't let him eat, he dumped the boss' food on the floor. The boss called the police a few times but the police couldn't do anything about it. So it continued like this for almost fifteen days and the boss finally gave in ... gave the worker 2,100 yuan a month (the average salary in the city) and sent him to the best hospital in town ... We can't totally rely on the law because we know it can be unfair. We have to think of other methods, taking individual actions to make it a bit fairer. But of course, I'm not teaching you to take these actions [eliciting chuckles from the audience].

(Participant observation, 2010)

By using these narratives as pedagogical tools, activists taught workers that when the weapon of the law failed, workers could resort to creative means to seek compensation.

In another narrative, a desperate factory worker recruited his nephew to impersonate a powerful businessman in order to intimidate the worker's boss into paying his wages. The worker instructed his nephew, who worked as a chauffeur, to drive up to the factory in the new BMW he drove for work. Sporting a crisp Western-style suit, the worker's nephew affected the mannerisms of a wealthy businessman who had a close relationship with the worker and demanded to negotiate directly with the factory boss. The boss, threatened by the worker's apparent connections to an individual visibly more powerful than himself, gave the worker the wages due to him (Participant observation, 2009). This narrative showed how deception could serve as an effective tactic for making rights claims.

DEPLOYING ATOMIZED ACTION

The following story of a worker-participant illustrates a successful case of claiming rights through the gradual escalation of atomized action. Activists later transformed this case into a narrative to inspire other workers. Li was a 26-year-old migrant worker who had injured her hand while working at a factory.[8] Despite her injuries, her boss had refused to pay for the second stage of her medical treatment. After Li attended one of Pay It Forward's workshops and learned of her legal right to injury compensation, she went to the township Labor Bureau to confront the bureau chief:

I only found out about injury compensation after I went to one of those workshops. The third time I went to the Labor Bureau, they tried to take my cell phone because I caught the Bureau Chief on voice recording saying, "I'm not going to help you. What are you going to do to me?" Then he hired a motorcyclist to take my cell phone as I was walking down the road. I just held on to my cell phone as best as I could and the motorcyclist dragged me down the street. After that, the Labor Bureau [officials] were afraid of me. They told the security guard to push me [when I waited outside of the Bureau Chief's office]. That guard was a guy so he was afraid to push me. I warned him, "If you push, I'll yell rape!" So he left me alone. I waited for the Bureau Chief to come out of his office, I knocked on his door and he finally opened, saying, "It's you again?!" I was furious and threw his computer keyboard out of the third-storey window.

(Interview, Li, 2010)

Throwing the Labor Bureau Chief's computer keyboard out of the window required an audacity that showed the Bureau Chief that she "feared neither sky nor earth" (*tianbupa dibupa*). However, because it did not yield immediate results, Li escalated her threats:

---

[8] Li is a pseudonym.

After I threw the keyboard out the window, I returned to my factory and pulled out the general electricity plug. That stopped all production ... the boss said he was going to call the police. I said, "I hope the police come!" He then called on the other female workers to shove me around, but nobody dared to touch me. He then ordered the security guard to harass me. I said, "If you touch me, you won't be walking out the factory in one piece!"

(Interview, Li, 2010)

Even after making a scene at both the offices of the Labor Bureau and the factory, Li did not receive compensation. With few other options, she further escalated the situation by threatening to commit suicide:

I became so angry, I went back to the factory dormitory and was going to jump off the building, take down the Labor Bureau with me, see if they die! Then somebody dialed 110. [The police] came and tried to mediate with the factory; [they] said that if someone dies from the dispute, the factory's going to have to pay. So they [the police] called up the district Labor Bureau; they were all there. A few days later, the Labor Bureau called to ask if I wanted to mediate in private or if I wanted to get my proof of industrial injury done [the first step of the legal channel for industrial injury compensation].

(Interview, Li, 2010)

Neither the police nor the Labor Bureau wanted to deal with a worker's suicide which would attract unwanted publicity and disrupt social stability. Working through mediators, Li and the factory boss finally agreed on 50,000 yuan (7,600 US dollars) in compensation. Activists played a pivotal role in providing tactical coaching and moral support to Li throughout this process.

RIGHTS BARGAINING

Deploying atomized action rarely resulted in employers providing full and immediate compensation to workers. Instead, it usually instigated an informal process of rights bargaining between the state, workers, and factory management. These negotiations resulted in compromises that frequently fell short of the full compensation guaranteed to workers under relevant labor laws. In this process, activists instructed workers on how and with whom to negotiate, and the amount of compensation they should accept. The following case illustrates the role that activists played in the disguised coaching of atomized action as well as in the ensuing process of bargaining over the price of a worker's rights.

Chang was a 31-year-old mother-of-two who worked at a small auto parts factory in the suburbs of a manufacturing city in Guangdong Province.[9] While using a drill, her upper arm and fingers got caught in the machine, resulting in severe wounds. Without immediate medical attention, Chang realized she could be permanently disabled and she rushed herself to the hospital. At first, the cost of her treatment was covered by her employer. Yet when the factory

---

[9] Pseudonym.

boss stopped paying her medical bills, Chang became desperate. She sought assistance from the township Labor Bureau, which arranged for mediation with the factory management. Chang felt she could not wait for the conclusion of the labor arbitration process (which would take at least forty-five days) as she needed the money to continue treatment at the hospital. Under these circumstances, Chang had two choices: either borrow money from relatives or seek immediate financial compensation from her boss.

Chang came into contact with activists from Pay It Forward at the legal workshop where she first learned of her right to injury compensation. With three surgically attached metal rods sticking out of her upper arm visible to all in attendance, she declared what she would do if the Labor Bureau continued to put her case on hold:

> I told them [the township Labor Bureau], if you don't solve my problem now I'm going to have to use extreme measures, and you'd have to deal with the consequences. I'm going to carry a bucket of gasoline there, what do you think? This is what I'm planning to do.
>
> (Participant observation, 2010)

The staff was at first unresponsive, but when she again sought the approval of her audience, an activist replied, "You can go ahead, but be careful not to hurt yourself." He encouraged her to first explore all the possible legal avenues before she took such extreme measures:

> Go to the labor office, then to the labor union, then to the Women's Federation. If all else fails, call up seven or eight of your hometown folks or relatives and stage a sit-in at the labor office. We had a case once before where an injured worker stalked his boss everywhere, ate with him, followed him to meetings, sat in front of his house, everywhere. For fifteen days he stalked and he ended up getting all the compensation owed to him for the injury.
>
> (Participant observation, 2010)

Chang left Pay It Forward with a final piece of advice from a staff member: "If they really don't help you, tell them your arm is rotting and that you can't wait any longer" (Participant observation, 2010).

Heeding the activists' advice, Chang again attempted to go through the formal dispute resolution channels. Perched on the seat of her husband's motorbike, Chang clutched a plastic bag filled with crumpled court documents as she rode to the township government building. Once inside the building, Chang grew uneasy; the building had no signs to direct visitors to the appropriate office. Only after asking several office workers did she arrive at the non-descript Women's Federation office. Though Chang had spoken boldly at the labor organization, she grew timid and confused in front of the Women's Federation official:

CHANG: Hi, are you the Women's Federation?
OFFICIAL: What's your situation?

CHANG: I'm an injured worker. A few days ago my factory stopped paying my medical
bills. What do you think I can do?
OFFICIAL: We don't have funding. We are not responsible for these kinds of issues.
CHANG: Aren't you responsible for women and children?
OFFICIAL: You're a migrant, right? We're only responsible for local [urban] female
workers.

(Participant observation, 2010)

Chang did not know how to respond to the official's claim that the ACWF
only served women with local household registration, not migrant women like
herself. The Women's Federation official directed Chang to the township labor
union located in the same building. The union official asked her to write down
a description of her case before filing it away.

Following these unsuccessful visits, an activist from Pay It Forward
instructed Chang to return to the township Labor Bureau. Chang took his
advice and once again approached the Bureau. Having recognized the official
in charge of processing her case, she inquired about its progress:

CHANG: Hi, what should be done about my problem?
OFFICIAL: Didn't I already tell you? There is no resolution! You can apply for arbitration.
CHANG: But my arm can't wait! If it becomes paralyzed, then even if you pay me
100,000 yuan it'll be useless.
OFFICIAL: [irritated and yelling] So, what do you want me to do? I can't take cash
straight out of the boss' drawers and give it to you!
CHANG: But you guys are responsible for doing something. If you're helpless, then I'm
even more helpless. *If you push me like this, then I can only take extreme actions!* I'm
not leaving [this office] today!
OFFICIAL: Be my guest!

(Participant observation, 2010)

Despite her best attempts, Chang's threat to sit-in at the Labor Bureau was not
enough to encourage the official to take action.

Through text messages and phone calls, activists instructed Chang to appeal
directly to the Labor Bureau chief. The chief was a young, bespectacled man
whose first reaction was to take out a blank piece of paper and ask Chang to
record her grievances. He then called in his subordinate, the labor officer whom
Chang had just confronted. What ensued was a process of rights bargaining in
which both officials pleaded with Chang to sympathize with the government's
position and entreated her to understand that both state and workers needed
to make allowances for one another (Participant observation, 2010).

BUREAU CHIEF: My knife is only so long, understand? [Referring to his capacity as a
bureaucrat]
CHANG: If you aren't willing to help me solve this ...
BUREAU CHIEF: It's not willingness; it's a matter of capacity. I can't rob the factory to
pay for your medical expenses; the state gave us limited powers.

CHANG: Okay, okay. So I said it wrong. Your knife can't slaughter that pig, right? If even you guys don't have that ability, then I am even more helpless. Aren't you here to serve workers? If you aren't willing ...
BUREAU CHIEF: Didn't I already say? It's not that we're not willing; it's that we don't have the capacity. You can only go the arbitration route ... We have to follow the law to resolve this case. The government only gave us such limited powers, what do you want me to do? You have to understand our work; we are also in a difficult place. You'd better wait patiently.
CHANG: I know, but you have to consider it from my point of view. I can wait but my arm can't. I've already been injured badly; this is going to affect me for life!
BUREAU CHIEF: See if you can borrow some money from friends or relatives.
LABOR OFFICER: Didn't your boss want to transfer you to a different hospital? That's not against the law.
CHANG: But [the boss] has connections there, they'll kick me out of the hospital before I heal. *If you push me to the edge then I will have to take extreme actions ...* then you'd have to bear the consequences.
BUREAU CHIEF: I'm not going to comment.

(Participant observation, 2010)

In this exchange, the bureau chief turned law enforcement into a matter of personal favors and exchanges. During the bargaining process between Chang and the bureau chief, the rule of law was not invoked. Instead, the legal right to injury compensation was turned into a personal favor bestowed upon Chang by benevolent officials. Under such circumstances, Chang resorted to an ambiguous but powerful verbal threat: "If you leave me with no other option, I'll take extreme actions." The bureau chief first denied any responsibility for her actions. Yet a few minutes later, he dispatched a team of labor inspection officers to investigate Chang's factory.

Chang immediately contacted the activist from Pay It Forward via her mobile phone and the activist agreed to accompany her to the factory under the guise of being her friend. The factory was composed of two dimly lit industrial garages, and the dozen workers who worked there did not wear protective gear, aside from gloves. The labor inspection team was led by the same labor officer that Chang had confronted earlier.

Chang did not see the inspection team go into the factory. Instead, the team and the factory boss went into a private room for an hour and a half-long conference that Chang was not privy to. The factory boss signed some papers with the labor inspector, but when the official came out, he motioned for Chang to negotiate with the boss and left the factory. The labor inspection team and factory management again spoke behind closed doors (Participant observation, 2010).

When their meeting ended, the factory boss came out to ask Chang to give him more time, claiming that he had no knowledge of her situation. Chang said this was not possible because she had sent him a threatening text message earlier in the week asking him if he "want[ed] to be in the news?" Just before

Chang left the factory, the activist directly threatened the factory boss: "If this is not resolved, she [Chang] might go to the Guangzhou Trade Fair to make a scene; this thing might escalate" (Participant observation, 2010). As we exited the factory, the Pay It Forward activist told Chang that she needed to take action and not just make empty threats.

Chang left the factory without a clear answer from her boss or the government official. However, two days later, the factory boss agreed to pay for her medical expenses. Staff members of Pay It Forward also connected Chang to a journalist who wrote a brief article about her case. Following coverage of her case in the local press, the district labor union representative visited Chang at the hospital, bringing a "gift" of 1,000 yuan and urged her to call the labor union's hotline in the future.

Chang's case demonstrated the instrumental role that Pay It Forward played in providing tactical and moral support for workers. When Chang's initial threat to a lower-ranked official failed to deliver any results, an activist advised her to target the bureau chief. Although the activist was not physically present at the Labor Bureau, he instructed Chang on how, when, and whom to target in escalating her threats. His moral support and tactical coaching was critical to Chang's eventual success. Nonetheless, this kind of activism was a risky process of bargaining for rights nominally guaranteed under China's labor law.

ORGANIZATIONAL AND PARTICIPANT OUTCOMES

Compared to the pedagogy of micro-collective action, the pedagogy of atomized action lowered organizational risks. By limiting the scale of contention to a sole individual, the organization refrained from becoming embroiled in mass incidents. Activists learned from previous experience that coordinating collective contention elicited state repression. In response, they devised the pedagogy of atomized action which disguised the coordination of contention behind a façade of individual action. To further reduce risk to the organization, activists typically refrained from accompanying participants to government offices and instead coached workers via text messaging or phone calls. When they did accompany participants to the sites of conflict, they assumed the role of a friend or a relative. Doing so allowed activists to hide their true identities from the officials in the Labor Bureau and local courts.

These precautionary measures did not eliminate all organizational risk. State Security continued to monitor their activities. Undercover agents occasionally infiltrated underground labor organizations by disguising themselves as workers in need of assistance. State Security also occasionally interrogated leaders and activists by inviting them to tea. During periodic crackdowns, authorities arrested leaders and disbanded their organizations. Nevertheless, the deployment of atomized action was far less risky than micro-collective action, which elicited immediate repression. By limiting the scale of contention, activists made a political compromise to censor their activism in exchange for greater space in which to maneuver.

Yet for participants, the pedagogy of atomized action further undermined workers' faith in local state institutions. Before contacting Pay It Forward, many workers attempted to resolve their disputes through informal processes of mediation with factory management, which bypassed the state altogether. After contacting the organization, workers were encouraged to first seek redress through the labor dispute system before attempting to deploy atomized action. After being repeatedly rebuffed by officials of the labor bureaus, labor unions, and courts, many workers became deeply disenchanted with these institutions. Repeated encounters with bureaucracies that failed to address their concerns produced in worker-participants a shared understanding of the local state as predatory. While they perceived central state authorities as possessing a moral conscience (*liangxin*), they viewed local state authorities as rent-seeking allies of local business interests. As one worker-participant declared, "The labor law has been passed but the local bureaus are not enforcing it! The local bureaus set traps for you. The Labor Bureau knows about the factories' violations but they don't do anything! But why don't people overthrow the Labor Bureau? Because it's the boss-man" (Interview with worker, 2010). As in other cases, such "informed disenchantment" (Gallagher 2007) paradoxically led to worker empowerment as they came to see themselves as having agency under the tutelage of activists. Workers learned that the best way to defend their interests was to make threats and threaten authorities into a negotiation over rights.

Paradoxically, participants' lack of faith in the local state's mandate to "serve the people" was accompanied by an ambivalent attitude toward civil society organizations. Unlike the participants of Solidarity in Action, who aspired to build a worker's platform for future collective mobilization, the participants of Pay It Forward had no such aspirations. Many did not believe in the power of civil society to create sustained, meaningful social change. They viewed organizations like Pay It Forward to be at the mercy of a powerful state. Many workers felt that without state recognition, organizations would inevitably be limited in their power to confront employers over labor abuses. Two workers at the organization's annual retreat made a case for why civil society organizations ought to be recognized by the state:

WORKER A: The grassroots organization's function is to be a backup; it can never be the main actor. The state doesn't recognize it [because it believes that] it is antigovernment. But if the state understood, then it would gain an extra hand to solve problems. In my ideal world, grassroots organizations should be in the open because they aren't distant from the people. The state should recognize these organizations instead of letting them stay in the dark; it should let them put up a sign [become officially registered].

WORKER B: There are a lot more of us migrant workers than there are of them [civil servants] so we should lend them a hand. Our organization should be like journalists;

if the government doesn't investigate, then journalists investigate. We see a lot more [problems] and we can report it to the government.

(Participant observation, 2010)

Even Chang, who gained compensation with the organization's aid, felt that civil society's power was limited: "The staff members are not as powerful as the government, in the end. It's just that you have to make a big enough scene. They [local officials] are afraid of losing their rice bowls [their positions], so they'll have to deal with it in the end" (Interview, 2010). When asked what she would do differently if she encountered a similar problem in the future, Chang said that she would turn to the activists for tactical advice. However, if she did not have access to them, she would turn to the formal labor dispute system. Her last resort would be to threaten to commit suicide. In short, the worker-participants of Pay It Forward viewed the organization as a weak institution that could provide moral support and tactical counsel on making rights claims when government institutions failed to implement laws. However, few participants aspired to build the organization into a larger mobilizing structure that could stage collective contention.

Despite the fact that few worker-participants aspired to stage collective action, the pedagogical process nevertheless fostered collective consciousness among them. This was embodied in Pay It Forward's mission to "increase migrant workers' rights consciousness and promote unity and mutual aid" (Organizational pamphlet, 2010). Accordingly, activists encouraged participants to disseminate their knowledge of labor rights to their co-workers, friends, and family. Moreover, activists recruited committed participants to become volunteers.[10] In 2010, Pay It Forward's volunteer network included several generations of workers, ranging from teenagers to retirees. These volunteers accompanied activists on recruitment visits, assisted at legal workshops, and provided moral support to participants. They also turned up to the court hearings of other workers in demonstrations of solidarity. Thus, although atomized actions were individualistic, the pedagogy called upon participants to "Pay It Forward" and to identify as part of a broader collective of workers advocating for rights, even if such collective consciousness did not translate into collective action.

CONCLUSION

This chapter examined the second tactical variation of mobilizing without the masses: the pedagogy of atomized action. Although atomized action appeared to be self-motivated, it was in fact the outcome of a pedagogical process led by

---

[10] Having formal membership would have sent a signal to the state that the organization was politicized, given the association of membership with political parties. Thus, these workers were called "volunteers."

civil society organizations. This process entailed two components: informing citizens about their legal rights and instructing them to deploy atomized action that threatened social stability. Atomized actions worked through two mechanisms: threatening social stability and challenging the moral authority of state officials. In contrast to everyday resistance (Scott 1987), atomized protestors staged ostentatious displays of defiance, which signaled their willingness to disrupt social stability. Such public spectacles attracted the attention of crowds and the media, which amplified a solo protestor's challenge to the state's moral authority. In response, otherwise unresponsive state officials were incentivized to address the grievances of the individual in order to pre-empt further unrest.

The pedagogy of atomized action sought to further reduce organizational risk by scaling down contentious activity to the action of a single individual. Whereas rallying a group of workers to protest would trigger immediate state repression, channeling these same workers into individualized forms of contention was a more tolerable form of activism in the eyes of the state. Moreover, unlike workers who engaged in symbolic micro-collective action, wielders of atomized action sought to gain monetary compensation for labor law violations. In this sense, activists played an active role in the state's routinization of protest by facilitating a tri-party negotiation over the price of rights between the worker, state official, and management. This negotiation essentially depoliticized the process of rights claiming by playing into the state's attempts to quell social unrest through paying off protestors (Lee and Zhang 2013; Chen 2012; Su and He 2010). In fact, it is even less costly for the state to pay off a single protestor than it is to placate a crowd of rabble-rousers. One could further argue that the lone atomized protestor is but a skillful manipulator of an informal state institution.

However, the outright confrontation between the rights claimants and the state constitutes only the "public transcript" – "open interaction between subordinates and those who dominate" (Scott 1990: 2). The "hidden transcript," which constitutes "gesture, speech, practices – that is ordinarily excluded from the public transcript of subordinates by the exercise of power" (Scott 1990: 27), took place between activists and workers during the pedagogical sessions. Through a long-term process of coaching, activists taught workers to articulate their individual problems as part of a broader set of structural inequities stemming from the collusion between state and capital. As the last chapter of this book argues, activists also constructed an alternative script for workers, one that subverted the state's dominant narrative of workers sacrificing to advance the nation's modernization. Such narratives were hardly ever openly articulated; they were instead rehearsed during legal workshops, social events, and other seemingly innocuous activities. Nevertheless, these ritualized scripts of subversion laid the foundations for what would later become a tactical escalation in terms of mobilizing *with* the masses (see Chapter 8).

7

Discursive Action

This chapter examines a third tactical variation of mobilizing without the masses: the pedagogy of discursive action. In closed polities where freedoms of association and speech are limited, subversive discourse criticizing the state and its policies can be a form of resistance (Johnston 2006: 198). Complaints about the ruling party, discussions about repression, kitchen talk, joke-telling, and informal conversations in bars and cafés about social or historical events all constitute "oppositional speech acts" (Johnston 2006: 199). Although informal, these discursive acts are contentious because they involve an audience that participates as listeners and partners in conversation (Johnston 2006).

Civil society organizations can play an instrumental role in constructing and disseminating a counter-hegemonic discourse that asserts the rights of their participants. In the pedagogy of discursive action, labor activists coach participants to contend with the state through constructing a counter-discourse that presents migrant workers as citizens deserving of the same rights as their urban counterparts. Deploying a range of cultural resources including written, performance, and visual arts, activists coach participants to identify as "new citizens" (*xin gongmin or xin shimin*)[1] rather than as subalterns (*diceng*). It is on this basis of equal citizenship that claims for labor rights are made. Activists attempt to persuade participants that the party-state and the business class not only materially exploit the working class, they also dominate workers through a hegemonic discourse that culturally and ideologically subjugates the less powerful.

In the context of labor organizations in China, the pedagogy of discursive action attempts to elevate workers to the status of citizens in a state in which

[1] The term *gongmin* translates as the "public citizen," and traces its origins to the Confucian celebration of public service. The term *shimin* translates as the "urban citizen" and was used in the urban uprisings accompanying the revolution of 1911 as well as in the protests of 1989 (Goldman and Perry 2002).

the status of the proletariat has precipitously declined. During the early years of the People's Republic, workers and peasants were hailed as the vanguard of the revolution. Yet massive lay-offs in state-owned enterprises in the early 2000s stripped workers of their social and economic security (Hurst 2009). At the same time, economic reform created employment opportunities for a new class of workers – migrants from rural China who flooded coastal cities to work largely in the manufacturing and service sectors. These migrant workers were economically exploited by their employers and treated as second-class citizens by the state (K. W. Chan 2010; A. Chan 2001; Zhang 2001; Solinger 1999). China's household registration system barred migrant workers living in the cities from enjoying equal access to key public services such as education, healthcare, and housing.[2] Even as a second generation of migrant workers has become increasingly rights conscious (Lee 2007b), they nevertheless continue to be socially marginalized.

Accompanying economic exploitation and social marginalization was the discursive domination of migrant workers. This is most clearly embodied in popular and political discourse in the use of the denigrating term "peasant workers" (*nongmin gong*) to refer to migrant workers.[3] This term is inherently discriminatory as it suggests that peasants are lacking in both culture (*wenhua*) and in quality (*suzhi*) compared to their urban counterparts. Moreover, the term signifies that migrant workers are quasi-farmers and quasi-workers (Pun and Lu 2010), thereby discursively tying them to their rural backgrounds. In a process that has been termed "unfinished proletarianism" (Pun and Lu 2010), migrant workers were unable to complete the transition into becoming a new class of urban proletariat and instead continued to be socially marginalized as "outsiders."

Civil society organizations can play a role in constructing a collective identity of the current generation of migrant workers as "new urban citizens" who, unlike their predecessors in the first generation of migrants, will not return to rural China. The pedagogy of discursive action subverts the dominant discourse of migrant workers as "peasant workers" by asserting that they are, in fact, permanent members of urban communities rather than transient subjects who will ultimately return to their native villages. In this discourse, migrant workers are a new class of citizens who deserve equal access to education, housing, healthcare, and other social services already provided to their urban counterparts. By constructing a new identity for migrant workers as citizens,

---

[2] The household registration system is undergoing reform as the party-state has promised to grant 100 million permits to urban residents by 2020. See: S. Tiezzi, China's Plan for "Orderly" Hukou Reform, February 3, 2016, *Diplomat*.

[3] For example, reports from the National Bureau of Statistics use the term "peasant workers" in estimating migrant workers' population. 2014 nian quanguo nongmingong jiance diaocha baogao [2014 Peasant Worker Monitoring and Investigation Report], April 29, 2014, National Bureau of Statistics of the People's Republic of China.

activists situate their struggles for labor rights, claims for compensation, and demands for public goods and services as part of a larger struggle for equal citizenship. This approach to labor advocacy is a departure from routine worker strikes and protests, which eschew the language of citizenship in favor of the more anodyne language of economic compensation.

CASE STUDY: WORKERS' WORLD

The case of the labor organization Workers' World illustrated how activists deployed the pedagogy of discursive action to advocate for a wide range of labor rights. The organization was founded in 2002 when an idealistic migrant musician and a few friends transformed an abandoned factory in a village near a major metropolis into a thriving labor organization.[4] The ten founding activists were male migrants in their thirties and forties who had quit their jobs to work for the organization full time.[5] Although they were paid a base salary, they were expected to work on a volunteer basis when funding was tight. By 2013, what had begun as a small, grassroots project had grown into a mature organization that was attracting national attention from the media and state officials alike for its work advocating a cultural approach to worker mobilization. Instead of threatening social stability or pressing for economic compensation through the legal system, activists advanced "migrant workers' culture" (*dagong wenhua*). Through a variety of visual and performance arts, activists sought to propagate a workers' culture that embraced socialist values, decried the corrupting influences of capitalism, and asserted migrants as a new working class. Workers' World used the promotion of migrant workers' culture as a point of entry when demanding broader rights for migrant workers, including the right to affordable housing, healthcare, and equal education for migrant children, as well as the right to form migrant workers' cultural associations. In 2011, Workers' World registered as a non-profit cultural development enterprise (*wenhua fazhan gongsi*) under the Bureau of Industry and Commerce.

The promotion of migrant workers' culture was evident from the physical layout and practices of the organization. After walking through a maze of dusty alleyways in the village in which Workers' World was based, one arrived at the entrance to the organization's compound. The Chinese national flag flew over a mural outside the building depicting industrial workers with the slogan: "All workers under heaven are one family" (*tianxia dagong shi yijia*). The organization's internal structure and culture harkened back to the socialist values of the Mao era. Activists lived in sparse communal dormitories reminiscent of the pre-reform era and shared meals at the organization's cafeteria. Activists' free time also revolved around the organization: they played ping-pong in the

---

[4] The names of individuals and the organization are pseudonyms.
[5] The only female staff member was a scholar-activist who led the organization's research initiatives, among other duties.

courtyard, watched films in the organization's makeshift movie theater, and sang songs praising the value of migrant labor.

Workers' World embraced two broad goals. The first was constructing and disseminating an alternative discourse that asserted migrant workers as new urban citizens. Activists did this by deploying cultural resources such as didactic dramas, songs, and visual arts that celebrated migrant workers' contribution to China's modernization and their need to work in solidarity to claim citizenship rights. In the director's words, it was critical for migrant workers to acquire an awareness of themselves as rights-bearing citizens:

China now has 400–500 million new industrial workers; they will be the primary force shaping the future of Chinese society. If they do not have any forms of organization, they will not gain an understanding of citizenship rights. In order to stay in the cities for the long term, migrant workers need to have an awareness of their rights as citizens, and they need an organization to help them realize this.

(Interview, director, 2011)

It was on the basis of claiming equal citizenship that worker-participants were coached to claim basic rights to the city and its public services.

A parallel goal was to persuade elite actors (including state officials, journalists, and scholars) to view migrant workers as citizens with a legitimate claim to equal rights. Activists sought to persuade elites that it was in the interest of the party-state to allow migrant workers to form cultural associations. These associations would promote migrant workers' culture within a nominally socialist polity dominated by the Communist Party. Although on its surface the right to form cultural associations might appear to be a politically "soft" demand, it in fact constituted a challenge to the state's monopoly on the cultural representation of the working class. By demanding that migrant workers be allowed to form their own cultural associations, Workers' World essentially contested the state's monopoly over the cultural representation of workers.

Activists attempted to persuade political and social elites that workers ought to be able to culturally represent themselves, and the director of Workers' World was well versed in pitching different stories to various stakeholders. To journalists, he recounted his personal story of giving up his life as an itinerant migrant worker musician in order to establish a platform for cultivating migrant workers' culture. For TV stations, he played his guitar and sang about migrant construction workers yearning for home. To scholars, he spoke in the language of Marxist philosophy and expressed his distaste for the capitalist mode of production and consumer society. To state officials, he highlighted the state's achievements in improving the lives of migrant workers and forged synergistic partnerships with state institutions in charge of culture and propaganda. These relationships with elites enabled Workers' World to initiate a policy discussion at the Central Party School, China's top institution of higher learning for Communist Party cadres.

CONTESTING DOMINANT DISCOURSES

Activists deployed a range of resources to construct an alternative discourse of migrants as citizens central to China's modernization. These included the construction of the nation's first museum commemorating the history and contribution of migrant workers to economic reform, as well as the production and performance of didactic dramas, songs, and poetry for both migrant workers and general audiences. These performances narrated migrant workers' marginalization and called upon workers to stand in solidarity with each other to advocate for greater protection of their labor rights. Finally, the organization invested in educational resources in the form of an elementary school for migrant children and a workers' college. These institutions propagated Workers' World's ideas concerning citizenship and workers' rights to a young generation of migrant workers.

Workers' World adopted a strategy of cultural mobilization that was reminiscent of the Chinese Communist Party's own use of cultural resources to mobilize individuals and govern the country (Perry 2013, 2012). During the pre-1949 revolutionary era, the Party mobilized the peasantry and the proletariat through deft usage of the arts, with Communist Party leaders – including Mao Zedong, Liu Shaoqi, and Li Lisan – using mass education, didactic dramas, and other activities to persuade workers to recognize their collective contributions to society and their revolutionary potential as a class (Perry 2012: 11). At Anyuan, the birthplace of the Communist revolution, the workers' club established by the Communist Party devoted its resources to proletarian education. Among the mobilization materials were textbooks, dramas, songs, and lectures which constituted a "cultural template" that was disseminated to other Communist bases across the country (Perry 2012: 10–11). After the revolution, the party-state continued to deploy cultural governance – the strategic use of propaganda and the active shaping of public opinion to legitimize its rule (Perry 2013).

Workers' World's use of cultural resources mimicked the Chinese Communist Party's own use of cultural mobilization as a means of governing workers. The scale of the organization's its cultural production efforts, and its power to disseminate their cultural products, paled in comparison to that of the party-state's propaganda machinery. Nevertheless, its cultural production represented a form of grassroots labor activism that at once challenged the party-state's monopoly over the cultural representation of workers and was reminiscent of the Party's own domination strategies. Activists sought to re-invent old cultural tools for the purposes of mobilizing workers to both reclaim the high social status of workers under socialism which they had lost, as well as to claim their right to equal treatment from a nominally socialist state.

To begin with, Workers' World, with the support of international donors, constructed China's first – and so far only – museum commemorating migrant workers' history. The museum was one of the prominent cultural resources that the organization deployed to challenge the popular narrative of migrants as uneducated peasant workers. It highlighted not only the historical contribution of migrants to China's miraculous economic development but also their social and cultural marginalization as a class. Located in the same compound as the organization's headquarters, the museum attracted a wide range of visitors, including government officials, scholars, journalists, as well as activists and workers from other labor organizations. The narrative of the permanent exhibit was couched in the language of the state yet defiant in its display of the egregious abuses that migrants had suffered during the decades of economic reform. Activists provided visitors with guided tours of the museum, but their narration of the exhibits changed according to the audience. To state officials and domestic journalists, guides highlighted milestones in the party-state's ongoing efforts to liberalize government policies directed at migrant rights. To workers, activists, and like-minded scholars, guides narrated the inadequacies of the legal protections afforded to workers and the injustice of state policies that rendered migrants as second-class citizens.

Walking into the first exhibition room, one saw a red banner emblazoned with a quote by former Premier Wen Jiabao: "Respecting the value of labor is the fundamental principle for a nation." When state officials visited the museum, the director would point to the banner and ask rhetorically, "Premier Wen has told us to live with dignity. How *can* we live with dignity?" (Participant observation, 2010). The question was left open as visitors walked through a chronological display of migrant workers' history that ran from the early years of the reform era to the present. Makeshift display cases exhibited the temporary residence permits that migrants were required to obtain in order to remain in the cities. The same display cases also showed tattered citations and fines that were issued to migrants who did not carry temporary residence permits – such migrants were often detained and abused by local authorities in a practice known as administrative detention.[6] The exhibit went on to showcase the notorious case of Sun Zhigang, a college student beaten to death by railway officials for not carrying his temporary residence permit. His case triggered a national outcry that precipitated reforms in the system of the administrative detention of migrants.[7] The exhibit also displayed photos and news clippings reporting state interventions to safeguard the rights of migrant workers, including media coverage of a famous 2003 incident in which former Premier Wen Jiabao aided a peasant woman in recovering wages owed to her husband, a construction worker.

When state officials and domestic journalists toured the museum, activists stood by this "public transcript" (Scott 1990) that applauded the party-state's

---

[6] Since 2015 migrant workers have not been required to hold temporary residence permits. Reuters 2015.

[7] M. Luo, Sun zhigang shijian yu huji zhidu gaige [The Sun Zhigang Incident and Household Registration System Reform], *Renda yanjiu*, 12.1, 2003.

advancements in safeguarding labor rights. However, in private conversations, activists viscerally critiqued the gap between state rhetoric and action. When two workers from another organization visited the museum, the activist who served as their guide remarked: "It takes a premier to recover the salary of one migrant worker? How embarrassing!" (Participant observation, 2010). The exhibition ended with the display of a single migrant child's twelve different school uniforms (one for each school he attended), a powerful symbol of the state's unequal treatment of migrants. Migrant children could only attend migrant schools, which often operated without official permits. A lack of affordable housing for migrant workers further disrupted the education of migrant children by compelling families to frequently move and change schools. The migrant workers' museum was one of the main forums for producing and disseminating an alternative narrative of China's economic development, one which placed migrant workers at the center. This alternative narrative was channeled domestically and internationally through alternative media outlets, with a version of the exhibit even traveling to Spain in 2011 to disseminate the story of Chinese migrant workers to a global audience.

Performance and literary arts served as other cultural resources deployed by Workers' World to contest dominant narratives about migrant workers. Composing songs and poetry, activists attempted to construct an identity for migrants as a new generation of industrial workers. These songs, recounting how China's economic modernization was built on the backs of hundreds of millions of migrant workers, were disseminated across the country through touring live performances and the distribution of CDs, DVDs, edited volumes, and poetry chapbooks.[8] Between 2002 and 2011, Workers' World staged over 200 performances and distributed more than 100,000 CDs. One of their most popular songs – *Labor Is Glorious*[9] co-opted an old party-state slogan to propagate a subversive message of worker solidarity:

> *Labor is glorious, hey!* (Repeat 3x)
> *We built the high rises, we paved the wide boulevards*
> *We work the filthiest, dirtiest jobs!*
> *We ought to stand up and be proud,*
> *We earn our meals through our labor.*
> *Labor is glorious, hey!* (Repeat 3x)
> *We are the laborers of a new era*
> *We are the pioneers of a new China*
> *Let us join hands, stand shoulder to shoulder*
> *We shall stand up tall and*
> *March forth with courage!*

---

[8] In my fieldwork in South China, I also saw these song lyrics posted on the walls of other labor organizations.
[9] Workers' World 2004 CD.

By asserting that migrant workers have been the engines of China's economic transformation, songs like *Labor Is Glorious* asserted workers as the proletarians of a new China and called for them to work together to fight for their collective interests. The organization's website promoted such messages by offering free downloads of music and videos, and by showcasing photographs of recent Workers' World-sponsored performances and events.

Workers' World disseminated this counter-narrative to diverse audiences. Since 2002, the director and his performing troupe (made up of the organization's core activists) have toured the country, performing for workers and managers on construction sites as well as for the general public and university students. For example, the organization participated in a 2010 concert at a construction site that brought Beijing university students and migrant workers together to celebrate the contributions of construction workers to China's economic growth. This was a unique event: although university student groups have supported research on peasants and rural China, they rarely engaged in labor activism. Yet in celebration of Construction Workers' Day, Workers' World collaborated with students at several Beijing universities to host a concert for workers at a nearby construction site. Workers' World performed popular songs like *Beijing, Beijing* and *Ode to Workers*. The audience included nearly 100 construction workers, as well as scholars invited by Workers' World and one representative from the construction company (Field notes, 2010). This concert, along with other concerts staged by the organization for workers, enabled Workers' World to disseminate their message of worker empowerment to their clientele without directly challenging the authority of the party-state. And by drawing upon cultural resources, the organization was able to motivate workers to value their labor and recognize their collective power without taking confrontational collective action.

The third cultural resource that Workers' World deployed were didactic dramas that personalized labor exploitation and illustrated the state's and society's unequal treatment of migrants. To this end, Workers' World forged a partnership with an urban district's Bureau of Culture, which gave the organization free access to a popular theater venue. Like their concerts, these didactic dramas straddled the boundary between subversion and political acceptability. In one play staged during the 2008 Beijing Olympics, Workers' World changed the official Olympics slogan "One World, One Dream" to "*Our* World, *Our* Dream." Through a series of vignettes, the play illustrated the desire of migrant workers to be free from police harassment and dangerous working conditions, to be respected by society, and to enjoy decent housing. Didactic dramas such as these illustrated the problems facing migrant workers and told a moral tale of the capitalist exploitation of workers. They provided a safe space in which migrant workers could "speak bitterness" (*suku*), just as Chinese peasants were encouraged to voice their grievances during village meetings in the Mao era (Perry 2002c: 112). However, these dramas stopped short of directly criticizing the party-state's role in such exploitation.

The final cultural resource of Workers' World was the compilation of a dictionary documenting the everyday language of migrant workers. This workers' dictionary was part of an attempt to subvert popular and official discourse surrounding "peasant workers" as belonging to a sub-class of urban residents. In collaboration with scholars from the Chinese Academy of Social Sciences, activists conducted research on common terms that workers used in their daily lives, as well as alternative labels to describe the migrant class. The dictionary advocated the use of a new term – "new industrial workers" (*xin chanye gongren*) – to refer to the second generation of migrant workers who, unlike their predecessors, intended to settle permanently in the cities where they worked. The organization hoped that the terms contained in the dictionary would be adopted by journalists, scholars, and state officials alike and that by compiling a workers' lexicon, they could encourage the state and society to recognize workers as equal citizens.

In each sphere of cultural mobilization, Workers' World strategically refrained from issuing a "call to arms" by avoiding direct critiques of the party-state. Departing from the modus operandi of other labor organizations, activists at Workers' World also refrained from giving workers legal counsel or representing them during labor dispute arbitration and mediation. They also steered clear of coaching workers to challenge social stability. By remaining in the realm of discursive struggle, Workers' World has been far more successful than many other organizations establishing partnerships with various branches of the state.

PERSUADING POLICY-MAKERS

One of the target audiences for the activists at Workers' World was policy-makers, who they hoped would grant more political space for migrant workers to form their own cultural associations. In this sense, Workers' World was one among a number of "policy entrepreneurs" in China that "occupy space from which they can articulate and amplify their issue in ways that engage the political process rather than existing outside of and in direct opposition to it" (Mertha 2008: 7). To this end, the organization forged strategic partnerships with political insiders including government officials, journalists, and scholars. These alliances created a network of political insiders that assisted Workers' World in disseminating migrant worker culture and amplifying the voice of migrant workers in policy-making.

Instead of demanding immediate legal or political reform, Workers' World strategically advocated for the broadening of cultural rights. This was in response to a political opportunity that emerged in 2009 when four ministries of China's central government jointly issued the nation's first policy document encouraging the development of grassroots cultural associations.[10] Seizing this

---

[10] These included the Ministry of Culture, the Ministry of Finance, the Ministry of Personnel, and the State Administration of Taxation. For the Chinese text, see Wenhuabu guanyu cujin

opening, Workers' World advocated for the right to form migrant cultural associations, a demand they believed was more innocuous than calls for legal reform. Many of the agencies that partnered with Workers' World were under pressure from the central government to develop new ways of serving marginalized communities and were therefore willing to engage with grassroots organizations.

In 2010, Workers' World established a unique partnership with a professor at the Party School of the Central Committee of the Communist Party of China (CPS), the nation's elite educational institution for Party cadres. The CPS professor had conducted research on migrant labor organizations across China and had an avid interest in their cultural activities. Eventually, she collaborated with the director of Workers' World to design a curriculum module on "new workers' culture" (*xin gongren wenhua*) which she later taught to Party cadres at the CPS. In partnership with the director and other Chinese scholars, the professor compiled an essay series on the origins, manifestations, and policy implications of new workers' culture. This series served as part of the core curriculum for her course and was published in an official magazine.[11]

These articles generated debate among Party cadres about the merits of grassroots migrant workers' organizations. Did these organizations stabilize society by channeling worker discontent into harmless cultural activities? Or did they instigate social instability by mobilizing the dispossessed? At the core of the debate was whether or not these grassroots labor organizations promoted an agenda that aligned with Party ideology. One essayist argued that these issues deserved the attention of policy-makers:

Over these last few years, a number of migrant workers have established their own organizations … [and] with the increase in horizontal networking among these grassroots organizations and transnational networking, [these groups] have a growing influence in society. How to view these new cultural phenomena, how to evaluate their significance, how to guide and manage these organizations in order to find a synthesis in the bottom-up and top-down forces of cultural construction, [these questions] deserve deep reflection.

(C. Liu 2010: 22)

The same contributor argued that the values espoused by grassroots labor organizations aligned with those promoted by the party-state:

Thus, the values advocated by migrant culture – including respect for labor and the glory of labor – are in line with the values of the socialist society advocated by the

mingying wenyi biaoyan tuanti fazhan de ruogan yijian [Recommendations by the Ministry of Culture on the Encouragement of Grassroots Performance Organizations' Development], June 6, 2009, Central People's Government of the People's Republic of China. This recommendation was China's first document directly encouraging the development of grassroots cultural associations.

[11] The authors included various Party cadres, scholars at the Chinese Academy of Social Sciences, and a migrant worker activist (Chinese Cadres Tribune) *Zhongguo dangzheng ganbu luntan*, 2010, 9, 22–6.

central party-state. As an innovative supplement, [these values] also extend the traditions of civilized people-oriented culture as advocated by the Party. It counters negative values in society such as worshiping wealth.

(C. Liu 2010: 22)

A migrant activist made a similar argument:

General Party Secretary Hu Jintao said on May 1 at the National Ceremony of the Labor Models and Advanced Workers that we should respect the value and dignity of labor. We believe that if labor is not respected ... then there is no way to realize mutual respect and harmonious relations between capital and labor. All of these things depend on cultural change. Culture must embrace the labor force's rise, and migrant workers' culture represented by Workers' World is a forerunner of this force.

(Activist, 2010: 33)

These contributors argued that migrant workers' associations were stabilizing agents which promoted the core values of the Chinese Communist Party.

In contrast, other officials argued that grassroots labor organizations must be closely monitored by the state because they promoted heterodox values. The Party Secretary of Henan University advocated for greater Party guidance of grassroots worker culture so that it could become "an instrument of communication between authorities and the masses ... enabling rulers to synthesize the psyche of society for policy in order to achieve the goal of stable rule." Without guidance from the party-state on moral values and aesthetic expression, he warned that "the culture of the subordinate class can often drift towards baseness, promoting sex, drugs, and violence – all psychological vices that grassroots culture easily incubates." His solution was to "incorporate, guide, uplift, and synthesize grassroots working culture so that it could become a part of advanced culture" (2010: 26). The Party Secretary and Director of the Shaanxi Bureau of Culture echoed this view and distinguished between "rational and irrational forms of [worker] demands." He argued that migrant workers' artistic productions showed signs of "an extreme [or irrational] mood." The Party Secretary cautioned that Party cadres should be wary of the "negative and destructive effects of irrational demands [of the subordinate class]" (2010: 27).

Workers' World participated in this deliberative process indirectly by partnering with key political insiders and brokers who could convey the organization's position to policy-makers. The CPS professor who had traveled across the country doing research on migrant workers' cultural associations served as one such broker. She found that initially, most local governments were skeptical of self-organized cultural groups composed of workers (Interview, 2011). However, discussions such as the ones that took place in her course were slowly changing the attitudes of Party cadres towards grassroots organizing:

Last year when I held the seminar, a number of people were surprised that there was such a voice [grassroots migrant organizations] in society. Many of [my students] had come from the countryside themselves. The individuals who were worried thought that these groups might be like Falun Gong ... this is an instinctive fear, but everybody is sympathetic towards commoners.

(Interview, 2011)

By introducing Party cadres to labor organizations, the professor hoped that these cadres would eventually create a more open environment in their own localities in which workers' cultural associations could operate.

Workers' World also forged a strategic partnership with a county government to set up China's first community-based trade union that was not a formal chapter of the ACFTU. As the director of Workers' World explained, the creation of the trade union emerged from an unexpected political opportunity:

A group of delegates from the national and municipal chapters [of the ACFTU] had taken American trade union delegates on a tour of Workers' World, signaling to the foreigners that China, too, had grassroots labor organizations. When the American trade unionists asked if China had any non-state unions, Chinese officials did not know what to say. A few weeks later, county government officials approached me to request that we establish an enterprise trade union, since we are a registered cultural enterprise. So we did. It was an opportunity to experiment with the community-based trade union model that could potentially be established nationwide.

(Interview, director, 2010)

By using their status as a registered cultural enterprise, Workers' World was able to establish a community-based trade union in the organization's compound in early 2011. With just over fifty members, the union provided workers with education, a free library, legal aid, reading groups, and legal consultation. This mutually beneficial partnership with the county government gave Workers' World a chance to experiment with a community-based trade union model while also boosting the political legitimacy of the organization. The director hoped that the creation of the union would lead to the future liberalization of state policies on worker representation. In the meantime, recognition by the ACFTU sent positive signals to other government agencies that Workers' World was an organization with which it was "safe" to be affiliated.

Finally, Workers' World also partnered with the local village committee (*cunweihui*) whose approval was critical to the organization's daily operations. The organization contributed to village administration by providing critical public goods: a non-profit elementary school for migrant children and a workers' college. The elementary school was an important service to a village composed mostly of migrant workers whose children faced high obstacles in enrolling in urban schools due to their rural registration status.[12] In addition, in collaboration with a university-based rural development center, Workers' World recruited young adult migrants from labor organizations across the country to attend training courses at the college. Each year, over twenty young adults

---

[12] For details on the obstacles that migrant children face in education, see: *China Labour Bulletin*, Migrant Workers and Their Children, June 27, 2013.

nominated by labor organizations across the country participated in a six-month intensive, boot camp-style training program in social work. These students lived in dormitories with staff members and were required to remain in the village for the duration of the program and abide by a strict work schedule.

To the public, the workers' college was advertised as a training program in response to the party-state's call for improving migrant workers' marketable skills. A state-run newspaper article in 2010 about the Beijing government's efforts to train young migrant workers applauded Workers' World's efforts:

Responding to the State Council's call for employment training for a new generation of migrant workers to propel their urbanization, [Workers' World] is amassing social resources in order to provide free training opportunities to this population. The training will include computer technician courses and urban citizenship education.[13]

On the surface, the training program was purely vocational, as it offered training in specific skills. Yet the curriculum used at the workers' college also conveyed an ideology that aligned with Workers' World's ultimate mission of training a new generation of migrant workers to work in other NGOs. Accompanying the training in marketable skills such as graphic design or computer maintenance was a curriculum that taught workers to grapple with their low position in society. In addition to practical skills, students learned to critique global capitalism and to value their own contribution as laborers. According to the director:

We teach them to recognize the value of labor. Capitalists are enslaved by money, but workers cannot share this value. Every Thursday, the students must put their knowledge to practice through community service … What can workers turn to? They must turn to the value of labor.

(Interview, director, 2011)

Getting young migrant workers to grasp the concept of civil society is difficult. According to the principal of the workers' college, being a citizen means recognizing that workers have innate rights which are not simply bestowed upon them by their bosses:

Civil society is a concept that came from abroad. A lot of [students] do not have a good grasp of it because, in the countryside, relationships matter more than the law … In the citizenship course, we will give students real-life scenarios to analyze. For instance, if a construction worker wins back his wages, many workers would thank their boss. But we teach them that it is your right [as a citizen]; it's not the boss who gives you rights.

(Interview, principal, 2011)

By teaching workers to recognize the value of their labor and to make rights claims, the school sought to instill in them a sense of citizenship and belonging.

---

[13] The full citation has been omitted to protect the organization's identity.

ORGANIZATION AND PARTICIPANT OUTCOMES

Deploying the pedagogy of discursive action enabled Workers' World to gain political legitimacy by partnering with various government bureaus. Workers' World experienced far less state harassment than its counterparts in the Pearl River Delta that threatened social stability. Since its founding in 2002, the organization operated without once being relocated or disbanded by the authorities. As of 2011, Workers' World continued to be registered as a non-profit cultural development enterprise (*wenhua fazhan gongsi*) under the Bureau of Industry and Commerce.

The organization's strategic choice to refrain from legal and political mobilization drew criticism from other labor organizations, particularly activists in the Pearl River Delta who criticized Workers' World for substituting direct action with "empty discourse" (*kong hua*). From their perspective, an organization that engaged solely in a discursive struggle neglected the material struggle aimed at improving the lives of China's working class. Critics believed that a genuine advocacy organization would fight for the legal rights of workers instead of retreating into the realm of cultural activism. To the critics of Workers' World, cultural mobilization was a soft form of advocacy that was far too abstract and intellectual to have a direct impact on workers' lives. The increased political legitimacy that Workers' World gained from cultural mobilization came at the expense of losing legitimacy in the eyes of some of its peers.

In spite of these criticisms, the migrant workers who participated in Workers' World felt that they gained a new collective identity for themselves as citizens. This was critical to the mobilization of China's second generation of migrant workers. On the one hand, these workers were no longer peasants because they worked in cities and adopted the consumer habits of urbanites. On the other hand, they were not considered full proletariats because of their rural registration status (Pun and Lu 2010: 17). In this "unfinished process of proletarianization" (2010), organizations such as Workers' World offered an alternative grammar of contention, entreating migrants to make demands of their employers beyond one-off acts of economic compensation. Activists hoped that once migrant workers came to identify as urban workers, they would unite in solidarity to press the government to guarantee their right to affordable housing, healthcare, and equal education for their children. While it is still too early to assess the impact of these forms of cultural mobilization, organizations such as Workers' World have forged the cultural resources necessary for future worker mobilization.

Besides constructing a collective identity for migrant workers as citizens, Workers' World also trained young migrants to become future civil society leaders through its workers' college. Workers' World may one day become an important actor in fostering labor organization growth across China. One of China's foremost advocates for peasant rights argued that the director of Workers' World and his followers will continue to have significant impact on the migrant working class in the coming decade:

> I like [the director] because he is a migrant worker himself; the working class comes from the peasantry. His organizational ideology is ahead of our times in many respects, but he is also cautious. He is neither an intellectual nor a peasant, so he can play off that identity when dealing with the government. In the future decade, he and his followers will be one of the most significant influences on the working class.
>
> (Interview, advocate, 2011)

Indeed, perhaps one of the most enduring participant outcomes for Workers' World is the cultivation of a generation of young migrant leaders who identify themselves as new proletariats.

CONCLUSION

This chapter analyzed the third tactical variation of mobilizing without the masses: the pedagogy of discursive action. Instead of coaching participants to challenge social stability, activists promoted migrant workers' culture as a point of entry into labor rights advocacy. They used a wide range of visual, performance, and literary arts to disseminate a counter-narrative of migrant workers as citizens. This narrative challenged popular and official discourses of migrants as "peasant workers" which marked them as marginal subjects in the city. By asserting that migrants are citizens, activists offered worker-participants a new grammar of labor contention, one in which labor grievances are set within the broader context of workers demanding their rights as citizens.

This case also showed that by engaging in cultural mobilization, organizations like Workers' World could influence policy-makers. Activists for Workers' World introduced a novel lexicon to officials and journalists alike who had previously conceived of migrants simply as "peasant workers." In addition, Workers' World's partnership with the Central Party School enabled the organization to ignite a debate among Party cadres over the legitimacy of migrant workers' cultural organizations. By framing the right to associate simply as part of broader efforts to promote migrant workers' culture, activists hoped to convince policy-makers that not all forms of grassroots organizations were threatening to social stability. Although it is too early to fully assess the impact of Workers' World's efforts on state policy, this mobilization strategy gave the organization an opportunity to directly influence the ideological outlook and rhetoric of elite Party cadres.

The pedagogy of discursive action is an attempt to reshape the grammar of migrant workers' rights claims and to encourage workers to participate fully in the social, cultural, and political life of their communities. Whereas the vast majority of migrant workers' protests and strikes in China are centered around immediate economic grievances, the pedagogy of discursive action teaches workers to aspire to a range of post-material demands, including the right to artistic self-representation (which has been traditionally reserved for the party-state's official propaganda apparatus). Moreover, this pedagogy aims to foster a new generation of workers who will become activists in civil society organizations across China. This new generation of worker leaders might be more likely to frame labor rights as citizenship rights.

8

A Political Compromise?

In illiberal regimes, contestation between the state and regime opponents rarely takes place in the open. There is often no neat dichotomy between a repressive state and heroic resisters (Hollander and Einwohner 2004), and the pattern of interaction between challengers and their opponents might fail to conform to the iterative "chess-like game" that characterized the civil rights movement in the United States (McAdam 1983). Cross-cutting relationships between state and civil society actors show that "[r]esistance is not always pure ... even while resisting power, individuals or groups may simultaneously support the structures of domination that necessitate resistance in the first place" (Hollander and Einwohner 2004: 549).

The repressive environment under which organizations operated constituted the form of civil society mobilization. Part I evidenced that the Chinese party-state deployed *flexible repression* to govern civil society organizations by simultaneously fostering the growth of aboveground civil society organizations while containing the development of underground organizations. The party-state kept the formal and informal institutions that governed civil society organizations in flux, thus permitting local states to experiment with diverse control mechanisms. In this operating environment, state and civil society were not always in opposition. Some state actors abetted organizations – even blacklisted ones – and helped to secure their survival. Activists also sought out state allies and competed with each other to win greater legitimacy and resources from local authorities.

Under flexible repression, mobilization was not only possible but also directly constituted by the political condition of high risks to organizing collective action. Part II analyzed three types of tactical innovations – the pedagogies of micro-collective action, atomized action, and discursive action – that germinated under the operating environment of flexible repression. Activists devised these tactics in order to lower the political risks that came with coordinating large-scale, public demonstrations of defiance. Their organizations thus served as mobilizing structures that amassed cognitive, strategic, and moral resources in order to advance migrant workers' rights. However, their strategic role in facilitating contention was partially hidden behind small-scale acts of rights claiming which afforded these organizations some protection.

Throughout this book, I have argued that this dynamic of disguising coordination behind individual or small group resistance is a form of mobilization – the amassing of resources for the purposes of contention. In this final chapter, I interrogate whether or not mobilizing without the masses enables weak groups to contest status quo power arrangements, thereby challenging regime stability, or if it is ultimately a political compromise with the state. What are the prospects for mobilizing without the masses to transform into mobilizing *with* the masses? If these organizations eventually mobilize popular, large-scale mobilization, then they may very well be able to contribute to a broader movement that challenges state power. If, however, they remain tethered to small-scale and under-the-radar mobilization, then their direct impact on institutional change may be limited, albeit not impossible.

I tackle this question by differentiating the short-term and long-term impact of mobilizing without the masses. I argue that by adopting this dynamic of mobilization, organizations have a paradoxical effect on popular contention and state power. In the short term, these organizations may end up buttressing state power by participating in the routinization of popular contention. Through channeling citizens into atomized forms of claims making, they inadvertently play into the party-state's control strategy of individualizing and depoliticizing claims-making behavior. It is difficult to see how this form of mobilization can challenge authority if these organizations are enhancing the state's ability to "buy off" protestors one by one.

However, political change is not an overnight process; it is a protracted struggle that takes place not only in the streets and inside government offices but also in the consciousness of citizens and state officials. Just as state domination relies on symbolic power (Wedeen 1999) and ideological hegemony (Gramsci 1971), so too does genuine mobilization also germinate in the consciousness of claims-makers. To this end, I argue that organizations adopting mobilizing without the masses can and do transform the grammar of contention in the long term. Through the pedagogical process, they shape the way citizens think and talk about their rights in a fundamental way that constitutes a core element of political change. By teaching their participants to articulate and attribute grievances to broader structural and political arrangements, these organizations and activists play an important role in countering the state's ideological domination.

POLITICAL COMPROMISE: STRENGTHENING STATE POWER

The Chinese party-state's regime resilience has been the subject of long-standing scholarly and popular debates (Shambaugh 2016; Fewsmith 2013; Li 2012; Heilmann and Perry 2011; Freidman and Wong 2008; Shirk 2007; Pei 2006; Nathan 2003). Scholars seeking to explain the relative longevity of the party-state have characterized the political system as an "adaptive authoritarianism" (Heilmann and Perry 2011). This means that the Chinese governance system has built-in flexibility mechanisms that allow it to respond agilely to external shocks and to domestic challenges (Heilmann and Perry 2011). One of the ways the regime has adapted has been to become more responsive (Distelhorst and Hou 2017) and consultative, creating channels that allow certain sectors of civil society to provide feedback and policy recommendations (Teets 2014).

Another important institutional adaptation is the regime's routinized absorption of popular contention. As previous studies have evidenced, local states across China have learned to routinize contention by buying off protestors with a mix of concession and repression (Lee and Zhang 2013; X. Chen 2012; Cai 2010). This adaptation is particularly critical to regime survival since post-1989 China has witnessed a surprising rise in the level of collective contention (Lorentzen 2013: 128; X. Chen 2012: 6). In 2007, there were approximately 80,000 mass incidents according to the regime's own count (Sun et al. 2010). By 2010, this number reached an estimated 180,000.[1] Chinese citizens – including migrant workers, urban homeowners, landless peasants, and pollution victims – are taking to the streets in greater numbers, protesting, striking, petitioning, and even storming local government offices (Friedman 2014; Ong and Goebel 2014; Cai 2010; F. Chen 2008; Hurst 2008; Perry 2002b).

To manage this tide of collective contention, local authorities have developed routine practices to demobilize contention by negotiating with protestors through a process that has been termed "bargained authoritarianism" (Lee and Zhang 2013: 1481). Such bargaining between the state and aggrieved citizens may take many different forms. The local state may distribute financial compensation to appease protestors, with many local states having a dedicated "stability maintenance fund" (Lee and Zhang 2013: 1485). In addition, local courts regularly place pressure on employers to distribute funds to purchase potential protestors' acquiescence and pre-empt worker protests (Su and He 2010). Alternatively, state agents can deploy "relational repression," a tactic whereby pressure is placed on the friends and relatives of contenders in order to demobilize protestors (Deng and O'Brien 2013). No matter the particular response of the state to popular contention, these forms of bargained authoritarianism are meant to absorb and depoliticize contention by facilitating an exchange between state and society over the price of rights.

[1] B. Demick, Protests in China over Local Grievances Surge and Get a Hearing, October 8, 2011, *The Los Angeles Times.*

Aggrieved citizens are "willing and willful players of these legal-bureaucratic games that lend legitimacy and protection to their actions and motivate them with a real chance of winning material or symbolic compensations" (Lee and Zhang 2013: 1481).

In its contained and relatively apolitical form, organizations that mobilize without the masses can actually buttress rather than undermine state power by facilitating this routinization of contention. By coaching citizens to demand their rights from the state either in small groups or as individuals, these organizations directly participate in the state's efforts to contain contentious collective action. The case studies in previous chapters reveal that organizations can facilitate an informal bargaining process between workers, state authorities, and factory representatives. In the pedagogy of atomized action, organizations coached aggrieved workers to become better strategic negotiators when bargaining over the level of compensation owed to them by their employers. Empowered by this training and the moral support given to them by activists, individual contenders – who may have otherwise balked at the prospect of fighting for their rights – were emboldened to bargain with officials and factory management over the acceptable amount of compensation for industrial injuries, unpaid wages, forced dismissals, and other labor violations. Activists discreetly took part in rights bargaining through the behind-the-scenes tactical coaching of workers or by disguising themselves as workers' relatives or friends and negotiating directly with factory managers. In doing so, they inadvertently helped to develop rights bargaining into an informal institution while simultaneously participating in the depoliticization of popular contention. In practice, they became complicit in local officials' attempts to transform rights into negotiable commodities.

The pedagogy of discursive action, in which activists refrained from directly challenging social stability in exchange for organizational survival, could be viewed as an even more explicit tactical compromise. At times activists withdrew from staging public events for fear of antagonizing the state or business interests. For example, whereas Workers' World previously performed live concerts for workers on construction sites, the leadership of the organization eventually phased out this practice in the face of employers' complaints that these concerts roused the emotions of workers and could lead to unrest (Interview, director, 2009). By 2011, the organization no longer performed at construction sites and restricted the dissemination of their music to CD sales, online downloads, and live performances in theaters or at the organization's headquarters. In addition, Workers' World refrained from becoming involved in direct confrontations, such as strikes and lawsuits, between workers and employers. The organization offered minimal legal counsel to aggrieved workers and did not hold workshops educating workers on their labor rights. These self-limiting strategies contributed to the survival of the organization, but at the cost of restricting its tactics to the realms of discourse and culture and avoiding participation in immediate material struggles for greater worker compensation.

Even the most radical of the tactics, the pedagogy of micro-collective action, could be seen as a political compromise with the state that strengthened state power. By reducing the scale of collective action to a handful of participants and limiting its duration to flash demonstrations, activists channeled workers into less disruptive forms of contention. Like other forms of mobilizing without the masses, the scale of micro-collective action paled in comparison to conventional factory-wide labor strikes. In this way, organizations adopting mobilizing without the masses essentially participated in the state's routinization and individualization of contention even as they empowered citizens to make rights claims, thus buttressing state power.

GENUINE MOBILIZATION: TRANSFORMING THE GRAMMAR OF CONTENTION

While mobilizing without the masses is a form of political compromise, it does not represent a complete surrender to state domination. Throughout the pedagogical process, organizations play a direct role in shaping the grammar of rights claims in ways that deviate from both official and popular discourses. Instead, they advocate for a framing of rights around citizenship, which marks a departure from the state's official rhetoric of workers as temporary urban subjects. Activists coach migrants to reject the term "peasant workers" and advise them to claim their rights as equal citizens.

Crafting an alternative discourse of rights based on citizenship is especially important in light of the history of the labor rights struggle in China. As Charles Tilly has suggested, citizenship is not merely a legal identity; it also entails a process of active negotiation and struggle between state and society (Tilly 1995: 385). Before the Communist Party took power in 1949, Chinese workers' struggle for labor rights was part of a larger cross-class struggle for citizenship rights. In Republican China (1912–49), workers mobilized alongside intellectuals and rallied around unifying issues such as national humiliation at the hands of foreign powers, price inflation, and political oppression (Perry 2002a: 133–58). In contrast, workers have been more reticent to mobilize as citizens alongside other social groups after the Communist Party took power, in part due to the Party's success in "isolating working-class resistance from intellectual dissent" (2002a: 155). This strategy of fragmenting interest groups has shaped the nature of labor activism in the post-1989 period: workers do not necessarily mobilize on the basis of broad claims as citizens but instead draw upon the language of a socialist moral economy (Lee 2007b) or on regionally specific "mass frames" (Hurst 2009).

Throughout the economic reform period (1978–present), workers' movements were limited not only by the state's direct repression of protests but also by their own grammar of contention which reproduced the state's dominant discourse of modernization. During the 1990s, worker protest persisted but was constrained in action and thought by what Mark Blecher described as the hegemony of the state and market (Blecher 2002). Chinese workers came to accept the state's logic that economic reform inevitably came with "losers" and that workers' lost privileges were an inevitable part of an irreversible trajectory towards modernization (Blecher 2002: 298–9). At the same time, the hegemony of the market atomized workers' protests, channeling them into the legal disputes and fragmenting solidarity (Blecher 2002: 295). Like their urban counterparts, migrant workers also reproduced the state's discourse of modernization, which asserted that workers should sacrifice themselves in order to advance the state's economic development (Fu 2009). Throughout the later stages of economic reform in the 2000s and 2010s, the party-state's steering of labor disputes into legal and bureaucratic channels continued to atomize the working class, with worker mobilization functioning as an "alarm system" that alerted the state to problems in a reactive manner (Gallagher 2014). Moreover, workers' rights-claiming behavior was shaped by the state's discourse on social stability and its accompanying logic of the market. The party-state essentially transformed rights claims into commodities as officials and citizens entered into a depoliticized "non-zero sum game" over the price of rights (Lee and Zhang 2013: 1495). Victorious claimants were the ones who learned to operate the market of social instability by depoliticizing their claims and targeting local officials who would be punished for their failure to maintain social stability (2013: 1493–5). In the process, workers' framing of contention was inevitably shaped by the discourse of the state and market, which demanded that they steer clear of political claims and honed in on the monetary value of individual rights.

The insertion of civil society organizations into the struggle for labor rights entailed a significant effort to transform the grammar of migrant workers' activism from narrow, depoliticized claims for wages and benefits to a broader set of claims for social, cultural, and political citizenship. Activists sought to coach migrant workers to articulate a discourse of new citizenship (*xin gongmin* or *xin shimin*)[2] to voice their demands for access to equal housing, education, decent treatment at work, and employment opportunities. In doing so, activists sought to shape the way that second-generation migrant workers – the "unfinished proletarians" (Pun and Lu 2010) – articulated their social positions. This younger generation of workers born in the 1970s and 1980s had experienced a "huge chasm … between their life expectation of becoming urban worker-citizens and their actual daily work experiences," a chasm which "precipitated anger, frustration, and resentment conducive to the emergence of workers' consciousness and their shared class position" (Pun and Lu 2010: 3).

---

[2] The term *gongmin* translates as the "public citizen," and traces its origins to the Confucian celebration of public service. The term *shimin* translates as the "urban citizen" and was used in the urban uprisings accompanying the revolution of 1911 as well as in the protests of 1989 (Goldman and Perry 2002).

In response, labor organizations attempted to channel migrants' expectations for a more permanent position in urban society into the basis for citizenship-based activism.

Thus, even as these organizations refrained from mobilizing large-scale collective contention, they still crafted an alternative pedagogy that taught subalterns to demand more from the state than simply economic compensation. First and foremost, labor organizations promoted equality in social citizenship, including the right to social services like public education, healthcare, and housing. According to T. H. Marshall, social citizenship entails the right to "live the life of a civilized being according to the standards prevailing in the society," including access to education and social services (Marshall 1950: 10–11). In China, social citizenship has been a cornerstone of state legitimacy since imperial times (Goldman and Perry 2002); "the idea that good governance rests upon guaranteeing the livelihood of ordinary people has been a hallmark of Chinese political philosophy and practice from Mencius to Mao – and beyond. It is reflected not only in government pronouncements and policies, but also in grassroots protests" (Perry 2008: 39). Since the founding of the People's Republic of China, the state has promised to fulfill its duty to ensure that the people enjoy the basic right to survival (Perry 2008: 43). Taking the state at its word, the labor organizations examined in this book taught migrant workers to demand social citizenship in contemporary China and claim *equal* social rights with urban residents. Equal treatment is an important issue because these workers live semi-permanently in the cities but continue to be treated as "second-class citizens" (K. W. Chan 2010; A. Chan 2001), or even as "non-citizens" (Solinger 1999: 1) by the state. Through strikes and other forms of collective action, migrant workers have fought for higher wages and greater benefits (Friedman 2014; Lee 2007b; Hurst 2009; A. Chan 2001). Yet other persistent issues – such as unequal access to housing and the lack of opportunities for migrant children to attend urban schools – are not easily resolved through one time pay-offs by the state or by employers.

In this context, civil society organizations play an instrumental role in advocating for equal social citizenship for China's migrant workers. In the pedagogy of discursive action, activists encouraged workers to construct a common identity as "new urban citizens" which would signify their permanent membership in urban society. The assertion of this urban identity suggested to worker-participants that it was imperative not only to fight for higher wages and greater benefits, but also to demand the right to send their children to the same schools as urban residents and to gain access to affordable urban housing and healthcare. In other words, activists worked to reframe a narrow struggle for basic subsistence as part of a broader, long-term struggle for social citizenship. Similarly, in the pedagogy of atomized action, activists trained workers to demand just treatment from government agencies. Perceiving Chinese society as a place where the rich are corrupt and exploitative, many activists thought of themselves as partaking in a moral mission to right social injustices and to empower worker-participants to speak loudly and boldly to the local state as citizens instead of supplicants. Even though this did not always bear out in the practice of rights bargaining between the workers, the state, and the employer, the pedagogical process of teaching workers to see themselves as citizens nevertheless had an impact on the way worker-participants understood themselves in relation to the state.

Second, these organizations advanced workers' cultural citizenship – the right to belong to a broader community and the responsibility to protect that community's dignity (Fong and Murphy 2006: 2). The promotion of cultural citizenship was important because migrant workers' subjectivity was marked by their cultural exclusion from mainstream society. Whereas the working class enjoyed high social status under the rule of Mao Zedong, since the beginning of the reform era in the early 1980s workers have experienced "the greatest downward mobility of any social group in China" (Hurst et al. 2009). Migrant workers, as a part of a new working class, continue to be culturally marginalized in official and popular discourses. Derided as lacking in culture and quality (civility) by urbanites, migrant workers are not considered full members of the urban community.[3] This social exclusion is not only geographically embodied by worker enclaves located at the fringes of the city and institutionally enforced through the denial of access to public goods and services, it is also discursively embodied by official and popular discourses about "peasant workers" and the "peasant worker problem" (*nongmin gong wenti*). Such terms reflect migrant workers' low social status and their cultural exclusion from urban communities.

In conventional labor strikes and protests, Chinese migrant workers rarely take to the streets to protest cultural exclusion. However, the labor organizations examined in this book advocated for broadening the scope of the claims made by migrant workers to include demands for cultural citizenship. Workers' World called on migrants to reclaim their dignity by taking pride in their labor and by viewing themselves as indispensable to China's economic transformation. In the pedagogy of discursive action, activists taught migrant workers that they ought to respect themselves and their social position vis-à-vis political and social elites. Activists aspired to uplift the cultural status of migrant workers by asserting that they belonged to a broader community of workers whose collective labor contributed to China's economic development. In addition, by disseminating migrant workers' culture to both the wider public and to policymakers, activists hoped to carve out a space for workers' cultural associations in China.

Finally, these labor organizations advocated for political citizenship – the right to participate in the political activities of the nation-state. In liberal democracies, political citizenship typically refers to the right of citizens to participate

---

[3] "Quality" or *suzhi* refers to the lack of civility and education of the population (Anagnost 1997).

in the exercising of political power, specifically the right to vote and to run for public office (Marshall 1950: 11). In China, where both of these rights are restricted, labor organizations' struggle for political citizenship entailed two components: pressing for the right to participate in the policy-making process, and for the right to form associations.[4] Chinese NGOs have become increasingly active participants in policy-making. NGOs are one among several kinds of policy entrepreneurs that partner with state agencies and the media to frame policy debates (Mertha 2008) and engage in authoritarian deliberation (He and Warren 2011). Many social organizations participate in "consultative authoritarianism" whereby local states learn from NGOs' experiences and observations, a process of learning that can lead to endogenous institutional change (Teets 2014: 6). This increased space for political participation reflects the interest of the party-state to collaborate with civil society groups to mitigate the effects of various social problems.

In this broad context, labor organizations have seized this opening to influence state policies on migrant workers. Social Engineering provided policy recommendations to the state concerning the treatment of workers suffering from occupational diseases, and through its collaborations with various local government agencies sought to promote participatory governance at the local level. Following its promotion to the status of a "supportive organization" (*zhichixing zuzhi*), Social Engineering assisted the Bureau of Civil Affairs in designing an overhaul of the regulatory framework governing the registration of social organizations. These forays into policy-making show how some labor organizations have been able to influence the process.

In addition, the very act of forming labor organizations without the explicit approval of the party-state constitutes a claim for political citizenship. The Chinese Communist Party (CCP) mobilized peasants and workers as core members of "the people," which came to substitute for the term "citizen" (Nathan 1985: 110), initially through forming workers' clubs. Prior to the success of the CCP-led revolution in 1949, these clubs produced cultural resources such as textbooks, dramas, songs, and lectures that were later disseminated to communist bases across the country (Perry 2012: 11). In light of this history, the formation of independent worker's organizations in the late 1990s and the 2000s embodied a yearning for political citizenship by migrant workers living under the CCP's continuing rule. Abandoning the socialist language of "the people" in favor of "citizens," these workers' organizations are claiming a more legitimate membership in a polity that has come to institutionally exclude them.

Founded by migrant workers disillusioned by their treatment in a nominally socialist state, these organizations sought to claim migrant workers' rights to

---

[4] According to Andrew Nathan, political rights have been important features in Chinese constitutions since imperial times (Nathan 1985: 107). He defines political rights as "rights to take actions to influence the choice of government personnel or policy" and argues that, in China, the root of rights has derived not from basic humanity but from the state's granting of citizenship.

participate in political life. This desire for political citizenship was captured in the struggle of the labor organizations that attempted to gain the legal right to form associations, a struggle shared by millions of other civil society groups in China. Solidarity in Action activists coached their participants to fight for genuine worker representation. Their adoption of micro-collective action represented a different kind of contention, one with civil society organizations at the center. Whereas more conventional strikes and demonstrations in China are facilitated by informal ties among participants, such as those between workers living in the same factory dormitories (Lee 2007a), micro-collective action was inspired by civil society organizations that harbored goals beyond immediate compensation for workers. Solidarity in Action's participants sought to use flash protests to demonstrate that workers from different factories could unite to fight for their collective rights. Such a goal stemmed from the organization's pedagogy that workers should not just seek one-time monetary pay-offs but instead should fight for freedom of association and the right to collective bargaining.

Likewise, organizations deploying a more moderate tactic of discursive action also fought for the freedom of association by self-censoring their contentious actions in exchange for the state's tacit toleration of their mobilizing activities. In persuading Party cadres to gain an understanding of migrant workers' culture, Workers' World pressed the state for the right to form more limited cultural associations and attempted to train the next generation of migrant workers who could form their own labor organizations across China. Although it is too early to assess the outcomes of this training, the organization nevertheless pioneered innovative forms of cultural advocacy – especially the staging of didactic dramas – that have been adopted by other labor organizations in China.

However, without the benediction of the party-state, these organizations' attempts to advocate for the social, cultural, and political rights of China's migrant workers have been a highly contested struggle. The state continues to circumscribe their sphere of activities and to contain their expansion. Mobilizing without the masses thus represents both the outcome of compromises made by civil society organizations in response to the structural constraints imposed on them by an authoritarian state, and the articulation by these same organizations of transgressive claims for citizenship-based rights. If one were to assess the success of mobilizing without the masses solely by the number of participants taking part in protests for political rights, then the organizations featured in this study would undoubtedly fall short.

Yet zooming in on the recruitment, ideological framing, and pedagogical processes of these groups reveals how mobilizing without the masses can lead to workers articulating a nuanced set of aspirational claims for equal citizenship. Unlike most popular protests in China, these claims are not limited to demands for economic compensation based on social citizenship; they embody claims for cultural and political citizenship as well. Insofar as these organizations are able to shape the grammar of rights of China's 270 million migrant workers, they are indeed engaging in genuine mobilization.

FROM RIGHTS DISCOURSE TO CONSCIOUSNESS CHANGE

Yet, articulating a discourse of rights and citizenship does not automatically translate into a deeper consciousness change on the part of contenders. Does mobilizing without the masses teach participants to challenge their fundamental dispositions vis-à-vis state authority, seeing themselves as citizens instead of supplicants? This cuts to the heart of an ongoing debate within Chinese politics about whether individuals making rights claims maintain a "rules consciousness" (Perry 2009) or if they are becoming increasingly rights conscious (Gallagher 2017; Lorentzen and Scoggins 2015; Li 2010). Elizabeth Perry has argued that while protestors in contemporary China might appear to be following a new script of rights and the rule of law, their underlying dispositions toward political authority remains unchanged. In her words, "although a discourse of 'rights' proclaimed by 'citizens' has replaced a Mao-era language of 'revolution' proclaimed by 'comrades,' it is not readily apparent that protesters today differ fundamentally from previous generations in either their mentality or their relationship to the authoritarian state" (2009: 19).

In response, a number of scholars have argued that while Chinese citizens may not have the rights consciousness as it is understood in a Western context, they nevertheless aim to change the rules of the game through insisting on political participation and demanding institutional changes (Gallagher 2017; O'Brien 2013; Li 2010). For instance, Mary Gallagher argues that workers' rights mobilization "is more than just a strategic ploy or rhetorical device." Although workers use the existing legal and political framework to press for their rights, their mobilization nevertheless yielded in the expansion of legal rights (Gallagher 2017). Other qualitative and quantitative studies have shown that both types of consciousness may exist at the same time (Lorentzen and Scoggins 2015; O'Brien 2013; Li 2010). Li Lianjiang draws a useful conceptual distinction between the rights consciousness and rules consciousness by arguing that "rules consciousness targets *rule-enforcement* [emphasis added] authorities, presumes skepticism toward them, and a sense of equality with them before central policies and state laws" (Li 2010: 64). In contrast, rights consciousness exhibits itself through skepticism towards *rule-making* authorities, which is usually the central state and might manifest itself in the "hidden discourses" between subjects rather than in their public dialogue with the state (2010).

The worker-participants I studied possessed both rules consciousness and rights consciousness. In their public transcripts with the state, workers and activists contending for their rights exhibited rules consciousness because they rarely openly questioned the legitimacy of laws. Instead, they demanded local authorities to grant them rights that were already guaranteed by the 2008

Labor Contract Law. When a worker threatens suicide in order to induce official action, he or she is almost always doing so in order to press for law enforcement, not to change the system. In this sense, their actions could be seen as a continuation of a long tradition of rebellion that has little to do with an emergent rights consciousness. In their public scripts, activists deftly reproduce the language of social stability and harmony from official discourse in order to emphasize their obedience to authority. In addition, they mainly target low-level officials, which accords with Perry's observation that this might be more "an indication of routine politics than a harbinger of some tectonic shift in state-society relations" (2009: 20).

Nonetheless, the activists engaging in mobilizing without the masses also harbor broader ambitions; they aim to instill in workers a nascent hope for institutional changes such as the right to collective bargaining and the freedom of association. In the more private spaces created by labor organizations, workers' "hidden transcripts" (Scott 1990) suggested a blossoming rights consciousness as activists led them in discussions that questioned the very legitimacy of unresponsive state authorities. A number of the organizations I studied dedicated workshops to educating workers on the importance of demanding collective bargaining, not just collective consultation as sanctioned by the party-state. In 2015, a number of labor activists in Guangdong organizations were at the helm of coaching striking workers to put what they learned into practice through collective bargaining, which resulted in their subsequent arrests.[5] In the case of Workers' World, activists also encouraged participants to claim rights that went beyond law enforcement, extending into the realm of demanding policy change. For instance, they asked workers to interrogate the legitimacy of the household registration system that barred migrants from enjoying equal access to housing, education, and other social services. They then organized workers to articulate these demands through the performance arts, the discourse of which reflected growing rights consciousness.

All of these actions suggest that labor activists and their organizations are attempting to mobilize a new generation of workers to change its consciousness, not just to articulate an empty rights discourse without challenging the ideological hegemony of the state and the market. Mobilizing without the masses attempts to transform the very consciousness of participants so that they see themselves as both deserving of the rights enshrined by the law and as citizens entitled to press for longer-term institutional changes such as the freedom of association. At the same time, activists and their participants are also bound by a rules consciousness because they recognize and accept that demanding law enforcement from local authorities is far more likely to yield immediate and tangible gains than changing the rules of the game. Thus, they

---

[5] D. Sevastopulo, China Charges Labour Activist after Yue Yuen Shoe Factory Strike, April 29, 2014, *Financial Times*. B. Eihorn et al., Hong Kong Isn't the Only Protest Chinese Leaders Are Worried About, October 2, 2014, *Bloomberg Business Week*.

continue to mobilize while simultaneously inhabiting both rules and rights consciousness.

FROM MOBILIZING WITHOUT TO *WITH* THE MASSES

When does mobilizing without the masses transform into mobilizing *with* the masses? During 2012, the last year of the Hu administration, labor organizations in Guangdong Province attempted a series of high-risk tactical maneuvers that marked a clear departure from mobilizing without the masses. Between 2012 and 2015, several labor organizations in Guangdong Province began to experiment with riskier forms of mobilization involving collective contention. Disenchanted with the long-term impact of their previous strategies that resolved workers' grievances on an individual basis, activists turned to mobilizing "worker-led collective bargaining" (Li 2016). At least seven labor organizations in Guangdong began to coach workers to engage in seventy cases of collective bargaining, according to Hong Kong-based labor activist Han Dongfang, who supported the endeavor.[6] Activists from labor organizations educated factory workers on what collective bargaining entailed and instructed them on how to elect their own representatives.

In the process, their tactics fundamentally changed from mobilizing without the masses to mobilizing *with* the masses. The scale of worker mobilization varied but ranged from just over 100 workers in the Luenshing Factory strikes in 2013 (Li 2016: ch. 1) to over 2,500 workers in the Lide Shoe Factory strike.[7] This was a drastic increase in the scale of labor organizations' mobilization compared to their earlier tactics described in Part II of this book. This move was decidedly risky because it transgressed the cardinal principle that had previously guided their organizing: steer clear of organizing collective action.

The Xi administration responded with a decisiveness that was unmatched by the previous Hu administration. Leaders of labor organizations became prime targets for harsh repression, including being placed under house arrest or detained as part of an unprecedented campaign targeting civil society groups across the country.[8] In December 2015, the police arrested at least twenty-five staff members and activists from five different labor organizations. Among them was the director of the province's first and largest organization, who, along with two of his co-workers, was detained and charged with "gathering a crowd to disrupt social order" and "misappropriation of funds."[9] In September

---

[6] Han Dongfang, Testimony, US House of Representatives, June 17, 2015, cited in Li 2016: 70.

[7] D. Sevastopulo, "China Charges Labour Activist after Yue Yuen Shoe Factory Strike," April 29, 2014, *Financial Times*. B. Eihorn et al., "Hong Kong Isn't the Only Protest Chinese Leaders Are Worried About," October 2, 2014, *Bloomberg BusinessWeek*.

[8] T. Phillips, Call for China to Free Labor Activists or Risk Backlash from Frustrated Workforce, December 10, 2015, *Guardian*.

[9] Y. Cao, Chinese Authorities Orchestrate Surprise Raid of Labor NGOS in Guangdong, October 12, 2015, *China Change. China Labour Bulletin*, Guangdong Labour Activists Detained Without Trial for Nine Months, January 9, 2016.

2016, the state sentenced the lead labor activist to three years in jail with four years of suspension and his co-workers to eighteen months of jail with two years of suspension.[10] The same lead activist also became the target of a smear campaign in the official media. In December 2015, the *People's Daily* published an article accusing him of engaging in fraud under the cover of philanthropic activities.[11] This was followed by China Central Television (CCTV) channel 13's airing of a special report titled "Investigating the Criminal Case of a Star of the Labor Movement" that accused the activist of criminal activities.[12] The report claimed that this particular activist's organization had been actively involved in at least twenty-nine cases of worker strikes and had developed a comprehensive organizational strategy for instigating workers' mass incidents. It described in detail the various steps that activists and members of his organization allegedly took to rile up factory workers. First, they researched the targeted firm, and then "enticed" aggrieved workers with small-scale pro bono services. Next, the organization would purportedly select workers with "radical dispositions" to become representatives, thus completing an organizational process (*zhuzhihua*). Activists would then hold training sessions on collective bargaining, including bringing worker leaders to other factories with labor conflicts to learn about activism on-site. Before striking, activists would teach workers to make certain "unreasonable demands and to reject legal routes for rights claiming," choosing instead "radical methods to force the employer to give in to workers' demands." Throughout this process, the organization would use micro-blogs, webchat, and direct communication with foreign media to publicize its influence. The CCTV report also accused the lead activist of misusing foreign funds for personal gain and for immoral personal behavior such as sexual harassment and identity theft. The report was released just after the activist and his co-workers were detained.

On the one hand, this uncompromising repression can be seen as part and parcel of a broad political campaign against civil society (Fu and Distelhorst, Forthcoming) in which the party-state targeted Hong Kong book publishers, feminist activists, and rights lawyers alike.[13] On the other hand, it can also be analyzed as a response to labor organizations' transgression from mobilizing without the masses to mobilizing *with* the masses. According to the *People's*

---

[10] Agence-France Presse, China Labor Activists Sentenced for Helping Workers in Wage Dispute, September 27, 2016, *Guardian*.

[11] *People's Daily*, "Gongsyunzhixing" Zenfeiyang Beizhua: dazhe gongyi huangzi liancai mose. ["Star of the Labor Movement" Zeng Feiyang: Money-Making under the Guise of Philanthropy], December 22, 2015.

[12] CCTV Channel 13 Law Online Program, Investigating the Criminal Case of a Star of the Labor Movement, December 25, 2015.

[13] M. Forsythe and A. Jacobs, In China, Books that Make Money, and Enemies, February 4, 2016. K. D. Tatlow, China Is Said to Force Closing of Women's Legal Aid Center, January 29, 2016, *New York Times*. Y. Cao, China's Shattered Dream for the Rule of Law, One Year On, July 8, 2016, *China Change*.

Daily article, the accused labor activist's most trangressive action was to surreptitiously instigate workers' collective action:

Although the organization is not registered with any administrative bureaucracy, it has in recent years been active in a number of labor conflicts in the Pearl River Delta. It has been planning, organizing, orchestrating behind the scenes to exacerbate labor conflict, seriously disturb social order, and trample upon workers' rights. In addition, it has been promoting its own positive image and influence in the foreign media while pointing the finger at the government for labor conflicts.[14]

The state's official recounting of labor activists' mobilizing strategy was fairly accurate, suggesting that the authorities had closely monitored the involvement of labor organizations in collective action throughout this period. A subsequent study of labor activism between 2012 and 2015 corroborated the fact that activists would train workers to elect their own representatives (Li 2016). It also revealed continuities in labor activists' strategies with the tactics described in Part II of this book. Just as activists had deftly used narratives to motivate workers to take atomized action (Chapter 6), so too did they tell stories of prior successful cases of collective bargaining to inspire factory workers to join in the collective bargaining (Li 2016: 152–5). Once a critical mass of workers came on board with collective bargaining, activists would guide them in specific strategies of negotiation. The official media's detailed reporting thus reflected the state's intimate knowledge of both labor organizations and workers' activism.

Evidently, the party-state's roundup of labor activists in 2015 was in response to labor organizations crossing from individualized contention into collective contention, which struck a sensitive nerve of the party-state. By actively coaching striking workers to take up collective bargaining, the activists had ventured into the state's forbidden zone of acting as "an invisible black hand" behind worker unrest. In doing so, at least some of the Guangdong organizations transitioned into a high-risk form of mobilization that represented a tactical escalation that the activists had aspired to and which the party-state feared.

The Xi's administration's response evidenced that the primary condition which induced organizations to turn to mobilizing without the masses in the first place remains highly relevant. Namely, organizations that implicate themselves in mass incidents would be subject to swift repression. If anything, the risks of organizing collective contention have increased due to Xi's political campaign against civil society as groups that were previously tolerated have been subject to ham-handed repression and demobilization. Under this administration, the Chinese government has not only pursued a form of "high-pressure" politics (*gaoya zhengce*) to purge corrupt leaders, it

---

[14] People's Daily, "*Gongyunzhixing*" *Zenfeiyang Beizhua: dazhe gongyi huangzi liancai mose.* ["Star of the Labor Movement" Zeng Feiyang: Money-Making under the Guise of Philanthropy], December 22, 2015.

has also launched an unprecedented campaign against grassroots civil society (Fu and Distelhorst, Forthcoming). Embarking on the largest ideological campaign since Mao Zedong (Zhao 2016), Xi views civil society as a conduit through which dangerous Western ideas flow into China. In a 2013 internal memo known as Document No. 9, Xi listed an independent civil society among the seven perils to the Chinese state.[15] Placing it in the company of media freedom and universal human rights, Xi saw civil society not only as a pragmatic threat to social stability but also as an ideological threat.[16]

Given a contracting space for activism and the dire consequences of labor organizations' audacious experimentation with mobilizing en masse, it has become even more imperative for civil society organizations to devise new tactics that fall under the dynamic of mobilizing without the masses. As the following section evidences, civil society actors including freedom of information activists, religious practitioners, pensioners, and feminist activists have also learned to mobilize without the masses.

CONTAINED MOBILIZATION IN COMPARATIVE PERSPECTIVE

How does mobilization without the masses "travel" to other contexts within China and beyond? Several key attributes of this broader mobilization dynamic can be observed across China in other civil society sectors during the Hu period (2002–12) as well as under the Xi Jinping administration (2013–present). First, the practice of *disguising the organizational process behind a façade of individualized action* has been adopted by civil society groups concerned with strengthening China's legislation on freedom of information under the Hu administration. Following the passage of China's freedom of information laws in 2008, one activist, Wu Junliang, organized a group of citizens to solicit the disclosure of information concerning national budgets from the central government. These information requests, however, were made in the names of individuals and not in the name of the organization. Wu financed a small staff of transparency activists who worked out of his office and submitted formal applications for information disclosure to a wide range of ministries and government agencies. However, Wu maintained in media interviews that he was not part of an organization: "We are a loose epistemic community. We don't have an organizational structure. If you identify with this work, you can participate."[17] He called the individuals he employed – who devoted up to ten hours per week to sending letters requesting transparency in government spending *in the name of individuals* rather than in the name of an organization – "volunteers" (*zhiyuanzhe*)

[15] ChinaFile, Document 9: A ChinaFile Translation, Section 3, November 8, 2013.
[16] Ibid.
[17] Z. Yang, Wujunliang Tuandui: Yusuan Gongkai Disan Tuili. Zhongguo Gaige [Wu Junliang Team: Open Budget's Third Push], April 5, 2010, *iFeng News*.

and not employees (Distelhorst 2013). By obfuscating the organizational element of their activism, freedom of information campaigners attempted to lower the risks of contention, just like their counterparts involved in labor activism. By declining to describe his group as an organization, Wu deployed a similar dynamic of disguising the organizational process behind a façade of individual action.[18] Moreover, just like the labor activists leveraged publicity to attract attention to workers' repertoire of atomized actions (Chapter 6), so too did information activists use the media to amplify institutional non-responsiveness, thus capitalizing on the state's "empty promise" (Distelhorst 2017).

In another parallel case, official Protestant churches that sought to indirectly contend with local authorities have also experimented with disguising the organized element of their activism. In the case of a small city whose religious leader was trying to convince the local authorities to overturn their decision to allow work units to use church property, the director of the church "skillfully instructed church staff to threaten street demonstrations by the whole congregation (while to religious affairs officials, he claimed to be unable to stop them) and eventually managed to pry government support for a new church building to be built elsewhere. *All this took place without ordinary congregants being involved* [emphasis added]" (Vala 2012: 48). The director's disguising of his coordination of small-group action is a key attribute of mobilizing without the masses. In this case, his implicit threat of collective action by the whole congregation was conveyed through sending only a handful of church staff to confront the authorities, much like the labor organizations that adopted the pedagogy of atomized action (Chapter 6).

A second attribute of mobilizing without the masses entailed *self-consciously limiting the scale of the organization*. In the labor groups examined in this study, activists strategically divided their main organization into smaller units instead of forming one large group. The organization Pay It Forward expanded by forming four separate offices across Guangdong Province, each with no more than one or two core activists. This "franchise model" protected the organization from being destroyed in a single act of government repression. If a district government shut down one of these offices, other branches in different jurisdictions continued to operate. An analogous case is that of unofficial Protestant churches which are not affiliated with the state-run Protestant church (the Three-Self Patriotic Movement, or *san zi jiaohui*) and thus operate illegally across China (Koesel 2014; Vala 2012; Cao 2010). The state views underground churches as threatening because they organize outside of state-sanctioned channels and have the potential to mobilize congregants to demand

---

[18] A similar case is grassroots activist lawyers in China who abet rights defenders who are embedded in networks and incipient organizations without directly engaging in collective action. These are "ordinary lawyers all over China who possess political liberal values and motivations but do not mobilize collectively due to unfavorable structural constraints" (Liu and Halliday 2016).

greater religious freedoms. Similar to underground labor organizations, these unofficial churches are careful to avoid appearing as strong institutions capable of mobilizing mass contention (Vala 2012). To signal that they are not a dire threat to the government, church leaders deliberately limit the size of their congregations by dividing their worshippers into smaller groups that attend services in different locations (Reny forthcoming: ch. 5). For example, the pastor of an unofficial Jiangsu church divided congregants into more than ten meeting points of fifty to sixty believers each, a practice that is also prevalent among college ministries (Reny forthcoming: ch. 5). In contrast, defiant churches in Wenzhou, Zhejiang – a city known as "China's Jerusalem" – did not restrict the size of their buildings or the size of the crosses hung on their steeples (Cao 2010). Consequently, the state forced the demolition of large churches in Wenzhou and placed restrictions on the size of church buildings as well as the size and placement of crosses on church facades in 2015.[19] Church leaders believe that restricting the size of the congregation lowers the risk of organizing by signaling to local authorities that each church has limited mobilizing potential. These churches would be more likely to avoid the harsh repression visited on churches with larger congregations.

Mobilizing without the masses also entailed *active organizational involvement in facilitating popular contention*. While previous research has generally minimized the role played by Chinese civil society in acts of contention, there are prominent exceptions. For example, environmental NGOs have coached citizens on how to resist dam-building projects. In their opposition to the Manwan dam in Yunnan Province, activists from the NGO Green Watershed organized a meeting of 150 representatives from local communities. Despite harassment from the local Public Security Bureau, the organizers managed to hold the meeting in a restaurant, thereby transforming a would-be public demonstration into a nominally private meeting in which people discussed and debated the issues at stake (Mertha 2008: 114). In another anti-dam campaign, activists from Green Earth Volunteers "organized a petition in which sixty-two people from the fields of science, arts, journalism, and grassroots environmental protection signed their opposition to the [Nu River Hydropower Project] at the second meeting of the China Environment and Cultural Promotion Society" (Mertha 2008: 119). These cases demonstrate the active role that environmental NGOs played in coaching contention in contemporary China.

In addition to environmental activism, emerging research on senior citizen associations shows how organizations coach contention in rural China. Old people's associations across villages in Fujian Province simultaneously mobilized and contained popular contention to demand the removal of corrupt officials (Hurst et al. 2014). One such association in Fujian Province "gathered 200 signatures to a petition and organized several protests (each of 20–30

---

[19] O. Geng and W. Kazer, China Province under Fire after New Rules on Churches, May 27, 2015, *Wall Street Journal*.

participants) in opposition, first at the Fujian Provincial letters and visits office in Fuzhou and then at city government offices" (Hurst et al. 2014: 468). Like underground labor groups, these organizations both facilitated contention and minimized its scale. Their protests were carried out "in small enough groups to avoid unduly escalating tensions" (Hurst et al. 2014: 468). Old people's associations actively fostered and sustained collective contention, but also "'virtuously' contained" it (2014: 470). In another case, similar groups in Zhejiang Province took the lead in mobilizing citizens to demand the closure of eleven factories that were polluting the community (Deng and O'Brien 2014). These groups – traditionally apolitical in nature – organized a range of acts of collective contention, including a petition drive and a tent sit-in at a chemical park. In the process, these groups transformed themselves into mobilizing structures.

These cases indicate that civil society organizations can play a more important role in mobilizing and sustaining contention in China than scholars have previously suggested. Yet there is important variation as well. Whereas some of the organizations mentioned above more closely resemble underground labor groups and largely eschewed collective action, others pursued larger-scale collective contention despite the risks that this posed. Under what conditions do organizations choose to mobilize collective contention as opposed to individual contention? One possibility is that the types of leaders, and their level of dependency on activism for their livelihood, explain these differences in strategies. For example, whereas old people's associations are led by former Party cadres and audacious senior citizens who, because of their age, may feel they have less to lose than younger people, labor organizations are mostly led by migrant workers whose very livelihoods depend on the survival of the organizations they command. This dependency may lead worker leaders to be more risk averse than activists whose livelihoods are not dependent on an organization. This caution might lead them to devise alternative tactics for coaching forms of contention that decrease the likelihood of organizational closure.

Another possibility is that it may be easier for rural associations to organize collective action because they are mobilizing constituents who already share kinship and communal ties. In contrast, mobilizing migrant workers in urban areas who come from diverse geographical, linguistic, and cultural backgrounds is a much greater challenge. Many of the labor organizations featured in this book were based in migrant residential communities near industrial centers. In these urban communities, friendship and communal ties were relatively weak and temporary, while the authority of the urban state was relatively strong. Thus, even if migrant worker-activists were willing to take on the risk of organizing collective contention, they faced higher barriers than rural activists when recruiting participants and establishing trust amongst them.

Finally, it might be the case that organizations allied with the media and with particular state agencies are more likely to coach collective contention. For example, the environmental activists who coordinated anti-dam campaigns had closer ties to political elites and the media than many of the labor activists featured in this study. In Andrew Mertha's study of environmental organizations, a large number of the officers and staff members of environmental NGOs had been trained as journalists or editors. This created an "almost seamless interface between the two groups" which allowed activists and journalists to work together to advocate for policy changes (Mertha 2008: 12). Media coverage might offer some protection against the most repressive responses of local governments, while being embedded in a network of state policy entrepreneurs might allow activists to secure more political cover than activists who work for organizations that are more socially isolated. Future research can fruitfully explore these relationships by comparing cases of organizations allied with state or media actors with organizations that lack these alliances.

Looking beyond China, mobilizing without the masses is likely to emerge as a dynamic of contention in polities where opportunities for associational life exist, but where the risks for organizations which coordinate collective contention are high. Limited opportunities for associating have emerged in economically liberalizing authoritarian and semi-authoritarian states across the Middle East (Lynch 2014; Schwedler 2012), Russia (Koesel 2014; Robertson 2009), and in Southeast Asia (Alaggapa 2004 Boudreau 2004). Recognizing that limited liberalization can actually bolster authoritarian regime adaptability (Heilmann and Perry 2011; Krastev 2011), some authoritarian incumbents have gradually loosened the regulatory frameworks governing civil society, thus allowing them to embrace more diverse forms of associational life while simultaneously managing these organizations' activities (Balzer 2003). In these illiberal polities, civil society organizations might be permitted to exist but are considerably constrained in their capacity to mobilize against the state (Alagappa 2004; Balzer 2003; Wiktorowicz 2000).

While in extraordinary times civil society organizations can overcome these constraints to mobilize the masses against an illiberal regime (Ekiert and Kubik 2001; Weigle and Butterfield 1992; Gold 1990), their limited, everyday struggles to gain political agency should not be discounted. In the vast political terrain between total immobility and revolutionary mobilization, civil society might invent novel tactics of mobilization that transform the grammar with which citizens demand their rights from the state.

Appendix

Political Ethnography

When I began my fieldwork in China in 2009, I was interested in how migrant workers organized to claim their collective rights. I initially assumed that they lacked effective organizational vehicles since independent unions are banned in China. Yet a fortuitous opportunity brought me face-to-face with some of the leaders of underground labor organizations. In 2009, I was invited to serve as an interpreter for a labor conference. Among the attendees of this conference were leaders of eight independent labor organizations based in the Pearl River Delta. Through informal conversations with these leaders, I realized that I was witnessing a new political process unfolding: migrant workers organizing themselves through founding their own NGOs. These conversations led me to a new research question: how do organizations that are repressed by the state mobilize citizen contention?

The primary challenge of studying labor organizations in China was access. My fieldwork took place during the Hu-Wen administration (2003–13), an administration that placed a high priority on maintaining social stability. The organizations I studied were, by definition, illegal: they either disguised themselves as commercial businesses or were completely unregistered. Because of their precarious legal status, their leaders were wary of disclosing information about their organizations to outsiders. Even after establishing contact with the leaders of an organization, it was difficult to gain the trust of the organization's activists. State security agents periodically infiltrated organizations or interrogated their leaders. As a result, activists were cautious about permitting outsiders (other than a small network of trusted domestic scholars and students) to observe their activities. It was only after months of relationship building with leaders and scholars embedded in the activist networks that I was permitted to study these groups.

CASE SELECTION AND CHARACTERISTICS

Based on a preliminary investigation of labor organizations distributed across China, I identified 72 unofficial labor organizations nationwide. I conducted on-site visits and interviews with the leaders and staff members of these organizations and also attended events held by these organizations whenever possible. Using snowball sampling, I sought additional organizations based on leads from these initial interviewees. This research helped to identify the two largest clusters of labor organizations in China: one in Beijing (composed of 15 organizations) and one in the Pearl River Delta (composed of 45 organizations). Organizations in the Beijing cluster were either registered legally as social organizations with the Bureau of Civil Affairs or registered illegally as businesses with the Bureau of Commerce. In contrast, many of the organizations in the Pearl River Delta were either unregistered or registered illegally as businesses with the Bureau of Commerce. Within the Pearl River Delta cluster, I further identified two networks of underground labor organizations: the Hong Kong network and the Mainland China network (see Chapter 2).

After initial interviews and participant observation inside these organizations, I selected four organizations – two from Beijing and two from the Pearl River Delta – and conducted three to four months of ethnographic study in each organization. Apart from these four case study groups, I conducted on-site visits, interviews, and participant observation at eleven organizations in Beijing and eleven organizations in the Pearl River Delta. Access to these organizations was gained through introductions provided by labor scholars who supported the organizations' work and knew their leaders. Although the organizations that granted me access were self-selected, they were typical of their respective networks, as discussed in greater detail in the sampling bias section. Obtaining access to these organizations allowed me to conduct the kinds of participant observation activities described in this book.

These small, grassroots organizations kept limited and incomplete records of their staff and activities. Reliable data on certain aspects of their work was therefore difficult to obtain.[1] Membership in the organizations I studied ranged from two to over twenty staff members. The organizations' founders and leaders typically made the major decisions about the organization's trajectory while staff members were in charge of daily operations such as running legal workshops, providing legal consultation, leading discussion groups, and organizing social activities. Larger organizations typically hired a staff lawyer who advised workers on navigating the formal labor dispute system, and a female staff member who served as secretary. In addition to

---

[1] A previous study of labor organizations in the PRD estimated an average of five staff members per organization (He and Huang 2008).

their formal staff, larger organizations also maintained a network of volunteers, who were typically former workers that became activists. These individuals were referred to as "volunteers" rather than "members," since formal membership implied the workers belonged to an illegal union. These volunteers assisted staff members in the organizations' activities and provided moral support to fellow workers.

Despite their limited size, these organizations were able to reach a sizable number of workers.[2] One organization in Beijing with over twenty staff members claims to have been able to serve more than 250,000 people, including the elderly, migrant children, and other marginalized populations, since its founding in 2003. Another organization with twenty full-time staff members and seven part-time staff was able to provide over 600,000 workers with services ranging from a consultation hotline, to personal intake of individual legal cases, to mediation assistance. The smallest organization in Beijing was a one-man hotline operation run out of a shack.

In the Pearl River Delta, the largest organization had twelve staff members and over a nine-year period (2005–13) provided over 30,000 workers with legal consultations, directly assisted in over 1,200 legal cases, and distributed over 200,000 organizational pamphlets to workers. A second organization with seven staff members provided over 6,000 workers with legal consultation, directly assisted 1,350 individuals with their legal cases, and distributed over 60,000 organizational pamphlets through hospital visits from 2006 to 2014.[3] During four months of observation inside one of these organizations, each branch conducted two legal workshops per month, with attendance ranging from forty to fifty workers at each event. In addition, each branch spoke with approximately fifteen to twenty workers in person or on the phone on a daily basis, seven days a week. Activists also made weekly recruitment trips to nearby hospitals to hand out pamphlets to injured workers. Because the level and type of an organization's activities fluctuated depending on the financial solvency of the organization and the political climate in which it operated, these data points could vary from year to year. Nonetheless, the combination of participant observation and self-reported data suggested that these organizations were able to reach a significant number of workers relative to their staff numbers.

INTERVIEWS

To place the participant observation data in context, I also conducted formal and informal interviews of labor organization staff and stakeholders across

---

[2] An exception is the Beijing Zhicheng Migrant Worker Legal Aid and Research Center which has twenty chapters across the country and is legally registered.

[3] Since activists have incentives to inflate the number of clientele served, these figures should be interpreted as the upper bounds of what the organizations actually achieved.

China. To avoid being trapped in a single network of interlinked respondents, I interviewed 123 individuals that represented a diverse cross-section of society with different relationships to labor organizations. These included forty-eight activists, nineteen workers, seventeen scholars, eight donors, six employers, three journalists, and three lawyers. The remaining nineteen interviews were conducted with government officials representing eight agencies and official organizations across six administrative levels.[4] I identified these interviewees through snowball sampling in which one interview subject became the source for identifying another interviewee (Bleich and Pekkanen 2013).

I found that interviews conducted after having established a degree of trust with participants yielded much richer accounts of their experiences. Activists more readily shared their world-views – including interpretations that contradicted the organizations' leadership and sensitive information about their own encounters with state security – with a researcher who was immersed in their daily work. Likewise, worker-participants were also more open to discussing their interpretation of the rights-claiming process with a researcher who had accompanied them to government offices or participated in the organizations' events. While initial interviews were open-ended, follow-up interviews were topically focused on organizational tactics and interactions with the state.

I found that labor activists had few incentives to reveal the hidden processes of mobilization to me during our initial interviews. They delivered rehearsed "public transcripts" (Scott 1990) about their organizations that highlighted their efforts to promote legal education and to assist the local state in providing social services to migrant workers. Activists invoked stock phrases such as "rights advocacy" (*weiquan*), "citizenship consciousness" (*gonmin yishi*), and "raising legal awareness" (*tigao falu yishi*), phrases which suggested compliance with the state's goals of maintaining social stability and promoting the rule of law. For this reason, I conducted extensive political ethnography, which attempted to uncover what the activists were *not* telling.

POLITICAL ETHNOGRAPHY

Political ethnography was the most advantageous method of studying the mobilization processes of difficult-to-access organizations. As a methodological approach, political ethnography can be useful for obtaining hidden data (Kapiszewski et al. 2015) and discovering new categories of phenomena (Schatz 2009b: 10–12). As a fundamentally interpretive exercise, it treats

---

[4] These agencies include: the Bureau of Civil Affairs; the Bureau of Human Resources and Social Security (Labor); the All-China Federation of Trade Unions (ACFTU); the All-China Women's Federation (ACWF); the China Association for NGO Cooperation (CANGO); Xinhua News Agency; the Social Organization Management Office; and the Government Development Research Center. The administrative levels include national, provincial, municipal/city, district, sub-district, and township.

insider perspectives and meaning-making practices as valuable forms of data (Wedeen 2010, 2009). When I began fieldwork in 2009, public data on these labor organizations and their activities came largely from studies by Chinese and foreign scholars.[5] However, public records concerning their geographical reach and even how many labor organizations existed were incomplete, as organizations either disappeared or relocated to other jurisdictions after being disbanded by state security. Since the universe of cases was unknown, ethnography provided a pathway to begin mapping out the organizational landscape. Immersing myself in a network of organizations allowed me to identify other types of labor organizations that existed throughout China.

Ethnographic fieldwork also produced "thick description" (Geertz 1973) of the mobilization processes of these organizations that would have been impossible to produce through ordinary interviews. Participant observation can help to compensate for potentially unreliable data gathered from interviewees who may provide false information or omit key events and details during formal interviews (Bleich and Pekkanen 2013: 88).

It revealed a host of activities that interviewees working in these labor organizations did not initially describe (such as the informal practices of recruitment, tactical coaching, and the dissemination of a new discourse of workers' rights) and which were crucial to the mobilizing process. I accompanied activists to hospitals where they would introduce themselves to injured workers whom they hoped to recruit. At meetings held by the organizations, I observed labor activists coaching participants on both legal and illegal tactics of contention. These activities differed from activists' "public transcripts," which omitted any extra-legal measures to advance and defend worker rights. I also observed how participants responded to these tactics, the questions they asked, and the words, gestures, and mannerisms they used to communicate with each other. In addition, participant observation took me outside of the organizations' headquarters to the sites of worker contention – the government bureaus, courthouses, and factory floors – where workers deployed the contentious tactics described in this study with varying degrees of success. These experiences provided me with the opportunity to observe this process of tactical deployment, and the attendant interactions between state officials and workers.

Outside of the organizations, I also attended eight formal conferences held between 2009 and 2011 where I observed activists networking with other activists, lawyers, and scholars from other regions of China. Through these conferences, as well as the informal conversations and meals I shared with labor activists, I observed activists liaise with donors and, on occasion, government officials who were sympathetic to their work. I took note of the informal conversations and rumors that circulated among activists, including which organizations' leaders may have been recruited as informants by the

---

[5] See Zhang and Smith 2009; He and Huang 2008; Huang 2006, 2012. Recent studies include Hsu 2017; Howell 2015; Franceschini 2014; Froissart 2011; Lee and Shen 2011; and Spires 2011.

state security apparatus. I also took note of the information they revealed or concealed from donors and the counsel that local scholars offered to them on strategies of organizational survival. These participant observation activities allowed me to examine the "hidden transcripts" of labor activists which included "gesture, speech, practices – that are ordinarily excluded from the public transcript of subordinates by the exercise of power" (Scott 1990: 27). Participant observation conducted in both formal and informal settings helped me to understand the differences between how activists *carried out* their work and how they *talked about* their work.

This "experience near" approach (Geertz 1973) also generated information about how different actors perceived the mobilization and claims-making processes (Schatz 2009b: 7). For example, activists in many organizations shared a common view of the central state as benevolent and the local state as predatory and corrupt. Yet while some activists saw their work as a step towards instigating political change (and even leading to the eventual democratization of China), others harbored ambivalent attitudes towards political reform and feared widespread social instability. During retreats or outings with worker-participants, informal conversations revealed that many activists perceived civil society as weak compared to the power of the state. Ethnography allowed me to probe how these actors' divergent interpretations of a shared political reality informed their strategic behavior.

RESEARCHER POSITIONALITY

Ethnography is an interpretative exercise that requires researchers to be attentive to how their engagement with human subjects affects knowledge generation (Schatz 2009b: 14–16). My findings should therefore be seen in light of my positionality vis-à-vis my research subjects. Throughout my fieldwork, I introduced myself as a Ph.D. student from a foreign university. However, activists did not always confer upon me the same power and authority that they would to researchers who were older, male, or ethnically foreign. The organizational culture of these labor organizations was male-dominated and leadership roles were largely occupied by men in their thirties and forties, with female staff usually holding secretarial positions. Being perceived as less authoritative than my male counterparts might have aided me in the participant observation process, as activists did not defer to me as an "expert." In addition, being ethnically Chinese and a native speaker of Mandarin meant that I did not attract undue attention from the organizations' clientele.

Nevertheless, my presence undoubtedly had some impact on the behavior of the activists whose organizations I was interested in studying. When I accompanied workers to government offices to confront officials, I was a source of moral support. When I visited workers on recruitment trips, potential recruits saw me as a volunteer for the organization. When I participated in social activities – outings, retreats, and meals – workers saw me as a friend, though not as an equal in terms of social status. Depending on the degree to which activists perceived me as a part of their organization, they may have concealed from me some of their criticisms of the organization's advocacy strategies. In these ways, in exchange for a textured analysis of the mobilization process of labor organizations, my immersion necessarily influenced the objectivity of these findings.

SAMPLING BIASES

Political ethnography seeks to study a problem from "the nearest possible vantage point" (Schatz 2009b: 307) in order to uncover new phenomena, capture heterogeneity, and provide an account of the lived experiences of human agents for the purposes of theory building (Scott 1985). Indeed, the goal of ethnography is not to generalize about a population but rather to construct novel theoretical concepts that may be applicable to other settings. Nevertheless, it is important to reflect on the degree to which the main findings of mobilizing without the masses are unique only to the organizations that I studied are indicative of a more widespread strategic approach adopted by labor organizations across China.

Snowball sampling tends to over-select similar organizations or those embedded in a certain network while under-representing those outside of these networks (Bleich and Pekkanen 2013: 87). It is also important to acknowledge the possible existence of other labor organizations, unknown and unconnected to the networks of subjects I interviewed and observed during my field research. The possibility that some organizations may be missing from my analysis is perhaps unavoidable given that these labor organizations often sought to operate under the radar.

However, there are reasons to believe that my findings are not limited simply to the particular organizations selected for in-depth case studies and might be applicable to other groups as well. First, the sample of organizations that I studied closely was typical of the larger Beijing and Pearl River Delta clusters. In Beijing, the two cases selected were typical in three dimensions: they were registered as social organizations or businesses; they were foreign-funded; and they had not been previously disbanded by the authorities. The two cases selected from the Pearl River Delta were also typical of their cluster along three dimensions: they were unregistered or illegally registered; they were foreign-funded; and they had been previously disbanded by the authorities. Second, within the Pearl River Delta cluster, the two selected cases included one from the Hong Kong network and one from the Mainland network. Third, organizations belonging to the same clusters were relatively homogenous in their goals and organizational tactics because many had been incubated within the same parent organizations.[6] Participant observation and interviews conducted

---

[6] See Chapter 2 for a discussion of the incubator effect.

at organizations within the same cluster confirmed this. For example, in the Mainland network, at least five founders of labor organizations had undergone informal training as volunteers at a parent organization, which served as a prototype for organizations in the Mainland network. In the Hong Kong network, at least six organizations had formed under the direct influence of a parent organization (Huang 2012). As a result, these organizations provided similar services, including pro bono legal consultation (in person and via a hotline) for workers taking part in labor arbitration and litigation, labor law workshops, hospital visits, social and cultural activities, and training workers to become volunteer activists. Organizations within the same network also communicated with each other. Their leaders often attended the same labor conferences and networked with the same scholars. On several occasions, I observed scholars counsel various leaders in the same network on how to represent themselves in a non-threatening fashion to state officials. Similarities in their founding stories, service portfolios, and social networks suggest that the tactics adopted by the organizations in which I did not conduct participant observation likely resembled the tactics used by those organizations I did directly observe.

There is also the question of selection bias of worker-participants. Were workers who contacted these organizations driven by activists to engage in mobilizing without the masses, or did the workers who visited these organizations constitute a self-selecting pool of individuals already predisposed to making rights claims? While it is difficult to establish the plausibility of a counterfactual argument in this setting, participant observation did produce a contextual understanding of these organizations and how they influenced workers' rights-claiming behaviors. In certain cases, participant observation and interviews suggested that strong-willed individuals may have deployed contentious tactics to claim their rights even without the assistance of an organization. However, most workers I observed during my fieldwork were deeply reluctant to engage in contention and only did so after being coached by activists during the rights-claiming process. For instance, in the pedagogy of micro-collective contention, worker-participants predisposed towards rights activism were drawn to participate in organizations like Solidarity in Action. Nevertheless, it was their involvement in the pedagogical process that enabled them to channel their resources into staging micro-collective action. Otherwise, these same individuals may have joined other workers in taking part in conventional forms of contention such as strikes or legal action.

In the pedagogy of atomized action, I personally accompanied worker-participants to sites of contention and observed the discrepancy between their stated ambition to "stand up to the authorities" and their actual hesitation in the face of powerful officials and managers. Workers needed active coaching and moral support from activists because it was both risky and emotionally costly to threaten state officials or factory bosses. Equipped with knowledge of local bureaucracies, activists instructed workers on which state officials to target and how. Activists also contacted journalists who amplified workers' claims and put pressure on officials and bosses to respond. In those cases I personally observed, workers received substantial instruction and encouragement from activists before deploying such actions.

Finally, in the pedagogy of discursive action, worker-participants who were directly involved in the organization likely already had an interest in artistic expression. Outside of the organizations, other migrant workers were also active in producing "migrant literature" (*dagong wenxue*) by writing poetry and narratives of their migrant experiences. Indeed, organizations such as Workers' World did not invent these forms of artistic expression. However, the organization's capacity to engage in cultural mobilization transformed these personal expressions into a form of discursive contentious action. By encouraging workers to adopt certain narratives and terminologies to voice their grievances, the organization played a critical role in shaping the grammar of migrant worker contention. In this sense, Workers' World mobilized workers to express themselves as a collective and to adopt a similar repertoire of discursive tactics to press for their rights. In short, while these findings do not claim generalizability to all labor organizations across China and there is selection bias, there is reason to believe that the sample cuts across a diverse range of labor organizations in different regions. But more importantly, mobilizing without the masses is about theorizing an innovative dynamic of organizing under duress.

Bibliography

ACADEMIC SOURCES

Alagappa, M. (2004). Civil Society and Political Change: An Analytical Framework. In M. Alagappa (Ed.), *Civil Society and Political Change in Asia: Expanding and Contracting Democratic Space* (25–57). Stanford, CA: Stanford University Press.

Alexander, P. and Chan, A. (2004). Does China Have an Apartheid Pass System? *Journal of Ethnic and Migration Studies*, 30, 609–69.

Almeida, P. (2003). Opportunity Organizations and Threat-Induced Contention: Protest Waves in Authoritarian Settings. *American Journal of Sociology*, 109, 345–400.

(2008). *Waves of Protest: Popular Struggle in El Salvador, 1925–2005*. Minneapolis, MN: University of Minnesota Press.

Anagnost, A. (1997). *National Past-times: Narrative, Representation, and Power in Modern China*. Durham, NC: Duke University Press.

Balzer, H. (2003). Managed Pluralism: Vladimir Putin's Emerging Regime. *Post-Soviet Affairs*, 19, 189–227.

Bayat, A. (2013). *Life as Politics: How Ordinary People Change the Middle East*. Stanford, CA: Stanford University Press.

Becker, J. (2012). The Knowledge to Act: Chinese Migrant Labor Protests in Comparative Perspective. *Comparative Political Studies*, 45(11), 1379–404.

Beinin, J. and Vairel, F. (Eds.). (2011). *Social Movements, Mobilization, and Contestation in the Middle East and North Africa*. Stanford, CA: Stanford University Press.

Beissinger, M. (2002). *Nationalist Mobilization and the Collapse of the Soviet State*. Cambridge: Cambridge University Press.

(2007). Structure and Example in Modular Political Phenomena: The Diffusion of Bulldozer/Rose/Orange/Tulip Revolutions. *Perspectives on Politics*, 5, 259–76.

Bellin, E. (2004). The Robustness of Authoritarianism in the Middle East: Exceptionalism in Comparative Perspective. *Comparative Politics*, 36, 139–57.

Benford, R. and Snow, D. (2000). Framing Processes and Social Movements: An Overview and Assessment. *Annual Review of Sociology*, 26, 611–39.

Bernhard, M. (1993). *The Origins of Democratization in Poland: Workers, Intellectuals, and Oppositional Politics, 1976–1980*. New York: Cambridge University Press.

Birney, M. (2013). Decentralization and Veiled Corruption under China's "Rule of Mandates." *World Development*, 53, 55–67.

Blecher, M. (2002). Hegemony and Workers' Politics in China. *The China Quarterly*, 170, 283–303.

Bleich, E. and Pekkanen, R. (2013). How to Report Interview Data: The Interview Methods Appendix. In L. Mosley (Ed.), *Interview Research in Political Science* (84–115). Ithaca, NY: Cornell University Press.

Boudreau, Vince. (2004). *Resisting Dictatorship: Repression and Protest in Southeast Asia*. Cambridge: Cambridge University Press.

Brook, Timothy and Frolic, B. Michael (Eds.). (1997). *Civil Society in China*. Armonk, NY: M. E. Sharpe.

Bunce, V. and Wolchik, S. (2011). *Defeating Authoritarian Leaders in Postcommunist Countries*. Cambridge: Cambridge University Press.

Cai, Y. (2008). Local Governments and the Suppression of Popular Resistance in China. *The China Quarterly*, 193, 24–42.

(2010). *Collective Resistance in China: Why Popular Protests Succeed or Fail*. Stanford, CA: Stanford University Press.

(2014). *State and Agents in China: Disciplining Government Officials*. Stanford, CA: Stanford University Press.

Cao, N. (2010). *Constructing China's Jerusalem: Christians, Power, and Place in the Contemporary Wenzhou*. Stanford, CA: Stanford University Press.

Carey, S. (2006). The Dynamic Relationship Between Protest and Repression. *Political Research Quarterly*, 59, 1–11.

Chan, A. (2001). *China's Workers under Assault: The Exploitation of Labor in a Globalizing Economy*. Armonk, NY: M. E. Sharpe.

Chan, A. and Siu, K. (2012). Chinese Migrant Workers: Factors Constraining the Emergence of Class Consciousness. In Beatriz Carrillo and David S. G. Goodman (Eds.), *China's Peasants and Workers: Changing Class Identities* (79–101). Northhampton: Edward Elgar Publishing.

Chan, C. (2010). *The Challenge of Labor in China: Strikes and the Changing Labor Regime in Global Factories*. New York: Routledge.

Chan, C. and Hui, E. (2014). The Development of Collective Bargaining in China: From "Collective Bargaining by Riot" to "Party State-led Wage Bargaining." *The China Quarterly*, 217, 221–42.

Chan, K. W. (2005). The Development of NGOs under a Post-Totalitarian Regime: The Case of China. In R. Weller (Ed.), *Civil Life, Globalization, and Political Change in Asia* (20–41). New York: Routledge.

(2010). The Chinese Household Registration System and Migrant Labor in China: Notes on a Debate. *Population and Development Review*, 36, 357–64.

Chen, F. (2008). Worker Leaders and Framing Factory-Based Resistance. In K. O'Brien (Ed.), *Popular Protest in China* (88–107). Cambridge, MA: Harvard University Press.

Chen, X. (2008). Collective Petitioning and Institutional Conversion. In K. O'Brien (Ed.), *Popular Protest in China* (54–70). Cambridge, MA: Harvard University Press.

(2012). *Social Protest and Contentious Authoritarianism in China*. New York: Cambridge University Press.

(2017). Origins of Informal Coercion in China. *Politics and Society*, 45(1), 67–89.

Davenport, C. (2004). Repression and Mobilization: Insights from Political Science and Sociology. In C. Davenport, Hank Johnston, and Carol Mueller (Eds.), *Repression and Mobilization* (viii–xli). Minneapolis, MN: University of Minnesota Press.

Della Porta, D. (1995). *Social Movements, Political Violence and the State.* Cambridge: Cambridge University Press.

Deng, Y. and O'Brien, K. (2013). Relational Repression in China: Using Social Ties to Demobilize Protesters. *The China Quarterly*, 215, 533–52.

(2014). Societies of Senior Citizens and Popular Protest in Rural Zhejiang. *The China Journal*, 71, 172–88.

Denoeux, G. (1993). *Urban Unrest in the Middle East: A Comparative Study of Informal Networks in Egypt, Iran, and Lebanon.* Albany, NY: State University of New York.

Diamond, L. (1994). Rethinking Civil Society: Toward Democratic Consolidation. *Journal of Democracy*, 5, 4–17.

Diani, M. and Bison, I. (2004). Organizations, Coalitions, and Movements. *Theory and Society*, 33, 281–309.

Dilla, H. and Oxhorn, P. (2002). The Virtues and Misfortunes of Civil Society in Cuba. *Latin American Perspectives*, 29, 11–30.

Dillon, N. (2011). Governing Civil Society: Adapting Revolutionary Methods to Serve Post-Communist Goals. In S. Heilmann and E. Perry (Eds.), *Mao's Invisible Hand: The Political Foundations of Adaptive Governance in China* (138–64). Cambridge, MA: Harvard University Asia Center.

Distelhorst, G. (2013). *Publicity-Driven Accountability in China: Qualitative and Experimental Evidence.* MIT Political Science Department Research Working Paper 2012–2014. Social Science Research Network.

(2017). The Power of Empty Promises: Quasi-Democratic Institutions and Activism in China. *Comparative Political Studies*, 50(4), 464–98.

Distelhorst, G. and Hou, Y. (2017). Constituency Service under Nondemocratic Rule: Evidence from China. *The Journal of Politics*, 79(3), 1024–40.

Earl, J. (2011). Political Repression: Iron Fists, Velvet Gloves, and Diffuse Control. *Annual Review of Sociology*, 37, 261–84.

Earl, J. and Soule, S. (2006). Seeing Blue: A Police-Centered Explanation of Protest Policing. *Mobilization*, 11, 145–64.

Economy, E. (2004). *The River Runs Black: The Environmental Challenge to China's Future.* Ithaca, NY: Cornell University Press.

Edin, Maria. (2003). State Capacity and Local Agent Control in China: CCP Cadre Management from a Township Perspective. *The China Quarterly*, 173, 35–52.

Ekiert, G. and Kubik, J. (2001). *Rebellious Civil Society: Popular Protest and Democratic Consolidation in Poland, 1989–1993.* Ann Arbor, MI: University of Michigan Press.

Elfstrom, M. and Kuruvilla, S. (2014). The Changing Nature of Labor Unrest in China. *Industrial and Labor Relations Review*, 67(2), 453–80.

Evans, P. (1995). *Embedded Autonomy: States and Industrial Transformation.* Princeton, NJ: Princeton University Press.

Evans, P. and Heller, P. (2015). Human Development, State Transformation, and the Politics of the Developmental State. In S. Leibfried, E. Huber, M. Lange, J. Levy, F. Nullmeier, and J. Stephens (Eds.), *The Oxford Handbook of Transformations of the State* (691–713). Oxford: Oxford University Press.

Fewsmith, J. (2013). *The Logic and Limits of Political Reform in China.* New York: Cambridge University Press.

Fincher, L.-H. (2016). China's Feminist Five. *Dissent*. Fall.

Fine, J. (2006). *Worker Centers: Organizing Communities at the Edge of the Dream.* Ithaca, NY: Cornell University Press.

Foley, M. and Edwards, B. (1996). The Paradox of Civil Society. *Journal of Democracy*, 7, 38–52.

Fong, V. and Murphy, R. (Eds.). (2006). *Chinese Citizenship: Views from the Margins.* New York: Routledge.

Foster, K. (2001). Associations in the Embrace of an Authoritarian State: State Domination of Society? *Studies in Comparative International Development*, 35, 84–109.

Franceschini, I. (2014). Labor NGOs in China: A Real Force for Political Change? *The China Quarterly*, 218, 474–92.

Francisco, R. (1995). The Relationship between Coercion and Protest: An Empirical Evaluation in Three Coercive States. *Journal of Conflict Resolution*, 39, 263–82.

Frazier, M. (2010). *Socialist Insecurity: Pensions and the Politics of Uneven Development in China.* Ithaca, NY: Cornell University Press.

Friedman, E. (2014). *Insurgency Trap: Labor Politics in Postsocialist China.* Ithaca, NY: Cornell University Press.

Friedman, E. and Wong, J. (2008). Learning to Lose: Dominant Parties, Dominant Party Systems and Their Transitions. In J. Wong and E. Friedman (Eds.), *Political Transitions in Dominant Party Systems: Learning to Lose* (1–13). New York: Routledge.

Froissart, C. (2011). "NGOs" Defending Migrant Workers' Rights: Semi-union Organisations Contribute to the Regime's Dynamic Stability. *China Perspectives*, 2, 18–25.

Frolic, M. (1997). State-Led Civil Society. In T. Brook and M. Frolic (Eds.), *Civil Society in China* (46–67). Armonk, NY: M. E. Sharpe.

Fu, D. (2009). A Cage of Voices: Producing and Doing Dagongmei in Contemporary China. *Modern China*, 35, 527–61.

(2017a). Disguised Collective Action in China. *Comparative Political Studies*, 50(4), 499–527.

(2017b). Fragmented Control: Governing Contentious Labor Organizations in China. *Governance*, 30, 445–62.

Fu, D. and Distelhorst, G. (Forthcoming). Grassroots Participation and Repression under Hu Jintao and Xi Jinping. *The China Journal*.

Fukuyama, F. (1995). *Trust: The Social Virtues and the Creation of Prosperity.* New York: Free Press.

Fung, A. (2003). Associations and Democracy: Between Theories, Hopes, and Realities. *Annual Review of Sociology*, 29, 515–39.

Gallagher, M. (2005). *Contagious Capitalism: Globalization and the Politics of Labor in China.* Princeton, NJ: Princeton University Press.

(2007). "Hope for Protection and Hopeless Choices": Labor Legal Aid in the PRC. In E. Perry (Ed.), *Grassroots Political Reform in Contemporary China* (196–227). Cambridge, MA: Harvard University Asia Center.

(2014). China's Workers Movement and the End of the Rapid-Growth Era. *Daedalus*, 143, 81–95.

Gallagher, M. (2017). *Authoritarian Legality in China: Law, Workers and the State.* Cambridge: Cambridge University Press.

Gamson, W. (1975). *The Strategy of Social Protest*. Homewood, IL: Dorsey.
  (1992). *Talking Politics*. New York: Cambridge University Press.
Gandhi, J. (2008). *Political Institutions under Dictatorship*. New York: Cambridge University Press.
Geertz, C. (1973). *The Interpretation of Cultures*. New York: Basic Books.
Gold, T. (1990). The Resurgence of Civil Society in China. *Journal of Democracy*, 1, 18–31.
  (1998). Bases for Civil Society in Reform China. In K. Brødsgaard and D. Strand (Eds.), *Reconstructing Twentieth-Century China: State Control, Civil Society, and National Identity* (163–88). Oxford: Clarendon Press.
Goldman, M. and Perry, E. (Eds.). (2002). *Changing Meanings of Citizenship in Modern China*. Cambridge, MA: Harvard University Press.
Goldstone, J. and Tilly, C. (2001). Threat (and Opportunity): Popular Action and State Response in the Dynamics of Contentious Action. In R. Aminzade, J. Goldstone, D. McAdam, E. Perry, W. Sewell, S. Tarrow, and C. Tilly (Eds.), *Silence and Voice in the Study of Contentious Politics* (179–94). Cambridge: Cambridge University Press.
Gordon, J. (2005). *Suburban Sweatshops: The Fight for Immigrant Rights*. Cambridge, MA: Harvard University Press.
Gramsci, A. (1971). *Selections from the Prison Notebooks: Antonio Gramsci*. New York: Columbia University Press.
Guang, L. (2005). Guerrilla Workfare: Migrant Renovators, State Power, and Informal Work in Urban China. *Politics and Society*, 33(3), 481–506.
Gurr, T. (1970). *Why Men Rebel*. Princeton, NJ: Princeton University Press.
He, B. and Warren, M. (2011). Authoritarian Deliberation: The Deliberative Turn in Chinese Political Development. *Perspectives on Politics*, 9, 269–89.
He, J. and Huang, H. (2008). NGOs Defending Migrant Labour Rights in the Pearl River Delta Region: A Descriptive Analysis. *Hong Kong Journal of Social Sciences*, 35, 41–71.
Heilmann, S. and Perry, E. (2011). Embracing Uncertainty: Guerrilla Policy Style and Adaptive Governance in China. In S. Heilmann and E. Perry (Eds.), *Mao's Invisible Hand: The Political Foundation of Adaptive Governance in China* (1–29). Cambridge, MA: Harvard University Asia Center Press.
Hess, D. and Martin, B. (2006). Repression, Backfire, and the Theory of Transformative Events. *Mobilization: An International Journal*, 11, 249–67.
Heurlin, C. (2016). *Responsive Authoritarianism in China: Land Protests, and Policy Making*. New York: Cambridge University Press.
Hildebrandt, T. (2013). *Social Organizations and the Authoritarian State in China*. New York: Cambridge University Press.
Ho, P. (2001). Greening Without Conflict? Environmentalism, NGOs, and Civil Society in China. *Development and Change*, 32, 893–921.
Hollander, J. and Einwohner, R. (2004). Conceptualizing Resistance. *Sociological Forum*, 19, 533–54.
Howell, J. (2003). New Directions in Civil Society: Organizing Around Marginalized Interests. In J. Howell (Ed.), *Governance in China* (143–71). Lanham, MD: Rowman and Littlefield.
  (2008). NGOs, Civil Society and Migrants in China. In R. Murphy (Ed.), *Labour Migration and Social Development in Contemporary China. Comparative Development and Policy in Asia* (171–94). Abingdon: Routledge.

(2012). Civil Society, Corporatism and Capitalism in China. *Journal of Comparative Asian Development*, 11(2), 271–97.

(2015). Shall We Dance? Welfarist Incorporation and the Politics of State-Labour NGO Relations. *The China Quarterly*, 223, 702–23.

Hsu, J. and Hasmath, R. (2014). The Local Corporatist State and NGO Relations in China. *Journal of Contemporary China*, 23, 516–34.

Huang, Y. (2006). Wailai gongzuzhi yu kuaguo laogong tuanjie wangluo – yi huanan diqu weili [Migrant Worker Organizations and Transnational Labor Solidarity Networks – A Case Study from South China]. *Kaifang Shidai*, 89–103.

(2012). Chuangzao Gongminquan: Laogong NGO de Hunhe Celue [Constructing Citizenship Rights: Labor NGOs' Variable Strategies]. *Guojia Xinzhengxueyuan Xuebao*, 4, 100–6.

Hurst, W. (2008). Mass Frames and Worker Protest. In K. O'Brien (Ed.), *Popular Protest in China* (71–87). Cambridge, MA: Harvard University Asia Center.

(2009). *The Chinese Worker after Socialism*. Cambridge: Cambridge University Press.

Hurst, W., Gold, T. B., and Won, J. (2009). Introduction. In T. Gold, W. Hurst, J. Won, and Q. Li (Eds.), *Laid-Off Workers in a Workers' State: Unemployment with Chinese Characteristics*. New York: Palgrave Macmillan.

Hurst, W., Liu, M., Liu, Y., and Tao, R. (2014). Reassessing Collective Petitioning in Rural China: Civic Engagement, Extra-State Violence, and Regional Variation. *Comparative Politics*, 46, 459–82.

Jeffries, J. (2002). Black Radicalism and Political Repression in Baltimore: The Case of the Black Panther Party. *Ethnic and Racial Studies*, 25, 64–98.

Johnston, H. (2004). Talking the Walk: Speech Acts and Resistance in Authoritarian Regimes. In C. Davenport, H. Johnston, and C. Mueller (Eds.), *Repression and Mobilization* (108–37). Minneapolis, MN: University of Minnesota Press.

(2006). "Let's Get Small": The Dynamics of (Small) Contention in Repressive States. *Mobilization: An International Journal*, 11, 195–212.

(2012). State Violence and Oppositional Protest in High-Capacity Authoritarian Regimes. *International Journal of Conflict and Violence*, 6(1), 55–74.

Jones, C. (1988). The Political Repression of the Black Panther Party, 1966–1971: The Case of the Oakland Bay Area. *Journal of Black Studies*, 18, 415–34.

Kang, X. and Han, H. (2008). Graduated Controls: The State-Society Relationship in Contemporary China. *Modern China*, 34, 36–55

Kapiszewski, D., MacLean, L., and Read, B. (2015). *Field Research in Political Science: Practices and Principles*. Cambridge: Cambridge University Press.

Kelliher, D. (1992). *Peasant Power in China: The Era of New Reform 1979–89*. New Haven, CT: Yale University Press.

King, G., Pan, J., and Roberts, M. (2013). How Censorship in China Allows Government Criticism but Silences Collective Expression. *American Political Science Review*, 107, 326–43.

Koesel, K. (2014). *Religion and Authoritarianism: Cooperation, Conflict, and the Consequences*. New York: Cambridge University Press.

Krastev, I. (2011). Paradoxes of the New Authoritarianism. *Journal of Democracy*, 22, 5–16.

Landry, P. (2008). *Decentralized Authoritarianism in China: The Communist Party's Control of Local Elites in the Post-Mao Era*. Cambridge: Cambridge University Press.

Lee, C. (1998). *Gender and the South China Miracle: Two Worlds of Factory Women.*
Los Angeles, CA: University of California Press.

(2007a). Is Labor a Political Force in China? In E. Perry and M. Goldman (Eds.),
Grassroots Political Reform in Contemporary China (228–52). Cambridge,
MA: Harvard University Press.

(2007b). *Against the Law: Labor Protests in China's Rustbelt and Sunbelt.* Berkeley,
CA: University of California.

Lee, C. and Shen, Y. (2011). The Anti-Solidarity Machine? Labor Nongovernmental
Organizations in China. In S. Kuruvilla, C. Lee, and M. Gallagher (Eds.), *From
Iron Rice-Bowl to Informalization: Markets, Workers and the State in a Changing
China.* Ithaca, NY: Cornell University.

Lee, C. and Zhang, Y. (2013). The Power of Instability: Unraveling the Microfounda-
tions of Bargained Authoritarianism in China. *American Journal of Sociology*, 118,
1475–508.

Lee, S. and Kleinman, A. (2003). Suicide as Resistance in Chinese Society. In E. Perry
and M. Selden (Eds.), *Chinese Society: Change, Conflict and Resistance* (221–40).
London: Routledge

Leung, J. and Xu, Y. (2015). *China's Social Welfare: The Third Turning Point.*
Cambridge: Polity Press.

Levitsky, S. and Way, L. (2010). *Competitive Authoritarianism: Hybrid Regimes after
the Cold War.* Cambridge: Cambridge University Press.

Li, C. (2012). The End of the CCP's Resilient Authoritarianism? A Tripartite Assessment
of Shifting Power in China. *The China Quarterly*, 211, 595–623.

(2016). *Unmaking Authoritarian Labor Regime: Collective Bargaining and Labor
Unrest in Contemporary China.* (Doctor of Philosophy Dissertation), Rutgers, The
State University of New Jersey, New Jersey.

Li, H. and Zhou, L. (2005). Political Turnover and Economic Performance: The Incentive
Role of Personnel Control in China. *Journal of Public Economics*, 89, 1743–62.

Li, L. (2010). Rights Consciousness and Rules Consciousness in Contemporary China.
The China Journal, 64 (July), 47–68.

Lichbach, M. and Gurr, T. (1981). The Conflict Process. *Journal of Conflict Resolution*,
25, 3–29.

Lieberthal, K. and Lampton, D. (1992). *Bureaucracy, Politics, and Decision Making in
Post-Mao China.* Berkeley, CA: University of California Press.

Liu, M. (2010). Union Organizing in China: Still a Monolithic Labor Movement?
Industrial and Labor Relations Review, 64(1), 30–52.

Liu, M. and Tao, R. (2007). Local Governance, Policy Mandates and Fiscal Reform
in China. In V. Shue and C. Wong (Eds.), *Paying for Progress in China: Public
Finance, Human Welfare and Changing Patterns of Inequality* (166–89).
New York: Routledge.

Liu, S. and Halliday, T. (2016). *Criminal Defense in China: The Politics of Lawyers at
Work.* Cambridge: Cambridge University Press.

Lorentzen, P. (2013). Regularizing Rioting: Permitting Public Protest in an Authoritarian
Regime. *Quarterly Journal of Political Science*, 8, 127–58.

Lorentzen, P. and Scoggins, S. (2015). Understanding China's Rising Rights
Consciousness. *The China Quarterly*, 223(September), 638–57.

Loveman, M. (1998). High-Risk Collective Action: Defending Human Rights in Chile, Uruguay, and Argentina. *The American Journal of Sociology*, 104, 477–525.

Lu, Y. (2009). *Non-Governmental Organizations in China: The Rise of Dependent Autonomy*. New York: Routledge.

Lu, X. and Landry, P. (2014). Show Me the Money: Interjurisdiction Political Competition and Fiscal Extraction in China. *American Political Science Review*, 108, 706–22.

Luo, M. (2003). Sun zhigang shijian yu huji zhidu gaige. [The Sun Zhigang Incident and Household Registration System Reform]. *Renda Yanjiu*, 12.

Lynch, M. (Ed.) (2014). *The Arab Uprisings Explained: New Contentious Politics in the Middle East*. New York: Cambridge University Press.

Ma, Q. (2006). *Non-Governmental Organizations in Contemporary China: Paving the Way to Civil Society?* New York: Routledge.

Manion, M. (1990). Reluctant Duelists: The Logic of the 1989 Protests and Massacre. In Michel Oksenberg, Lawrence Sullivan, and Marc Lambert (Eds.), *Beijing Spring, 1989: Confrontation and Conflict. The Basic Documents* (xiii–xlii). New York: M. E. Sharpe.

Marshall, T. H. (1950). *Citizenship and Social Class and Other Essays*. Cambridge: Cambridge University Press.

Mattingly, D. (2016). Elite Capture: How Decentralization and Informal Institutions Weaken Property Rights in China. *World Politics*, 68(3), 383–412.

McAdam, D. (1982). *Political Process and the Development of Black Insurgency, 1930–1970*. Chicago, IL: University of Chicago.

(1983). Tactical Innovation and the Pace of Insurgency. *American Sociological Review*, 48, 735–54.

McAdam, D., Tarrow, S., and Tilly, C. (2001). *Dynamics of Contention*. Cambridge: Cambridge University Press.

Melucci, A. (1989). *Nomads of the Present: Social Movements and Individual Needs in Contemporary Society*. Philadelphia, PA: Temple University Press.

Mertha, A. (2008). *China's Water Warriors: Citizen Action and Policy Change*. Ithaca, NY: Cornell University Press.

(2009). "Fragmented Authoritarianism 2.0": Political Pluralization in the Chinese Policy Process. *The China Quarterly*, 200, 995–1012.

Michels, R. (1911). *Political Parties: A Sociological Study of the Oligarchical Tendencies of Modern Democracy*. New York: Collier Books.

Nathan, A. (1985). *Chinese Democracy*. Berkeley, CA: University of California Press.

(2003). China's Changing of the Guard: Authoritarian Resilience. *Journal of Democracy*, 14(1), 6–17.

Nathan, A. and Link, P. (Eds.). (2001). *The Tiananmen Papers*. New York: Public Affairs.

O'Brien, K. (2003). Neither Transgressive Nor Contained: Boundary-Spanning Contention in China. *Mobilization: An International Journal*, 8(1), 51–64.

(2013). Rightful Resistance Revisited. *Journal of Peasant Studies*, 40(6), 1051–62.

O'Brien, K. and Deng, Y. (2015). Repression Backfires: Tactical Radicalization and Protest Spectacle in Rural China. *Journal of Contemporary China*, 24(93), 457–70.

O'Brien, K. and Li, L. (2006). *Rightful Resistance in Rural China*. Cambridge: Cambridge University Press.

O'Donnell, G. and Schmitter, P. (1986). *Transitions from Authoritarian Rule: Tentative Conclusions about Uncertain Democracies.* Baltimore, MA: Johns Hopkins University Press.

Oi, J. (1992). Fiscal Reform and the Economic Foundations of Local State Corporatism in China. *World Politics,* 45(1), 99–126.

Olson, M. (1965). *The Logic of Collective Action.* Cambridge, MA: Harvard University Press.

Ondetti, G. (2006). Repression, Opportunity, and Protest: Explaining the Takeoff of Brazil's Landless Movement. *Latin American Politics and Society,* 48, 61–94.

Ong, L. (2015). "Thugs for Hire": State Coercion and Everyday Repression in China. Cambridge, MA: Paper presented at Workshop on Collective Protest and State Governance in China's Xi Jinping Era: Harvard-Yenching Institute.

Ong, L. and Göbel, C. (2014). Social Unrest in China. In K. Brown (Ed.), *China and the EU in Context: Insights for Business and Investors* (178–213). London: Palgrave Macmillan.

Opp, K. and Roehl, W. (1990). Repression, Micromobilization, and Political Protest. *Social Forces,* 69, 521–47.

Ortiz, D. (2007). Confronting Oppression with Violence: Inequality, Military Infrastructure and Dissident Repression. *Mobilization,* 12, 219–38.

Pearson, M. (1997). *China's New Business Elite: The Political Consequences of Economic Reform.* Los Angeles, CA: University of California Press.

Pei, M. (2006). *China's Trapped Transition: The Limits of Developmental Autocracy.* Cambridge, MA: Harvard University Press.

Perry, E. (2002a). From Paris to the Paris of the East – and Back: Workers as Citizens in Modern Shanghai. In M. Goldman and E. Perry (Eds.), *Changing Meanings of Citizenship in Modern China.* Cambridge, MA: Harvard University Press.

(2002b). *Challenging the Mandate of Heaven: Social Protest and State Power in China.* New York: M. E. Sharpe.

(2002c). Moving the Masses: Emotion Work in the Chinese Revolution. *Mobilization: An International Journal,* 7, 111–28.

(2008). Chinese Conceptions of "Rights": From Mencius to Mao – and Now. *Perspectives on Politics,* 6, 37–50.

(2009). A New Rights Consciousness? *Journal of Democracy,* 20(3), 17–20.

(2012). *Anyuan: Mining China's Revolutionary Tradition.* Berkeley, CA: University of California Press.

(2013). Cultural Governance in Contemporary China: "Re-Orienting" Party Propaganda. Harvard-Yenching Institute Working Paper Series.

Perry, E. and Goldman, M. (Eds.). (2007). *Grassroots Political Reform in Contemporary China.* Cambridge, MA: Harvard University Press.

Piven, F. and Cloward, R. (1978). *Poor People's Movements: Why They Succeed, How They Fail.* New York: Vintage Books.

Policzer, P. (2009). *The Rise and Fall of Repression in Chile.* Notre Dame, IN: University of Notre Dame Press.

Posner, D. (2003). Civil Society and the Reconstruction of Failed States. In R. Rotberg (Ed.), *When States Fail: Causes and Consequences.* Princeton, NJ: Princeton University Press.

Pringle, T. and Clarke, S. (2011). *The Challenge of Transition: Trade Unions in Russia, China and Vietnam*: Basingstoke: Palgrave Macmillan.

Pun, N. (2005). *Made in China: Women Factory Workers in a Global Workplace*. Hong Kong: Hong Kong University Press.

Pun, N. and Lu, H. (2010). Unfinished Proletarianization: Self, Anger, and Class Action among the Second Generation of Peasant-Workers in Present-Day China. *Modern China*, 36, 493–519.

Putnam, R., Leonardi, R., and Nanetti, R. (1993). *Making Democracy Work: Civic Traditions in Modern Italy*. Princeton, NJ: Princeton University Press.

Read, Benjamin. (2008). Assessing Variation in Civil Society Organizations: China's Homeowner Associations in Comparative Perspective. *Comparative Political Studies*, 41(9), 1240–65.

Reny, M. E. (Forthcoming). *Authoritarian Containment: Public Security Bureaus and Protestant House Churches in Urban China*. Oxford: Oxford University Press.

Reny, M. E. and Hurst, W. (2013). Social Unrest. In C. Ogden (Ed.), *Handbook of China's Governance and Domestic Politics* (210–20). Abingdon: Routledge.

Rev, I. (1987). The Advantages of Being Atomized: How Hungarian Peasants Coped with Collectivization. *Dissent*, Summer, 335–50.

Robertson, G. (2009). Managing Society: Protest, Civil Society, and Regime in Putin's Russia. *Slavic Review*, 68(3), 528–47.

Saich, T. (2000). Negotiating the State: The Development of Social Organizations in China. *The China Quarterly*, 161, 124–41.

Schatz, E. (2009a). The Soft Authoritarian Tool Kit: Agenda-Setting Power in Kazakhstan and Kyrgyzstan. *Comparative Politics*, 41, 203–22.

(Ed.) (2009b). *Political Ethnography: What Immersion Contributes to the Study of Power*. Chicago, IL: University of Chicago Press.

Schmitter, P. (1974). Still the Century of Corporatism? *The Review of Politics*, 36, 85–131.

Schwedler, J. (2012). The Political Geography of Protest in Neoliberal Jordan. *Middle East Critique*, 21(3), 257–70.

Scoggins, S. E. and O'Brien, K. (2016). China's Unhappy Police. *Asian Survey*, 56(2), 225–42.

Scott, J. (1985). *Weapons of the Weak: Everyday Forms of Peasant Resistance*. New Haven, CT: Yale University Press.

(1987). Resistance without Protest and without Organization: Peasant Opposition to Islamic Zakat and the Christian Tithe. *Comparative Studies in Society and History*, 29, 417–52.

(1990). *Domination and the Arts of Resistance: Hidden Transcripts*. New Haven, CT: Yale University Press.

(1998). *Seeing Like a State: How Certain Schemes to Improve the Human Condition Have Failed*. New Haven, CT: Yale University Press.

(2009). *The Art of Not Being Governed: An Anarchist History of Upland Southeast Asia*. New Haven, CT: Yale University Press.

Shambaugh, D. (2016). *China's Future*. Boston, MA: Polity Press.

Shieh, S. (2009). Beyond Corporatism and Civil Society: Three Modes of State-NGO Interaction in China. In J. Schwartz and S. Shieh (Eds.), *State and Society Responses to Social Welfare Needs in China: Serving the People* (22–41). New York: Routledge.

Shirk, S. (2007). *China: Fragile Superpower. How China's Internal Politics Could Derail Its Peaceful Rise.* New York: Oxford University Press.

Shue, V. (2004). Legitimacy Crisis in China? In P. Gries and S. Rosen (Eds.) *State and Society in 21st Century China: Crisis, Contention, and Legitimation* (24–49). New York: Routledge.

Simon, K. (2013). *Civil Society in China: The Legal Framework from Ancient Times to the "New Reform Era."* New York: Oxford University Press.

Simon, M. (1994). Hawks, Doves, and Civil Conflict Dynamics: A "Strategic" Action-Reaction Model. *International Interaction*, 19, 213–39.

Singerman, D. (2004). The Networked World of Islamist Social Movements. In Q. Wiktorowicz (Ed.), *Islamic Activism: A Social Movement Theory Approach* (143–63). Bloomington, IN: Indiana University Press.

Slater, D. (2010). *Ordering Power: Contentious Politics and Authoritarian Leviathans in Southeast Asia.* Cambridge: Cambridge University Press.

Slater, D. and Wong, J. (2013). The Strength to Concede: Ruling Parties and Democratization in Developmental Asia. *Perspectives on Politics*, 11(3), 717–33.

Snow, D. (2013). Identity Dilemmas, Discursive Fields, Identity Work and Mobilization: Clarifying the Identity/Movement Nexus. In J. Van Stekelenburg, C. Roggeband, and B. Klandermans (Eds.), *The Changing Dynamics of Contention* (263–80). Minneapolis, MN: University of Minnesota Press.

Snow, D. and Benford, R. (1988). Ideology, Frame Resonance, and Participant Mobilization. *International Social Movement Research*, 1(1), 197–217.

Solinger, D. (1999). *Contesting Citizenship in Urban China.* Berkeley, CA: University of California Press.

Spires, A. (2011). Contingent Symbiosis and Civil Society in an Authoritarian State. *Journal of Sociology*, 117, 1–45.

Stern, R. (2013). *Environmental Litigation in China: A Study in Political Ambivalence.* New York: Cambridge University Press.

Stern, R. and O'Brien, K. (2012). Politics at the Boundary: Mixed Signals and the Chinese State. *Modern China*, 38(2), 174–98.

Stockmann, D. and Gallagher, M. (2011). Remote Control: How the Media Sustain Authoritarian Rule in China. *Comparative Political Studies*, 44(4), 436–67.

Su, Y. and He, X. (2010). Street as Courtroom: State Accommodation of Labor Protest in South China. *Law and Society Review*, 44, 157–84.

Sun, L., Shen, Y., Guo, Y., Jin, J., Ying, X., and Bi, X. (2010). *Yi liyi biaoda zhiduhua shixian changzhi jiuan* [Institutionalizing channels for interest expression will lead to long-term stability]. *Lindaozhe*, April, 33.

Sun, Y. and Zhao, D. (2008). State–Society Relations and Environmental Campaigns. In K. O'Brien (Ed.), *Popular Protest in China* (144–62). Cambridge, MA: Harvard University Press.

Tanner, M. S. (2000). Shackling the Coercive State: China's Ambivalent Struggle against Torture. *Problems of Post-Communism*, 47(5), 13–30.

Tarrow, S. (2011). *Power in Movement: Social Movements and Contentious Politics.* 3rd edn. Cambridge: Cambridge University Press.

Teets, J. (2009). Post-Earthquake Relief and Reconstruction Efforts: The Emergence of Civil Society in China? *The China Quarterly*, 198, 330–47.

  (2012). Reforming Service Delivery in China: The Emergence of a Social Innovation Model. *Journal of Chinese Political Science*, 17, 15–32.

(2014). *Civil Society under Authoritarianism: The China Model.* New York: Cambridge University Press.

Thornton, P. (2002). Framing Dissent in Contemporary China: Irony, Ambiguity and Metonymy. *The China Quarterly,* 171, 661–81.

Tilly, C. (1976). Major Forms of Collective Action in Western Europe 1500–1975. *Theory and Society,* 3(3), 365–75.

(1995). *Popular Contention in Great Britain, 1758–1834.* Cambridge, MA: Harvard University Press.

(2006). *Regimes and Repertoires.* Chicago, IL: University of Chicago Press.

(2008). *Contentious Performances.* Cambridge: Cambridge University Press.

Tilly, C. and Tarrow, S. (2015). *Contentious Politics.* 2nd edn. New York: Oxford University Press.

Tocqueville, A. de (2001). *Democracy in America.* New York: Penguin Putnam.

Tsai, L. (2011). Friends or Foes? Nonstate Public Goods Providers and Local State Authorities in Nondemocratic and Transitional Systems. *Studies in Comparative International Development,* 46, 46–69.

Tsui, K. and Wang, Y. (2004). Between Separate Stoves and a Single Menu: Fiscal Decentralization in China. *The China Quarterly,* 177, 71–90.

Unger, J. and Chan, A. (1995). China, Corporatism, and the East Asian Model. *The Australian Journal of Chinese Affairs,* 33, 29–53.

Vala, C. (2012). Protestant Christianity and Civil Society in Authoritarian China: The Impact of Official Churches and Unregistered "Urban Churches" on Civil Society Development in the 2000s. *China Perspectives,* 3, 43–52.

Vala, C. and O'Brien, K. (2008). Recruitment to Protestant House Churches. In K. O'Brien (Ed.), *Popular Protest in China.* Cambridge, MA: Harvard University Press.

Walder, A. (1984). The Remaking of the Chinese Working Class, 1949–1981. *Modern China,* 10, 3–48.

(1986). *Communist Neo-Traditionalism: Work and Authority in Chinese Industry.* Berkeley, CA: University of California Press.

(2009a). *Fractured Rebellion: The Beijing Red Guard Movement.* Cambridge, MA: Harvard University Press.

(2009b). Political Sociology and Social Movements. *Annual Review of Sociology,* 35, 393–412.

Walder, A. and Gong, X. (1993). Workers in the Tiananmen Protests: The Politics of the Beijing Workers' Autonomous Federation. *The Australian Journal of Chinese Affairs,* 29(Jan), 1–29.

Wallace, J. (2014). *Cities and Stability: Urbanization, Redistribution, and Regime Survival in China.* New York: Oxford University Press.

Wang, S. (2006). Money and Autonomy: Patterns of Civil Society Finance and Their Implications. *Studies in Comparative and International Development,* 40, 3–29.

Wang, S. and He, J. (2004). Associational Revolution in China: Mapping the Landscapes. *Korea Observer,* 35, 1–65.

Wang, Y. and Minzner, C. (2015). The Rise of the Chinese Security State. *The China Quarterly,* 222, 339–59.

Way, L. (2015). *Pluralism by Default: Weak Autocrats and the Rise of Competitive Politics.* Baltimore, MD: Johns Hopkins University Press.

Weber, M. (2004). *The Vocation Lectures.* Indianapolis, IN: Hackett Publishing.

Wedeen, L. (1999). *Ambiguities of Domination: Politics, Rhetoric, and Symbols in Contemporary Syria*. Chicago, IL: University of Chicago Press.

(2009). Ethnography as Interpretive Enterprise. In E. Schatz (Ed.), *Political Ethnography: What Immersion Contributes to the Study of Power* (75–94). Chicago, IL: University of Chicago Press.

(2010). Reflections on Ethnographic Work in Political Science. *Annual Review of Political Science*, 13, 255–72.

Weigle, M. and Butterfield, J. (1992). Civil Society in Reforming Communist Regimes: The Logic of Emergence. *Comparative Politics*, 25, 1–23.

Weller, R. (2012). Responsive Authoritarianism and Blind-Eye Governance in China. In Nina Bandelj and Dorothy J. Salinger (Eds.), *Socialism Vanquished, Socialism Challenged: Eastern Europe and China, 1989–2009* (83–99). New York: Oxford University Press.

White, G., Howell, J. and Shang, X. (Eds.). (1996). *In Search of Civil Society: Market Reform and Social Change in Contemporary China*. Oxford: Clarendon Press.

White, R. (1989). From Peaceful Protest to Guerrilla War: Micromobilization of the Provisional Irish Republican Army. *American Journal of Sociology*, 94, 1277–302.

Whiting, S. (1991). The Politics of NGO Development in China. *Voluntas: International Journal of Voluntary and Nonprofit Organizations*, 2(2), 16–48.

Wiktorowicz, Q. (2000). Civil Society as Social Control: State Power in Jordan. *Comparative Politics*, 33, 43–61.

(2003). Islamic Activism and Social Movement Theory. In Q. Wiktorowicz (Ed.), *Islamic Activism: A Social Movement Theory Approach*. Indiana, IN: Indiana University Press.

Wong, C. (2009). Rebuilding Government for the 21st Century: Can China Incrementally Reform the Public Sector? *The China Quarterly*, 200, 929–52.

Wood. E. (2003). *Insurgent Collective Action and Civil War in El Salvador*. Cambridge: Cambridge University Press.

Wood, L. (2012). *Direct Action, Deliberation, and Diffusion: Collective Action after the WTO Protests in Seattle*. New York: Cambridge University Press.

Wright, T. (2001). *The Perils of Protest: State Repression and Student Activism in China and Taiwan*. Honolulu: University of Hawaii Press.

Xu, Y. (2013). Labor Non-Governmental Organizations in China: Mobilizing Rural Migrant Workers. *Journal of Industrial Relations*, 55, 243–59.

Yang, G. (2009). *The Power of the Internet in China: Citizen Activism Online*. New York: Columbia University Press.

Yasuda, J. (2017). *On Feeding the Masses: An Anatomy of Regulatory Failure in China*. New York: Cambridge University Press.

Zald, M. and McCarthy, J. (1987). *Social Movements in an Organizational Society: Collected Essays*. New Brunswick, NJ: Transaction Books.

Zhang, H. and Smith, M. (2009). Navigating a Space for Labor Activism: Labor NGOs in the Pearl River Delta of South China. In J. Schwartz and S. Shieh (Eds.), *State and Society Responses to Social Welfare Needs in China: Serving the People* (66–88). New York: Routledge.

Zhang, L. (2001). *Strangers in the City: Reconfigurations of Space, Power, and Social Networks within China's Floating Population*. Stanford, CA: Stanford University Press.

Zhang, X. and Baum, R. (2004). Civil Society and the Anatomy of a Rural NGO. *The China Journal*, 52, 97–107.

Zhao, D. (2001). *The Power of Tiananmen: State-Society Relations and the 1989 Beijing Student Movement*. Chicago, IL: University of Chicago Press.

Zhao, S. (2016). Xi Jinping's Maoist Revival. *Journal of Democracy*, 27(3), 83–97.

Zhi, Q. and Pearson, M. (2016). China's Hybrid Adaptive Bureaucracy: The Case of the 863 Program for Science and Technology. *Governance: An International Journal of Policy, Administration, and Institutions*. DOI: 10.1111/gove.12245

Zhou, K. (1996). *How the Farmers Changed China: Power of the People*. Boulder, CO: Westview Press.

Zhou, X. (1993). Unorganized Interests and Collective Action in Communist China. *American Sociological Review*, 58, 54–73.

OTHER SOURCES

2014 nian quanguo nongmingong jiance diaocha baogao [2014 Peasant Worker Monitoring and Investigation Report]. (2014). April 29. *National Bureau of Statistics of the People's Republic of China*.

Agence-France Presse. (2016). China Labor Activists Sentenced for Helping Workers in Wage Dispute. September 27. *Guardian*.

Barboza, D. (2010). New Strike Threat at a Honda Parts Plant. June 15. *New York Times*.

Bradsher, K. (2010). A Labor Movement Stirs in China. June 10. *New York Times*.

Buckley, C. (2011). China Internal Security Spending Jumps Past Army Budget. Reuters. www.reuters.com/article/us-china-unrest-idUSTRE7222RA20110305

Cao, Y. (2015). Chinese Authorities Orchestrate Surprise Raid of Labor NGOs in Guangdong. October 12. *China Change*.

(2016). China's Shattered Dream for the Rule of Law, One Year On. July 8. *China Change*.

CCTV Channel 13 Law Online Program. (2015). Investigating the Criminal Case of a Star of the Labor Movement. December 25.

Chakrabortty, A. (2013). The Woman Who Nearly Died Making Your iPad. August 5. *Guardian*.

ChinaFile. (2013). Document 9: A ChinaFile Translation. Section 3. November 8.

China Labor Watch. (2007). The Long March: Survey and Case Studies of Work Injuries in the Pearl River Delta Region.

China Labour Bulletin. (1999). Victims of the 1993 Zhili Fire. December 31.

(2010). Guangdong's New Labor Regulations Open the Door to Worker Participation in Collective Bargaining. July 26.

(2013). Migrant Workers and Their Children. June 27.

(2014). China's Labor Dispute Resolution System. October 30.

(2015). Five Years On, Nanhai Honda Workers Want More from Their Trade Unions. May 20.

(2016a). Guangdong Labour Activists Detained Without Trial for Nine Months. January 9.

(2016b). Guangzhou Chef Goes to Court Again in Gender Discrimination Battle. August 22. *China Labour Bulletin*.

[Chinese Cadres Tribune] *Zhongguo dangzheng ganbu luntan*, 2010, 9, 22–6.

Demick, B. (2011). Protests in China over Local Grievances Surge and Get a Hearing. October 8. *The Los Angeles Times*.

Economist. (2009). Open Constitution Closed. July 25.

Economist. (2015). Out, Brothers, Out: Guangdong Province Pioneers a New Approach to Keeping Workers Happy. January 31.

Eihorn, B., Roberts, D., and Larson, C. (2014). Hong Kong Isn't the Only Protest Chinese Leaders Are Worried About. October 2. *Bloomberg Businessweek*.

Forsythe, M. and Jacobs, A. (2016). In China, Books That Make Money, and Enemies. February 4. *New York Times*.

Fu, D. (2017). Why Is China Afraid of Chinese Feminists? July 27. *Washington Post: Monkey Cage*.

Geng, O. and Kazer, W. (2015). China Province under Fire after New Rules on Churches. May 27. *Wall Street Journal*.

Gongzi jiti xieshang shixing banfa [The Implementation of Collective Wage Mediation]. (2000). Ministry of Human Resources and Social Security.

Guomin jingji he shehui fazhan dishierge wunian guihua gangyao 2011–2015. [The 12th Five-Year Plan on Economic and Social Development, 2011–2015].

Han, D. (2012). A Chance to Help Build Grassroots Democracy in China. July 5. *China Labour Bulletin*.

Hui, W. (2010). Government Procurement Promotes Social Work Agencies. February 7. *China Development Brief*.

Jacobs, A. (2015). China Raids Offices of Rights Group as Crackdown on Activism Continues. March 26. *New York Times*.

Jacobs, A. and Buckley, C. (2014). Chinese Activists Test New Leader and Are Crushed. January 15. *New York Times*.

Jiu ming shehuixuezhe fa gongkaixin; dujue fushikang beiju [Nine Sociologists Publish Open Letter, Put a Stop to the Foxconn Tragedy]. (2010). May 19. *Sina News*.

Johnston, I. (2013). Picking Death over Eviction. September 8. *New York Times*.

Langfitt, F. (2013). Desperate Chinese Villagers Turn to Self-Immolation. October 23. *National Public Radio*.

Luo, W. (2015). Ministry Encourages Increase in Social Workers, Community-Based Services. November 22. *China Daily*.

Minzhengbu F. (2011). Nian Shehui Fuwu Fazhan Tongji Gongbao [Ministry of Civil Affairs Publishes the 2011 Statistical Report on Social Service Development]. (2012). June 21. Ministry of Civil Affairs of the People's Republic of China.

Minzhengbu guanyu kaizhan shehuigongzuo rencai duiwu jianshe shidian gong-zuo de tongzhi [Notice from the Ministry of Civil Affairs Regarding Setting Up Experimental Sites for the Construction of a Corps of Social Workers]. (2007). February 15. Ministry of Civil Affairs of the People's Republic of China.

The Nanhai Honda Strike and the Union. (2010). July 18. *China Labor New Translations*.

Nanhaiqu zonggonghui, shishanzheng zonggonghui zhi bentian yuangong de gong-kaixin [Open Letter from Nanhai District Union and Shishan Township Union to Honda Workers]. (2010). June 3. *Sohu Business*.

People's Daily. (2015). "Gongyunzhixing" Zenfeiyang Beizhua: dazhe gongyi huangzi liancai mose ["Star of the Labor Movement" Zeng Feiyang: Money-Making under the Guise of Philanthropy]. December 22.

Phillips, T. (2015). Call for China to Free Labor Activists or Risk Backlash from Frustrated Workforce. December 10. *Guardian*.

Reuters. (2015). China to Scrap Temporary Residence Permits. February 16. *Reuters*.

Sevastopulo, D. (2014). China Charges Labor Activist after Yue Yuen Shoe Factory Strike. April 29. *Financial Times*.

Shieh, S. (2016). Charity Law Facts. March 29. NGOs in China Blog.

Tatlow, K. D. (2016). China Is Said to Force Closing of Women's Legal Aid Center. January 29. *New York Times*.

Tiezzi, S. (2016). China's Plan for "Orderly" Hukou Reform. February 3. *Diplomat*.

Wang, S. (2011). Minzhengbu cheng san lei shehui zuzhi you wang yunxu zhijie dengji [The Ministry of Civil Affairs Declares Three Types of Social Organizations May Be Permitted to Directly Register]. November 24. *Caixin*.

Wenhuabu guanyu cujin mingying wenyi biaoyan tuanti fazhan de ruogan yijian [Recommendations by the Ministry of Culture on the Encouragement of Grassroots Performance Organizations' Development]. (2009). June 26. Central People's Government of the People's Republic of China.

Woetzel, J., Mendonca, L., Devan, J., Negri, S., Hu, Y., Jordan, L., Li, X., Maasry, A., Tsen, G., and Yu, F. (2009). *Preparing for China's Urban Billion*. McKinsey Global Institute.

Wong. (2015). Five Women's Rights Activists Are Formally Detained in Beijing. March 13. *New York Times*.

Xinhua News. (2011). Chinese President Urges Improved Social Management for Greater Harmony, Stability. February 19.

Xu, C. (2008). *Zhusanjiao laogong weiquan NGO jubu weikun* [Pearl River Delta Labor Weiquan NGO Faces Difficulty Each Step of the Way]. February 21.

Yang, Z. (2010). Wujunliang Tuandui: Yusuan Gongkai Disan Tuili [Wu Junliang Team: Open Budget's Third Push]. April 5. *iFeng*.

Zhonggong Zhongyang Bangongting, Guowuyuan Bangongting Guanyu jinyibu jia-qiang minjian zuzhi guanli gongzuode tongzhi [General Office of the Central Committee of the CPC, State Council General Office's Notice on the Work of Strengthening Management of Grassroots Organizations]. (1999). November 1.

Zhou, B. (2011). Zou Zhongguo tese shehui guanli chuangxin zhilu [Take the Path of Innovative Social Management with Chinese Characteristics]. *Qiushi*, 10.

Zhou, Y. (2011). Jiaqiang he chuangxin shehuiguanli, Jianli jianquan zhongguo tese shehuizhuyi shehui guanli tixi [Strengthen and Innovate Social Management, Fully Establish Social Management System with Chinese Socialist Characteristics]. *Qiushi*, 9.

Index

Books in the Series (continued from p. iii)

Printed in the USA
CPSIA information can be obtained
at www.ICGtesting.com
LVHW050921211223
766986LV00003B/127